The poor in England 1700–1850

An economy of makeshifts

edited by Steven King and Alannah Tomkins

Manchester University Press
Manchester and New York

distributed exclusively in the USA by Palgrave

Published by Manchester University Press
Oxford Road, Manchester M13 9NR, UK
and Room 400, 175 Fifth Avenue, New York, NY 10010, USA
www.manchesteruniversitypress.co.uk

Distributed exclusively in the USA by
Palgrave, 175 Fifth Avenue, New York,
NY 10010, USA

Distributed exclusively in Canada by
UBC Press, University of British Columbia, 2029 West Mall,
Vancouver, BC, Canada V6T 1Z2

British Library Cataloguing-in-Publication Data
A catalogue record for this book is available from the British Library

Library of Congress Cataloging-in-Publication Data applied for

ISBN   0 7190 6159 8 *hardback*

First published 2003

11 10 09 08 07 06 05 04 03   10 9 8 7 6 5 4 3 2 1

Typeset in Baskerville and Stone Sans
by Carnegie Publishing Ltd, Lancaster
Printed in Great Britain
by Biddles Ltd, Guildford and Kings Lynn

The poor in England
1700–1850

MANCHESTER
UNIVERSITY PRESS

Steven King: for L. and a Baldon picnic

Alannah Tomkins: for Liam and Edward

Contents

List of tables

List of figures

Acknowledgements

This book has been a number of years in the making. Its origins lie in a conference entitled 'Making shift', organised by Steve Hindle at Warwick amd attended by both editors, which brought us together for the first time. A subsequent meeting in a coffee shop in Stafford in 1997 ended with a realisation that, despite its obvious importance, relatively little had been published on the detailed economy of makeshifts in England. So the idea for this edited volume was born. We have been blessed with excellent and very punctual contributors, and to them our thanks for making the editorial process so easy. Collectively, we feel that this volume will help to set a new theoretical and empirical framework for advancing our understanding of the economy of makeshifts. Alannah Tomkins owes particular thanks to Mrs Rita Freedman of the York City Archives for her generous assistance in microfilming the pawnbroker's pledgebook, and to colleagues, students and friends at both Keele University and Oxford Brookes University for their comments and questions about earlier drafts of the chapter. Steven King owes thanks to archivists at Rawtenstall, Kendal, Bolton and Manchester, who responded with good humour and generosity to a multitude of requests for help. He also owes thanks to Professor Dr Dietrich Ebeling, who arranged a Visiting Professorship in Germany, where some of this volume was written. Finally, we would both like to thank Alison Whittle at Manchester University Press for running with this book right from the start, despite the growing resistance to edited volumes.

1
Introduction
Alannah Tomkins and Steven King

Historiography of parish poor relief

Olwen Hufton could hardly have realised her future impact on the history of welfare when in 1974 she titled two of her chapters on the poor in France 'The economy of makeshifts'.[1] It is a phrase which neatly sums up the patchy, desperate and sometimes failing strategies of the poor for material survival and has been much repeated since 1974. Other phrases (discussed below) may try to represent the same essential idea but none have been so successful in capturing the imaginations of historians. Furthermore 'the economy of makeshifts' has become the organising concept for a number of historians of English welfare who wish to stress the disparate nature of income for poor households, in contrast to a concurrent research trend which would allow parish poor relief a predominant role. This is important given the past preoccupation with particular places and single forms of income. Such approaches have been successful in their own terms but now seem rather insular or parochial in the context of the recognisably varied and integrated reality of poor incomes.

The success of 'the economy of makeshifts' during the last twenty-five years is partly explained by the increasing interest shown by historians in the experiences of poor people rather than accounts which deal exclusively with government policy, elite or at least literate opinions of poverty, or the administrative machinery built up to deliver welfare. Histories of poverty initially (and understandably) tended to address the welfare measures and organisations which left the largest paper trail. For England, this has meant repeated, detailed studies of parish poor relief. In the first instance, parish papers were annexed for information relating to local policy and the power of individuals or governing groups, treating the recipients of relief en masse. Thus the monumental histories compiled by Sidney and Beatrice Webb [2] (significantly as part of a larger project on the history of many aspects of local government) and by Dorothy Marshall [3] set the pattern for multiple, shorter, works on the intricacies of local parish management. [4] Paupers made regular appearances in these works, but as illustrations of policy in practice rather than as individual people with an existence outside the framework of parochial relief. It is implied that the relief dispensed to these characters, and the experiences of the characters themselves, were static whereas it is more plausible to consider relief as a process rather than an event, and the experience of poverty as mutable according to age, employment and other factors.

The emphasis of these early works was decidedly critical; the old poor law was examined and found wanting. Many local examples of cruelty, mismanagement, undue thrift or inappropriate largesse were taken as indications that the system was faulty in design and negligently executed. The Webbs undertook a painstaking progress through 400 years of welfare history spread over two volumes and found much to criticise at every point. They concluded that legislation was merely cited to bolster local autonomy in matters of relief, leading to severity of attitude and no continuity of treatment towards the poor, while an absence of legal amendment was castigated as neglect. Marshall in contrast focused fairly consistently on the eighteenth century and charted the development of the legal framework that sustained and amended parish relief, the manifestations of outdoor relief and the ebb and flow of enthusiasm for setting the poor to work. In particular she grappled with the issue of *how* different parishes implemented the law and although she accorded limited success to some of the outdoor relief measures tried by parishes, she repeatedly labelled most of their efforts as 'failure'.

In both works, the charges levelled at the statutory framework and the host of local variant practices were broadly twofold. First, the poor law was incapable of making a significant dent in the misery of poverty and even inflicted new suffering of its own devising, particularly in the form of the mixed, general workhouse and the stringent application of settlement law. Second, developments at the end of the eighteenth century were guilty of contributing to the increase of poverty, by tending to draw greater numbers of people into the remit of the poor law in the short term and by supporting demographic changes which would in-crease the number and size of pauper families in the long term. The worst culprit was identified as the income supplement system which created a sliding scale of benefits for families based on the price of bread, the number of children in the family and an estimate of the total nutritional requirements of that family. Earn-ings which were insufficient to purchase the estimated minimum of food were topped up by poor relief funds. It was surmised that this practice gave workers no incentive to earn enough to keep their families, since the poor law would step in to pay for food, and gave encouragement to early marriage and independent household formation because the relief system seemed to remove the risk of hunger and suffering if employment failed (or even if the form of employment on offer was unpalatable).[5]

The latter judgement constituted an endorsement of the con-clusions reached rather earlier by the Hammonds, who twinned the enclosure movement with developments in parish relief to account for the desperate plight of the agricultural poor, and the 'Swing' riots, in 1830. The Hammonds had condemned the allow-ance system as 'the prison of the poor' in rural England.[6] They effectively confined their consideration of urban poverty to the post-1800 period, and then chiefly in the context of mechanised industry and factory establishments: the classic manifestations of the 'Industrial Revolution'.[7]

Alternative sources of assistance for the poor were addressed largely as free-standing exercises, giving rise to separate, parallel strands of enquiry relating to very poor, disadvantaged or marginal people. Jordan's attempt to evaluate the contribution of endowed charity endeavoured to grasp the issue of comparability between parish relief and non-statutory gifts, but the flaws in his research blinded historians to the merits of his approach and the important, if limited, implications of his findings for a long time.[8] Other works catalogued the genres of charity and changes to their operation and scope over time; these either did not attempt an evaluative exercise [9] or made judgements on the basis of thin evidence which were subsequently easy to challenge.[10] The conse-quence of these researches and their rejection led to the perception in the 1960s that welfare aside from poor relief meant 'charity' and that charity was a sham which did little to alleviate poverty and served the needs of donors rather than acting sensitively or helpfully towards recipients. Similarly, research on activities which were not overtly related to welfare but which effectually gave rise to alternative income strands for the poor comprised discrete studies of, for example, work, crime, or common rights without consciously connecting their findings to a broader picture of poverty and survival via manipulation, ingenuity and desperation.[11]

The early twentieth-century assessments of the old poor law and charity are unsurprising in that they reflect strongly the priorities and preoccupations of the decades in which they were written. In the 1920s, when the Webbs and Marshall were published, there was a tendency to view past experiments as faulty forerunners of the then modern, liberal welfare policies. By the 1950s and 1960s, the 'welfare state' had been established and the state's legitimate role aimed at nothing less than comprehensive provision for all legitimate needs, making the role and future of voluntary organisations and charities uncertain. Indeed the major development in the history of poverty in the 1960s was to rescue the old poor law from some of the opprobrium cast by the Webbs, and shed a more positive light on past efforts by the state. Mark Blaug's close examination of the demography of late eighteenth-century England argued that poor law measures such as the income supplement were implemented in response to change rather than supplying a major cause of change.[12] While the philosophical basis for his research, results and inferences have subsequently been challenged, the tenor of his work struck a chord with many welfare historians and even Blaug's critic, Williams, thought it 'futile to condemn the poor law in the 1800s for not paying universal full subsistence allowances when these were only put on the agenda in the 1940s'.[13]

In the last thirty years two strands of thought have emerged, generating a profusion of books and articles clustering round the issue of the poor law and its adequacy. Blaug's work cleared the way for an optimistic interpretation of statutory poor relief under the old poor law, which stresses material generosity, in both the amounts of money redistributed and the types of assistance countenanced by local authorities, and the humanity of a face-to-face, parochial system. At first this up-beat line was followed rather diffidently, by work such as Geoffrey Oxley's positive if slightly pedestrian survey,[14] but it was taken up more vigorously in the 1980s. Keith Snell's detailed research on agricultural labourers' quality of life in southern England in the eighteenth and nineteenth centuries surmised that the seasonality of rural unemployment and consequential population mobility pointed up the crucial importance of uncomplicated access to poor relief. He saw the poor law in the eighteenth century as a miniature welfare state, offering generous, comprehensive security and relief.[15] This view was consolidated by Paul Slack, whose studies of the parish relief dispensed in seventeenth-century towns demonstrated how individuals experienced relief and the relative liberality with which they were treated.[16] His most recent work moves away from the circumstances of the individual poor but finds virtue (where the Webbs would have found fault) with the flexibility of local responses to poverty and the energy with which the urge to reform both the law and the poor was taken up.[17] Perhaps the most outspoken, ambitious exponent of the view that the old poor law provided an effective welfare safety net, Peter Solar, argues that parishes manipulated their implementation of the poor laws in accordance with local perceptions of labour supply and demand.[18] He considers that this tailoring of the poor law to labour needs produced a near-universal welfare system which supported a mobile, responsive workforce and so facilitated early industrialisation. As yet this thesis still awaits a convincing body of empirical evidence.

Writers in this positive vein have made assumptions about the expansive capacity of poor relief, and its consequential dominance in the incomes of poor households. Tim Wales argued that in the second half of the seventeenth century parishes increasingly used extraordinary relief to plug gaps in the needs of households that were not filled by parish pension income. This argument holds that poor relief became the sole or dominant source of income for more and more people, but without confirming that extraordinary relief was routinely given to the *same* people who took regular parish payments.[19] Subsequent research has suggested that there was no stable relationship between the poor who were taking regular weekly or monthly relief and the people who received occasional monies for rent, fuel and other necessaries.[20] Still, Wales's work has been very influential in that he elaborated the significance of 'lifecycle' poverty, which was implicit in much previous work but rarely spelled out. He grappled with the extent to which individuals and families became saturated by impoverishment at different stages in their lives, which he gauged in line with the intensity of their impact on parish relief accounts.

Indeed, in the last twenty years the concept of life-cycle poverty has been almost as influential as the 'economy of makeshifts'.

Barry Stapleton has undertaken one of the very few studies to look at life-cycle poverty for a whole community and for more than one generation. According to his findings the early nineteenth century in rural Hampshire saw increasing numbers of people in lifetime poverty; the birth of a first child precipitated families into some sort of dependence for the rest of their lives.[21] Marjorie McIntosh has also approached the topic at the level of community, to show how the responsibility for care of the needy in the period prior to the formalisation of the poor laws fell variably on institutions, families and neighbours.[22] The emphasis on life-cycle has also inspired work on the stress points of childhood and old age. Pam Sharpe is unusual in that she has addressed both of these epochs in different places;[23] widows and the elderly have tended to attract most attention of late.[24] Thane's work has explored the expedients of the aged poor in relation to those listed in the Report of the 1832 Poor Law Commission. She found that poor relief was often a component expedient for survival but was usually 'residual and complementary', utilised along with friendly society payments, small-scale savings or bequests, kinship support and crops from allotments. She does not, however, attempt to prioritise the significance of these alternative resources for the elderly people who used them.[25] Few studies or individuals have tackled an overview of the whole life-cycle, although Susannah Ottoway and Samantha Williams have emphasised the necessity of prosopography for an adequate examination of individuals over their whole lives.[26] There is now room for a refinement of ideas about lifecycle poverty, particularly in relation to children and to men of all ages.

The records generated by parish administration have been used imaginatively to gain some access to the poor and their versions of events, both as individuals and groups. Snell has used settlement examinations to approach experiences of work and unemployment among cohorts of the rural labouring poor.[27] Other historians have glimpsed experiences of poverty via readings of pauper letters. This new attention to an overlooked source possibly represented one of the most refreshing developments in the history of welfare of the 1990s. Whether they are used to look at the interactions between an extended family and its parish,[28] the experience of a life-cycle stage,[29] or another aspect of impoverishment they provide one of the very few ways to investigate poverty using some of the words of the individual poor. Still, the results of this line of enquiry

so far have been limiting in some respects. Steven Taylor's categorisation of the voices of pauper authors (into formal, informative,
insistent and desperate) [30] has provided a useful initial survey but
should not be read as a comprehensive schema into which all
narrative voices fit. As a starting point the identification of four
types of voice has been helpful, but as a system of classification it
would be unhelpfully restricting. Similarly, the stories which unfold
from such letters provide some of the most poignant evidence we
have for the cruel exigencies of hardship and as such give accounts
which are rightly advertised. Yet such treatments have inevitably
given much weight to the prominence of parish relief; the rhetoric
of powerlessness adopted quite sensibly by pauper correspondents
has sometimes been accepted fairly uncritically by historians. [31]
While we would not want to make the mistake of according
significant empowerment to the poor via their interactions with
authorities it is also too bland to accept accounts of prostration.
A scratch at the surface of a pauper letter-writer's story can reveal
a much more complex (though not necessarily less heart-rending)
situation. [32]

Any acceptance of alleged powerlessness at this juncture is
surprising, given that recent developments have seen historians
increasingly according agency to the parish poor. This has been
achieved by stressing the face-to-face nature of parish government
(at least in the rural south and midlands parishes) and supposing
that they used local knowledge of people and resources, along
with powers of persuasion, to negotiate welfare deals. [33] In a related
though tangential literature, Thompson has emphasised the vigour
with which ordinary people defended and exercised their perceived
rights in his 'pre-histories of class formation', [34] collected as *Customs
in Common*. These essays chart the 'imperfect empowerment' [35]
open to ordinary people by their assertion of customary culture
(often in the teeth of technical or legal opposition). The concept
of a moral economy was central to this thesis, whereby high grain
prices, enclosure, game laws and other impositions by authority
were challenged with some temporary success, by people acting
together to obtain a measure of justice.

Therefore the positive school of thought has partly taken on
board the challenge (urged by Thompson and others) to confront
seriously the problem of writing history from below. Rebarbative
sources produced by administrative practices have been used with
some success to recover the partial biographies and stated views

of paupers. Nevertheless, some of the conclusions drawn from this work are unwarranted, based on the limitations of the research and the sources. Some challenges have been launched on the basis that authors have been insufficiently sensitive to the context of source production, a thorny question to which we return later in this chapter. Norma Landau, for instance, has questioned Snell's apparent assumption that the laws of settlement were employed solely to remove people who were nearly or actually destitute. She asserts that, prior to 1795, the laws were used by parishes to regulate the mobility of individuals and families who were not already impoverished. Such challenges to received opinion are valuable correctives.[36]

A recent exemplification of the positive view of the old poor law may be found in the textbook by Lynn Hollen Lees.[37] Unusually she covers the poor laws 1700 to 1948, thereby jettisoning consideration of the early emergence of the poor laws (so popular with pioneers in the subject) and implying the essential continuity between the old poor law, its 'new' reincarnation, and ultimately the twentieth-century welfare state. She has written of the widespread acceptance of parish relief by taxpayers and recipients alike before 1800, but after that date she identifies a hardening of attitude which saw the ratepayers become resistant to paying for relief and made the poor more reluctant to apply for it. Her chronology essentially endorses the mainstream view that the old poor law was marked by liberality (of attitude and payment) and the new poor law was implemented with a hard-nosed utility.

Therefore the first strand of recent research has been optimistic about the forms and influence of parish poor relief under the old poor law and the independence of the poor. Conversely a second strand, defined broadly, comprises work on the limits of poor relief, the variety of assistance available to the poor from other sources and the persistent necessity to exploit any and every source available. This line of thought derives from a number of complementary apprehensions about the lives of the poor and the trajectory of the historiography of parish relief. First, it has become very clear that poor households cobbled together incomes from a wide variety of sources and benefits, ranging from ultra-legitimate wage labour to the fragile advantage gained when a landlord withheld foreclosure. Second, an imbalance has been detected in the geographical basis of orthodox views about parish relief, in that understandings have been extrapolated from research that concentrates on the southern counties, particularly from south-eastern locations. Even this research on the south-east has opened the possibility that poor relief was insufficient on its own to sustain a majority of poor individuals and families.[38] Third, there is some doubt about the timing of changes in attitude from generous and expansive to mean and restrictive. Deborah Valenze and others date 'the deterioration of goodwill towards the poor' from 1780 or earlier.[39]

This corrective, cautionary sometimes pessimistic strand of thought is receiving increasing (though not overwhelming) endorsement by welfare historians. Joanna Innes has given the strand a national perspective by examining contemporary debates about the efficacy of relief, charity and other formal props.[40] Steven King has directly challenged Solar's thesis by conducting detailed research on parishes in the neglected north and west of England and demonstrating that the poor laws did not necessarily result in the formation of a reliable relief 'system'.[41] Essentially the poor law (and indeed other types of welfare) was resourced by a finite line of supply in the face of potentially infinite demand. There is some evidence that parish authorities in different places were well aware of both parochial and non-parochial sources of relief and set the supply of parish relief (or other controllable resources) at very different levels. The result of this control, be it conscious or unconscious, was a wide variation in provision within the same ostensible poor law 'system'. The aggregate effect of these controls was that there could be as many or more differences between relief, broadly defined, within England as there was between some English parishes and continental units of authority. Access to welfare was pitched accordingly, via a stringent or relaxed set of entry criteria. Pessimists conclude that, instead of marvelling at the extensive *range* of different benefits which could technically accrue to separate subsections of the poor, historians should in fact emphasise the *insufficiency* of welfare en masse.

In part this pessimistic re-evaluation of parish relief has involved a resurrection of charity, a trend in research with has emerged since 1980, although much of this focus on philanthropy continues to be directed at donors and their concerns.[42] Recipients rarely take centre stage. Nonetheless, the most sensitive accounts successfully mesh the charitable motive with the explication of a charity's operation.[43] Recently John Broad has stressed the importance of a holistic approach to welfare which takes account of both the

...ins of charity, whether deriving from landowners, clergy, other individuals or endowments derived from enclosure, and the power relations governing the scope of action (by either parish officials or charity distributors/managers).[44] Crucially he directs attention at the pre-1780 period, before population growth and the broadening reach of deep poverty diminished the relative contribution of charity to welfare. He corrects the apprehension of parish charity as ripe for embezzlement by observing the efficient flexibility with which the majority of parish funds were probably administered.[45]

This divergence between the primacy of state relief versus the complex efforts of the individual poor is unsurprising given the current unease in both government circles and wider society about the appropriate role of the state and the balance it should strike in welfare provision with (once again) proliferating voluntary organisations and charities. Yet the picture of welfare in England in 2003, of a large, unwieldy social security bill combined with eloquent proof (in the forms of evident homelessness and other sorts of visible hardship) that the state is patently not meeting even all the basic welfare needs of the modern population, introduces an interesting possibility for the earlier period being studied here. Increasing state intervention in the problem of poverty 1700–1850, either in terms of new initiatives or money spent, is not necessarily at odds with widespread involvement in the economy of makeshifts by the poor. Central or local government may have made efforts which were suspected of being too generous, but the impact of these measures at the individual or household level might have remained insufficient or even minimal (necessitating recourse to other incomes or strategies).

None of the recent research on English welfare has conclusively unseated the orthodox view that parish poor relief under the old poor law constituted a systematic welfare provision, which may not have been perfect or uniform but was recognisably functional throughout England. We want to argue that a 'system', that is to say a coherent, predictable pattern of relatively reliable relief supplying comprehensive benefits to individuals, has not been proved to exist for the whole of England. The old poor law was statutory only in as much as it compelled the propertied to contribute towards the maintenance of the poor; it did not proscribe the format of distributions or the sufficiency of its benefits. While some types of relief became 'typical' in the south-east, securing any relief, or adequate relief, was entirely uncertain in other regions. The portrait of relief in the south-east as a convincingly integrated system becomes more patchy and attenuated the further north and west the historian looks. Jordan made the unwise and sweeping assumption that only those parishes with surviving poor law accounts actually distributed poor relief in the years up to 1660. While it would be plainly unjustifiable to argue the reverse, that relief was probably dispensed even where there are no accounts, we should perhaps re-examine our assumptions about the spread and efficiency of the relief which was being given.

Origins and variants of the 'economy of makeshifts'

Explicit acknowledgement of the gaps in the poor relief 'system' and the consequent search for alternatives has been slow to take hold. As early as 1926 Dorothy Marshall referred to the 'patchwork' of relief supplied by parishes without elaborating on the characters of either the patches or the stitching. The concept was taken no further with the result that in 1981 Karel Williams too found parish relief in 1802–3 'selective, discontinuous and supplementary';[46] fuller consideration had to wait for an account of the continental European poor, which took a more inclusive approach to the question of 'welfare' by considering all avenues pursued for survival.

It is no accident that the influential expression 'economy of makeshifts' was devised to summarise the French experience of marginality. France in the later eighteenth century possessed nothing that could be described as a system of welfare. The Catholic Church in France retained some responsibility for the relief of the poor, and the foundation of charities and work schemes such as the lace factory in Bayeux undoubtedly provided a measure of relief or a route to self-help for some groups.[47] The efforts of the Church combined with the provisions of large, institutional charities in some of the larger French cities amounted to piecemeal demonstrations of goodwill but no more. The majority of people in difficulties were thrown back on their own resources. Conversely a phrase like 'economy of makeshifts' could not have been formulated to describe the distribution of welfare in the Protestant Netherlands, for example, which arguably possessed one of the most definite if decentralised 'systems' in Europe in the late seventeenth and eighteenth centuries. A partnership between the municipalities and the State Church ensured that there was a genuine safety net waiting to catch the Dutch poor.[48]

Hufton identified two basic strands to the French economy of makeshifts, corresponding to the two fundamental categories of able-bodied and impotent poor.[49] The first was physical mobility on a regional or national scale, the temporary response of under-employed agricultural labourers to seasonal jobs available in different regions (or in dire straits a permanent move, from seasonal agricultural work to unskilled urban employment), as a key survival-strategy for the healthy, adult poor. Such movement was a matter of effective coercion in that people were faced with 'the impossibility of making a living' at home.[50] Subsistence migration was clearly not new to France in the eighteenth century; what was unusual was the 'increasing dependence of communities upon these outward movements'[51] and the rising numbers of people involved.[52] The advantages were not simply or directly financial, since the net cash gain for migrant workers was typically very small, but arose from the removal of adult men from consumption of food at home, institutional support of families while men were absent, and (in the case of grain harvests) the importance of gleaning rights which accrued to wives.[53] There was also a significantly relaxed attitude to migrants surviving *en route* by begging.[54] Migrants found work as harvesters of grain or grapes, as navvies or pedlars, or as beggars with a *pique* (an account of loss or misfortune endorsed by some official or priest).

Therefore the first strand of the French 'economy of makeshifts' comprised the variety of strategies employed by the migrant/vagrant. The second strand was the practice of localised begging, mostly conducted by groups of the deserving poor. Children were effectively apprenticed in begging and varieties of gleaning, experiences which ranged from pleading for windfall fruit in the countryside, or putrefying food from market stalls, through to collections of shellfish at the coast. The elderly begged for their lives in old age, while lone mothers begged to augment earnings insufficient for themselves and dependent children. Crucially, Hufton originally detailed these makeshifts separately from formal and informal relief, and from types of marginal criminality such as petty theft or prostitution. Her makeshifts can be characterised as akin to work and other economic activities, and different to survival via external welfare assistance, subsistence crime or strictly legal self-help.

The concept of an 'economy of makeshifts' was quickly adopted by English welfare historians but came to mean something rather different from its original French definition. English makeshifts included geographical labour mobility but did not privilege it as a means of survival in the way that Hufton seemed to do, perhaps as a consequence of the English settlement laws and the absence of a *widespread* tradition of seasonal migration.[55] Similarly begging fell within its compass but was merely the most desperate of all possible makeshifts. In England the phrase has become a convenient shorthand to represent all of the ways which the mainly settled labouring poor made ends meet, the range of usually short-term strategies which might be brought into play when a family experienced unusual difficulty or was slipping into destitution. Making shift in the English context has therefore evolved into a perception of use of numerous, often local, resources by the poor over time to ensure the survival of individuals and families.

Refinements to this concept of 'makeshifts' have emerged in recent years, to tailor the original continental label to the English context and to clarify the terminology.[56] Perhaps the most subtle of these has been Joanna Innes's 'mixed economy of welfare' which shifts the focus somewhat from the proactive element or 'aggressive independence'[57] implicit in French makeshifts towards the English picture of multiple, overlapping authorities providing a plethora of benefits to differently-defined groups of the needy. Other alternatives have been suggested, but focus on the process of making a living amongst the labouring poor most widely defined. Thus Deborah Valenze's phrase 'The economics of survival' is directed at identifying the role that women in particular had in generating and holding on to an economy of makeshifts between 1700 and 1850. Robert Malcolmson's review of 'Ways of getting a living' was the first sophisticated attempt at relating the life-cycle to the economy of makeshifts for the labouring classes.[58] And Richard Wall's 'Adaptive family economy' focused on both the diversity of coping strategies available to the labouring poor and the way in which issues of life-cycle and household structure could limit or expand the options available.[59] Inevitably, periodic failure of all options must have bedeviled the survival strategies of the poor, the 'fasts ... which obviously operate as a dole in aid of wages'.[60]

Uncovering an English economy of makeshifts: the issue of sources

Elegant revisions of the rough and ready theoretical and termino-logical basis of the concept of the economy of makeshifts have thus been made to take account of the peculiar circumstances of the English welfare scene. Yet what is clear from the historiography is that empirical identification, quantification and analysis of the integrated economy of makeshifts at local and regional level has not kept pace with refinements in the conceptual basis of the phrase. How did the poor and the poor law balance the different elements of the economy of makeshifts in response to different life-cycle stages or different causes and durations of poverty? What was the particular place of work and kinship in the economy of makeshifts? How important was working-class self-help in an economy of making do? What impact did the rapid transition of the English population from a rural to an urban industrial population have on the value and composition of the economy of makeshifts? What were the regional differences in the flavour and value of the economy of makeshifts? What was the impact of gender? Was the economy of makeshifts quite fragile and in need of constant remoulding or was it resilient in the face of changes in land tenure and work location? What was the total value of the economy of makeshifts at local level, and what sort of living could its exploi-tation yield? How was the constant tension between supply of welfare from a widely conceived economy of makeshifts and poten-tially wide demand, notably at times of trade cycle stress, reconciled? In particular, what impact did access criteria have on the usefulness of the economy of makeshifts? Did different elements of the economy of makeshifts have the capacity to respond to local need at radically different speeds? How did perceptions of the role of, and eligibility for, the economy of makeshifts differ between people caught in grinding whole-life poverty and those who only experi-enced the odd incident of need? How did individuals and the family as a unit interact in garnering resources from a local economy of makeshifts? Did middling people recognise the importance of an economy of makeshifts and go out of their way to create extra strands to this economy, as they did for instance in Italy? [61]

In contrast to that on the continent, the English historiography provides only partial and limited answers to these important

questions for the central period (1700–1850) covered by this book.[62]
The limitations and complexities of the source base available to
the English welfare historian goes some way to explaining this
situation. Thus research on the economy of makeshifts is compelled
to exploit a source base which is both voluminous and patchy,
particularly if the future agenda wishes to move beyond the con-
jectural scope of makeshifts towards at least a partial quantification
for different strands of that economy. The most significant sources
for English welfare in terms of their survival quantity, the papers
generated by parish poor relief, can be exploited for this purpose
but they are both enticing and problematic. The documentary trail
outside parish collections is more sparse, more difficult to unearth
and highly variable in quality. This section will consider these two
(admittedly artificial) categories in turn.

Volumes and papers depicting parish welfare can also contain
fugitive evidence of alternative survival strategies by the poor who
asked for, received or were denied relief. Such evidence is usually
found in those documents created at the start of a relationship
between the poor and their parish, or where the responsibility to
relieve was subject to ongoing negotiation, such as settlement
examinations, petitions for assistance,[63] or vestry minutes. The
content of these genres is unreliable for two reasons, namely
the precise nature of their content and the manner of their
interpretation. First the survival of ostensible 'vestry minutes', for
example, is no guarantee of a sure route into the criteria employed
for welfare decision-making or to insights into applicants' circumstances. All too often a repository catalogue will indicate the
presence of minutes, only to conceal the paucity of their content.
At their thinnest, vestry minutes will be confined to the revelation
that meetings were held on specific days, appointed named officials, or took managerial decisions at parish rather than individual
level such as the periodic determination to sweep all poor children
into apprenticeships. Such material cannot be turned to any
purpose in the historiography of makeshifts. It is relatively unusual
to find minutes which account for the fine tuning of applications
by the poor and vestry responses over a period of time (in other
words, not just for the duration of one or two meetings), but these
do exist. Minutes from the early nineteenth century for the vestry
of Garstang, a small Lancashire town with a stringent attitude to
relief, reveal the full potential of the source for makeshifts.[64] The
minutes comprise a compilation of poor people's circumstances,

in terms of their family and dependants, their employment record and their immediate perception of deprivation requiring intervention, and the vestry's rejection, acceptance or conditional terms with which the request was met. For example, in November 1815 John Pedder 'attended and wanted some relief. He admits being in constant employ at the castle and earning 6s a week plus meat. He has only a wife and 3 children. His rent is paid by the town. Resolved that he is to have no further relief.' Minutes like these can be utilised to illuminate the interplay between parish relief and other props such as earnings (or perceptions of earning potential), kinship support, pawning, friendly society membership and the use of apprenticeship to lighten the family burden from adolescent consumption. Regrettably, like pauper letters before 1800, their survival is rare.

Second, any source which is essentially a veiled or direct request for money or other help is suspect, raising interpretative problems, because the applicant had a direct material interest in its success. Therefore the originator of the request may be supplying a cool, impartial account or be responsible for some manipulation in presenting their case, ranging from mild exaggeration and emotive language to outright lies (of assertion or omission). This is a suspicion which hangs over all formal and informal petitions, and research relying heavily on, say, pauper letters requires considerable caution and dexterity if historians want to attempt anything other than an analysis of the language of request. Taylor, Sokoll and Andrew have argued for some reliance on the surveillance powers of contemporaries to ensure that gross misrepresentation did not occur in begging letters.[65] It was certainly the case that parishes might conduct checks, either by their own officers or via a third party, to verify the basic premise of a petition, but these checks were ad hoc rather than a compulsory element of the relieving process. All styles of petition 'had to be credible to be effective',[66] but a depiction might be theoretically credible without being applicable to the case where it was employed. It is not clear that there is any satisfactory answer to this dilemma, but a measure of verification might rely on proof that a case was endorsed or investigated at the time, assumptions about proximity to the relevant welfare agency giving rise to fear of detection (or distance, potentially enabling a less accurate account), and external evidence such as parish registers (for checks on measurable matters, for example, did the family comprise the number of children cited by an applicant?). Even setting aside the degree of veracity of any one request, genres of petition contain insistent refrains which strongly suggest that there was an unofficial format being followed by writers/composers derived from the character of their need/request and that there were tacit limits on the material included. Petitions for clemency from convicted criminals, for example, unsurprisingly and routinely asserted a previously good character. They also maintained a demure, subordinate tone and were seemingly less volatile in their mode of expression than pauper letters.[67] Therefore it is unclear how reticent historians should be in utilising these attractive if slippery sources. Peter Mandler has argued that charitable reluctance to relieve the able-bodied meant that 'some emergency or mitigating circumstance had to be manufactured' by applicants, whose stories were consequently 'theatrical'.[68] Natalie Davis found that letters of request contain much material suited to tangential studies (in this case, such as kinship support, employment, or crime as a choice for economic survival) without the need for undue hesitation arising from worries about 'literary construction'.[69] Finally, uncertainties about authorship raise questions about whose account is being given. Is the written version an attempt by a barely literate person to write a convincing request or a fluent and persuasive piece of propaganda written by a well-educated and skilful manipulator? Is it a dictated account from an illiterate petitioner written down by a friend or neighbour, or the creative composition of a third party? It will not always be important to know for sure which of these origins applied in any one case, but such ambiguities make it necessary to proceed with a measure of caution and qualification when dealing with requests of any kind. Such lessons also apply to other sorts of English sources.

The extant sources outside of parish collections have survived and been catalogued erratically. This phenomenon is clearly the result of a wide variety of people and officials being responsible for document collections and changing decisions over time. What mixture of impulses prompts one family or business to retain every scrap of paper despite pressures on space and doubts about utility, and another to burn them, or give in to external injunction, for instance submitting them to wartime paper reclamation projects? It is probably attributable at least in part to an emphasis (an assumed interest by source retainers and preservers prior to professional archival interest) on the supply side of welfare or material benefits. In the case of formal charity, for example, it is possible to infer from repeated patterns of document retention and omission that there has been an assumption of enduring interest in the legal right of a charity to its income (via ownership of land or investments) and much less concern with the nature of demand (who applied for disbursements); 'charity was a business of giving but not receiving'.[70] Similarly, gauges of earnings by the poor are reliant on business records beyond deeds of ownership and accounts of operation, requiring those meticulous daily records of employment most likely to have been discarded after their immediate obvious use had expired. This sort of bias is also detectable in sources relating to most, if not all, other formal organisations with a role in the economy of makeshifts. Pawnbroking is perhaps an extreme example of a survival strategy for which very little detailed evidence survives. The pledgebook used in this volume by Alannah Tomkins is one of the only known examples of this type of source for England, revealing the internal workings of a pawnbroking business, relevant before 1800. Alternative external avenues for approaching the topic survive in the forms of references to pawning in the records of criminal prosecutions (either in court papers or in newspaper reports of crimes committed or trials prosecuted), in redemptions by third parties (usually overseers of the poor) and the existence of formal pawnshops may be traced in early directories. However, the full potential of these possibilities has yet to be explored, and the feasibility of such exploration is only now improving via electronic cataloguing of source content.[71] But it is also true that none of them affords comparable material on the day-to-day usage of pawnshops as a component in the economy of makeshifts.

Furthermore, multiple strands of this economy were composed of resources which were never supposed to be backed up by any records at all. Kinship and neighbourly support is probably the most obvious example here, where help must be inferred from demographic potential (families having co-resident kin, or with kin living in the same or nearby communities) or from direct, although often coincidental confirmation within letters, diaries, wills or accounts. Wherever proof of minute detail is found, it is inevitably partial and discontinuous; one family member might record their gifts to poorer kin for a matter of months or years without revealing the practice of the whole family or their own impulses outside the chronology of the surviving record. It is for these reasons that Sam Barrett in his contribution to this volume uses nominal record linkage to try and infer the character of family and kinship support in the economy of makeshifts from large-scale demographic and poor law data.

These considerations of source quantity and quality have inhibited a fuller exploration of the English economy of makeshifts. But there are routes forward which will permit a more subtle weighing of makeshifts at the level of household, community and region, particularly in relation to the better-documented strands of that economy. Leigh Shaw-Taylor has recently demonstrated the value of revisiting apparently well-known sources, published comments on agriculture in the late eighteenth and early nineteenth centuries, to argue that most labourers did not have common rights and therefore could not have been proletarianised by the loss of rights at the time of parliamentary enclosure.[72] Lyn MacKay has used Old Bailey Sessions Papers to show the potential connections between petty theft and pawning as extensions of neighbourly borrowing and exchange which went wrong.[73] Energetic pursuit of unused sources, and particularly creative use of familiar sources, will contribute to a better appreciation of the English economy of makeshifts in the future.

Uncovering an English economy of makeshifts: the lessons of the historiography

For now though, we must focus on the current lessons of the English historiography. As a starting point, it is important to recognise that our most comprehensive perspective on the day-to-day operation of the economy of makeshifts comes from cultural and oral historians focusing on urban Britain in the late nineteenth and early twentieth centuries. Carl Chinn, Elizabeth Roberts and Ellen Ross, for instance, have variously emphasised neighbourhood networks, pawning, petty work opportunities, kinship networks and imaginative engagement with the poor law as central coping strategies for the urban poor in a series of challenging methodological and empirical books and articles.[74] In similar vein, urban historians of seventeenth-century England have emphasised the importance of neighbourhood, kinship and work as coping strategies both for recent migrants and native town dwellers.[75]

The eighteenth and early nineteenth centuries have generated a more disparate direct literature on the economy of makeshifts. Thus welfare historians have often drawn an implicit (and sometimes explicit) contrast between the potential dimensions of the economy of makeshifts in the rural south and that in the west, midlands and north. The early poor law historians who dealt with the emergence of an allowance system and associated institutionalised coping strategies such as the roundsman system in the rural south, east and midlands were in effect pointing to an economy of makeshifts that had been denuded of key foundations by the later eighteenth century.[76] Keith Snell in 1985 put more flesh on these bones and made the comparison more explicit.[77] He traced the decline of the potential of the economy of makeshifts in the eighteenth-century south, noting the disintegration of its central components. Enclosure (and the associated termination of customary rights on the fields and in the forests), the decline of dynamic proto-industrial structures, the lethargic growth of southern towns, changes in work practices that prevented men and women being a foil to each other in earning terms and changes in the scale of charity, combined to generate fragile household economies at the very bottom of the social scale. Detailed analysis of household budgets subsequent to 1985 has apparently confirmed the justice of Snell's analysis.[78] Faced with the breakdown of the family economy in the rural south and midlands, as well as inexorable population increase, the poor law intervened in a major way to guarantee welfare. It became 'the' core plank on the welfare scaffold.

By contrast, work on the economy of makeshifts in the north and west by Richard Smith and others has emphasised its continued vibrancy.[79] Here, very considerable areas of waste and common remained, rural industry was much longer lived, towns were more dynamic, northern families (according to Eden[80]) were less demanding about diets, clothing and housing than their southern counterparts, and traditional perquisites, even in very advanced agricultural areas such as the East Riding,[81] were more widely and firmly entrenched. Of course, the starkness of this contrast must be tempered. An allowance system or some variant of family support was common even in the north and west, where the economy of makeshifts was nominally stronger.[82] The period covered by this volume also sees the transition from rural to urban makeshift economies at national level and it is hard to be sure that we are comparing like with like when attempting to reconstruct the role of the economy of makeshifts in the north and south. And, as we are now well aware, intra-regional variation in the role and character of the poor law (and by implication the role and character of the economy of makeshifts) could be very considerable indeed. Nonetheless, a broad difference in the strength and composition of the economy of makeshifts between north and south has remained an enduring part of the literature and its most significant organising framework. It is important to remember, however, that this writing on the economy of makeshifts emerges not from specific attempts to look at the subject itself, but as a mechanism for understanding perceived spatial differences in the scale of poverty and the response of the poor law to that poverty in terms of the number of people recognised as poor and the generosity of its treatment.[83]

Some local, rather than regional or comparative regional, studies have picked up rather more directly on the strongly held view of contemporary politicians and pamphleteers that there was a link to be fostered between collective welfare provision through the poor law and alternative ways of making ends meet such as work, charity and kinship at community level.[84] Roger Smith, in his study of Nottingham between 1800 and 1850, points to 'that modest area of poor relief that lay outside the orbit of the poor law guardians' and lists friendly societies, endowed charities and voluntary charities as the main coping strategies outside the poor law. By the 1830s and 1840s, some 16 per cent of the population in Nottingham were contributing to friendly societies, there was a co-operative shop with 64 members, almost 1,000 people were members of a Provident Medical Aid Society, endowed charities had invested assets of £37,000 plus land and houses, the hospital and dispensary were spending £4,000 per annum on health care and the Quaker Benevolent Society was distributing £1,000 per annum to the needy. In total the aggregate, calculable economy of makeshifts in the town in 1840 (i.e. that derived from charity and self-help) amounted to around £9,000 per annum, almost one half of the amount spent on poor law expenditure in that year. This comprehensive study mirrors the best studies of urban communities on the continent.[85] Jean Robin too has specifically addressed the economy of makeshifts in her study of Colyton, albeit at the very end of the period considered by this volume. She suggests that 'welfare' in the village had three (partly overlapping and partly discrete) strands – the poor law, the charitable funds administered by the Feoffees and two Mutual Provident Societies – and that by the 1890s over 90 per cent of the cohort born in the 1850s had turned to either the poor law or charity, or both.[86] At the other end of our period, John Broad has emphasised the pressure that movements such as disafforestation could place on the local economy of makeshifts and shown how attempts to create alternative planks in that economy of makeshifts might backfire. His analysis implies that navigating a yearly living when on the margins of poverty was an acquired skill and one which required familiarity with the seasonal and life-cycle manipulation of different welfare avenues.[87]

Most community studies, however, deal with aspects of the economy of makeshifts (and often the welfare process more widely) as a tangential issue. Keith Wrightson and David Levine, for instance, have traced the micro-impact of the development of the coal industry in the seventeenth-century north-east, noting for the village of Whickham [88] that industrialisation created a conflict between coal mine owners who wanted to exploit common and waste land through open cast mining and the building of tramways, and rural people or seasonally unemployed coal miners who depended upon such land for a significant part of their subsistence.[89] Similarly, Barry Reay uses a raft of linked nominal data for villages in nineteenth-century rural Kent to suggest that while kin did not offer support in the economy of makeshifts by varying their residential arrangements, they did live very close to each other, forming *de facto* extended families which could share resources, care obligations and negotiate more effectively with poor law authorities, employers and vendors of goods.[90] Pat Hudson and Steve King pick up on these sorts of themes in their study of industrialising communities in eighteenth- and nineteenth-century West Riding, stressing that kinship was a key factor in keeping people off poor relief but also highlighting the fact that proto-industrial communities had a unique capability to generate and regenerate earning opportunities for women and children even when movements such as technological redundancy spread across entire districts.[91]

Historians of rural and industrial popular protest have also displayed a tangential interest in the economy of makeshifts given that unrest was frequently a reflection of challenges to traditional perquisites, work patterns, the withdrawal of access to certain resources or the decline of traditional obligations and relationships which had been engendered by the presence and management of makeshift resources. Thus Freeman contends that the taking of deer in Whichwood forest continued to be regarded as a right by the very poorest elements of the villages around the forest even when law and ownership transition brought a nominal ending of such rights.[92] In the same vein, embezzlement, the ability to create time in the working week for alternative welfare opportunities, and regulated access to foodstuffs sold in the market-place (which was in effect part of the economy of makeshifts for urban workers) were vigorously defended when they came under pressure.[93] Family historians too have found it necessary to engage with strands of the economy of makeshifts. Will Coster's finding that bequests in wills came to be concentrated ever more strongly on the nuclear family during the eighteenth century has consequences for our appreciation of the economy of makeshifts, both because it implies a restriction of the amount of resources available through inheritance to poorer family members and because it is symbolic of the shrinking role of kinship in that economy of makeshifts.[94] Richard Wall's analysis begins to address the question of the practical value of the economy of makeshifts more systematically, though in the context of understanding the size and structure of the early modern family. He concludes that the work of women could add 30 per cent to the yearly household income and that receipt of poor relief could provide a further supplement of 9 per cent of the annual income of poor labouring families. If we add the 8–13 per cent that families might also gain from their gleaning activities, a point which is reviewed again below, we can begin to get a broadly quantitative view of the economy of makeshifts from family history research.[95]

Historians of religious groups, such as the Methodists and Quakers, have also tackled the economy of makeshifts indirectly, noting that such groups usually provided informal charitable aid to those who shared their views and often, as we saw from the work of Smith on Nottingham, to the wider community as well. Rex Watson's analysis of Quaker charity in the Marsden area of north-east Lancashire in the first half of the nineteenth century is exemplary, demonstrating that from their own resources and local charitable collections the Quakers were able to distribute clothing, food, cash and other relief to considerable numbers of the marginal families who combined work with petty selling and other income generation strategies because they were not eligible for poor relief in the harsh poor law regime of this county.[96] Finally, historians of gender have engaged particularly vigorously with the theoretical and practical idea of the economy of make-shifts. Valenze's gendered account of the Industrial Revolution, for instance, identifies poor women as ubiquitous. She suggests that such poor women were regarded as a pressing social and economic problem at the same time as some contemporary com-mentators were identifying their ability in bringing together and managing the different strands of the economy of makeshifts as the way to solve an endemic poverty problem in eighteenth- and nineteenth-century England.[97] Penelope Lane deals more directly with one of the strands, offering a gendered view of what she calls the 'informal economy' of resource generation beyond the limits of the law. Using material from Leicestershire and Derbyshire, Lane suggests that because of their demo-economic position, because they did not always get the access to poor relief that their objective economic position might have warranted and because they were hit particularly hard by movements such as enclosure or rural industrial decline, women had a particular need to engage with earning opportunities in the borderland between work and crime. This borderland was complex, encompassing former cus-tomary rights such as embezzlement and gleaning or wood gathering and other activities such as stealing and/or selling stolen goods, defrauding the poor law and petty brewing beyond the law of licensing, and it was movable according to national legislative changes and the broad thrust of case law in petty and quarter sessions. Ultimately, however, engagement with the informal econ-omy could provide all or most of family welfare, particularly at times of stress such as trade downturns or bad harvests which drove up food prices.[98]

More work on all of these themes could be reviewed. The key point, however, is that there has been relatively *little work directly on the economy of makeshifts as a collection of coping strategies* in either a theoretical or analytical sense. The detailed balancing of the potential resources available to those enmeshed in the economy of makeshifts undertaken by Catharina Lis for Antwerp is missing. Even rarer are attempts in micro-studies to use nominal linkage techniques in order to trace individuals through different 'welfare' sources (charity accounts, crime records, pawnbrokers' account books, etc.) at different life-cycle points, the starting point for creating the typologies of individual and family strategies which would really revolutionise the discussion of English welfare patterns and allow us to address some of the rhetorical questions with which we started this section. This neglect is frustrating in two senses. First, because, as Roger Smith shows in his study of Nottingham, it is possible both to identify the individual strands of the economy of makeshifts for any place or at any time, *and* to find the sources to say something useful about these individual strands. Second, because many of these individual strands have their own distinctive historiography which has rarely been linked to other aspects of the economy of makeshifts in either a theoretical or empirical sense.

The literatures dealing with kinship, crime and pawnbroking are reviewed elsewhere in this volume – by Sam Barrett, Heather Shore and Alannah Tomkins respectively – and we return to the literature on coping strategies such as demographic realignment in the conclusion. To move further, and provide an all-embracing overview of the multiple literatures touching somehow on the economy of makeshifts, would be an enormous task for which there is no space here. We hope, however, that we have shown how little work has been done on relating single coping strategies to the wider economy of makeshifts and to creating a generalised methodological or analytical framework of the sort that Hufton has suggested for France or Catharina Lis for the Netherlands. Collectively, our contributors make some headway on these issues, and it is to the lessons from their chapters that we now turn.

Cultures of poverty and making do – the contribution of this volume

The chapters in this book represent the single most significant attempt in print to supply the English 'economy of makeshifts' with a solid, empirical basis and to advance the concept of make-shifts from a rather woolly label (used all too often without thought for its meaning) to a more precise (if inclusive) delineation. The themes which emerge pertain to geographical regions and com-munities, both material and cultural considerations in the composition of makeshifts, the quantification of multiple strands of makeshifts and (less wholeheartedly) to life-cycles for the poor.

In chapters 2 and 3 Steve Hindle and Margaret Hanly deal with the general and particular ways in which 'makeshifts' might be constructed. In the only chapter to deal explicitly with the rural agricultural poor, Hindle unpicks the interrelations between the benefits derived from access to (including technically illegal assertion of) common rights alongside parish poor relief and voluntary charity. By focusing attention on three parishes in Rockingham Forest (Northamptonshire) and looking at three successive attempts to achieve parliamentary enclosure, he reconstructs the shifting hierarchy of 'Fuel, dole and bread' (an explicit case study of Innes's 'mixed economy of welfare'). The centrality of common rights for survival is extrapolated from their vigorous defence by propertyless cottagers in 1607 and again in the 1720s. But the value of those rights was in decline (the commons risked exhaustion in the early eighteenth century) as was the ability of the cottagers to mount an effective protection campaign, such that cottagers's actions in the 1790s were 'futile'. Similarly the chapter looks at the delicate role of a local bread charity, hedged about with stringent and persistent access requirements, which sustained a welfare role so far but no further. The material value of the charity fell, prompting a decline in its symbolic significance. These long-term trends are set against the rising importance of the parish dole; expenditure increased sharply after enclosure signalling a waning of the independence conferred by access to commons and a rising, forcible dependence on relief. Hindle concludes that the gradually changing balance of these elements gave rise to a distinctive 'forest' economy of makeshifts which may have been precarious but could be predictable. In studying the sweep of income props which were technically available over a lengthy period, in the face of patchy manuscript survivals, the chapter provides a model of what might be accomplished elsewhere at the community level. Still it is not in the business of unpicking the minute experiences of individual households, such as the impact of a charity loaf on a household budget.

The family and household perspective is picked up by Margaret Hanly. Focusing on Lancashire, and using a combination of early nineteenth-century censuses of the poor and the record books of Quaker women who dispensed charity, she deals with people labelled as 'poor' by their communities. Her observation that many 'poor' people had little or nothing to do with the communal welfare system has resonance with many recent trends in welfare historiography. Working out from this observation, she is able to begin the process of tracing the intricate and (at household level) diverse relationship between poor relief, kinship support, work and charity. She suggests that, in Lancashire at least, work was the mainstay of the family-based makeshift economy, even for those on poor relief. It was relatively rare for anyone labelled as 'poor' by their communities to be undertaking no paid work at all. Indeed, in the sense that the poor law itself was a big employer in most localities, relief was tied to work through the institution itself. Other avenues in the makeshift economy also loom large in the censuses of the poor, and Hanly is able to suggest that kinship and (more widely) social credit, were deemed by contemporaries to be important elements in their makeshift economies. Such observations link well with later contributors to the book. Moreover, Hanly also confirms the paltry allowances awarded through the poor law and implicitly contrasts them with the relatively generous schemes operated by individual and institutionalised charities such as the Quakers in Lancashire rural communities.

This theme – the place of formal, voluntary charity in the makeshift economy, particularly in the form of assistance conferred upon the poor by the prosperous – is developed further in chapter 4 by Sarah Lloyd, who begins to unravel the material and cultural implications of incorporating charity within survival strategies. She employs the records of the Welsh charity school in London (opened 1718) to exemplify both the benefits and meanings drawn from charity by recipients. An initial survey of the short- and long-term material gains accrued from charity schooling (primarily in the form of clothing worn by children or otherwise used by families, or as a route to an apprenticeship) is followed by a broader consideration of charity as a means of coping and the contextual rhetoric of charitably-disposed commentators. The chapter concludes that charity donors had little interest in any economy of makeshifts (even if they were essentially aware of its operation), being wholly concerned with the apparatus of giving (committee meetings, portraits of founders, celebratory feasts) and the creation of social distance (via patronage and deference). Nonetheless, it also argues that it is unhelpful and unsubtle to reduce the poor 'to a set of objects in search of objects'. Involvement in charity as a recipient inspired participation and belonging, which might be valued intrinsically and used to generate further opportunities and sources of protection.

Meanwhile, the deployment of crime as a means to get by, on

the part of the idle and disorderly, was a standard theme in eighteenth-century pamphlet literature (which established something of an artificial dichotomy between criminals and the 'honest' poor). In the second of our chapters touching on London and its environs, Heather Shore tackles the complicated relationship between poverty and social crime in the capital by looking at both contemporary published opinion and the evidence of the courts. Networks of criminal contact were demonised by contemporaries, but it is now plausible to emphasise the similarities between criminal networks and the more familiar (and less contentious) meshing of family, friends and neighbours into a physically and emotionally sustaining community. Even in London criminals were far from being anonymous loners or strangers; rather, they belonged. In such a setting the commission of crime, as either a response to a crisis or a long-term solution to discontinuous employment, was a rational, everyday and minor occurrence involving an unsurprising 'overlap' of poor/criminal populations. Yet it must be acknowledged that these were communities with a unique feature which could limit the lifespan of any grouping; informants regularly impeached their fellows, shutting down partnerships or gangs and forcing realignments of loyalty. Furthermore the chapter identifies the importance of life-cycle to induction into crime and its continuance. Contemporaries held up apprenticeship as a vulnerable time replete with temptations to dishonesty, but the records of crimes prosecuted give prominence to thefts by servants and prostitutes. As these labels suggest late adolescence and early adulthood were key periods for prosecution. The London evidence also indicates that women between 30 and 45 were prone to indictment for receiving, but were peculiarly difficult to convict as a direct result of their being embedded within a partially protective community. In this way Shore reworks familiar sources to stress the integrated nature of poor and criminal populations.

Little is known about the function of pawnbroking for the survival strategies of the urban poor, beyond the stereotypical complaints in print of the connection between pawnbrokers and criminal receiving and depictions of the role of pawnbroking for the later nineteenth-century poor. In the first of two chapters grappling with nominal linkage exercises, Alannah Tomkins uses the only known pawnbroker's pledgebook surviving for the eighteenth century to unravel patterns of use by pawnshop customers and their connections with the parish poor. A survey of pamphlet literature touching on credit, debt and pawnbroking reveals that outspoken, damning criticisms of pawnbrokers were often repeated but rarely qualified by any consideration of the cash flow exigencies of poverty. The example of a pawnshop in York, run by a reputable urban citizen, demonstrates a broader usage of its credit facilities than was conceived in the literature. A significant minority of the city's population found their way to the shop over the eighteen-month period of the surviving pledge-book; many used it only once, while others slipped into a pattern of frequent or regular use. These usages suggest that the shop acted like a relatively respectable bank for the poor rather than a shameful recourse. Crucially there were only slender, discernible connections between the pawning poor and parish paupers; the pawnshop and the parish were used successively rather than concurrently in a downward spiral of impoverishment.

Sam Barrett uses similar techniques to examine the theoretical and actual place of kinship support in the survival strategies of the poor. The historiography of kinship in the context of welfare has tended to circle around the measurable presence of kin, particularly co-resident kin, and to handle more cautiously the topic of effective kin (latterly including fictive kin) as welfare agents. Barrett surveys the contradictions in the existing literature before embarking on an assessment of the functionality of kin in six townships in the West Riding of Yorkshire 1700–1820. Family reconstitution data is linked to poor relief payments to show an unmistakable inverse relationship between presence of kin in a community and the receipt of poor relief, but it also exposes some of the subtleties in the family/parish support nexus. In these townships selected individuals with a high density of kin in the *neighbourhood* (which in this study was not mechanically defined as the township but included adjacent administrative blocks) took poor relief as a short-term aid, between the onset of a crisis and the emergence of effective support from families. Furthermore the presence or absence of lateral male kin had a substantial impact on neediness; people who lacked brothers, and uncles on the father's side of a family, were disproportionately likely to need relief for a protracted period. In an attempt to gauge the connectedness of people who were poor but did not apply to their parish, a cross-reference of those receiving relief with the recipients of formal charity shows that charities favoured applicants with good kinship connections. This finding points up the potential importance of the extent of kinship links for supplying or easing access to other sources of support. Still, the levels of kin-connectedness in Yorkshire contrast sharply with those found in Essex and Surrey, suggesting that these findings are regionally viable but that it would be unwise to extrapolate them automatically to geographical communities beyond the West Riding.

In his contribution to this volume, Steve King pulls the discernible threads of the economy of makeshifts together to present the aggregate welfare picture in the rural industrial north-west. An analysis of the scope and sufficiency of poor-relief payments in the locale finds the parish provision lacking in most respects. The evidence from vestry minutes points to a sizeable population who asserted claims to relief but were not awarded any, and shows that successful applicants faced chronically inadequate poor-relief payments and relief dispensed in an unexpected or unpalatable form. The chapter isolates the strands of the makeshift economy most pertinent to survival in the region and weighs their changing significance over the period 1750 to 1834. Two strands in particular, charity and work (in the latter case managed in conjunction with relief to yield a predictable income), generated monetary benefits which rivalled or outstripped parish payments alone. Finally a micro-study of the Lancashire township of Cowpe illustrates both the quantity and complexity of the makeshift economy. The 'poor' individuals revealed in payments from the parish and from both formal and informal charity funds are linked up to the employees collecting wages from mill work or 'putting out' work, and to the people carrying end of year debts at the local mill shop. Clearly this sort of nominal linkage exercise is unusual and ambitious. It has entailed making a number of assumptions about additional payments, such as the informal charity practised by local mill-owners who did not keep meticulous personal accounts, but the survival of a couple of excellent sources pertaining to Cowpe obviate the need for over-stretched extrapolation. The result is the only research thus far to demonstrate conclusively the relative significance of each makeshift and the concomitant minority role played by poor relief.

The overall contribution of these chapters is the furtherance of concepts crucial to the appreciation of makeshifts. Regional differences stand out strongly as a central mediator in the hierarchy of makeshifts, both in the extent to which welfare needs were mopped up by poor law solutions and in the range of available alternatives. In the latter case, these might be defined very obviously by geography (such as proximity to a resource like Rockingham Forest) or in less immediately visible ways (such as kinship and work cultures). Clearly any attempt to quantify the resources available through the different strands of the makeshift economy at community level, possibly through econometrics, will depend on the survival of numerous extraordinary sources; all too often the survival of one is rare enough. Still, the chapters here show conclusively, we hope, that it is possible to identify key players in the assembly of makeshifts and to anticipate the impact of urban-rural/rural-industrial shifts on the balance and access conditions of the economy of makeshifts. These contributions work either at the level of resources technically available for the community according to contemporary accounts or actually garnered by individuals via nominal linkage; future work may hope to discover whether it is possible to engage with the knottier problem of the individual-family dichotomy.

Notes

1 O. H. Hufton, *The Poor of Eighteenth-Century France 1750–1789* (Oxford, Clarendon, 1974).

2 S. and B. Webb, *English Local Government volume 7: English Poor Law History part 1: The Old Poor Law* (London, Green, 1927).

3 D. Marshall, *The English Poor in the Eighteenth Century* (London, Methuen, 1926).

4 For an early, substantial example of this genre see E. M. Hampson, *The Treatment of Poverty in Cambridgeshire 1597–1834* (Cambridge, Cambridge University Press, 1934); there are numerous examples of local history articles taking a similar theme and stance.

5 In this way the early writers bought in to Malthus's interpretation of early nineteenth-century population growth and, by implication, his advocation of sexual restraint: T. R. Malthus, *An Essay on the Principle of Population* (London, 1803).

6 J. L. and B. Hammond, *The Village Labourer* (London, Longman, 1978), p. 110.

7 J. L. and B. Hammond, *The Town Labourer* (London, Longman, 1978).

8 W. K. Jordan, *Philanthropy in England 1480–1660* (London, Allen and Unwin, 1959); W. G. Bittle and R. T. Lane, 'Inflation and philanthropy in England: a re-assessment of W. K. Jordan's data', *Economic History Review*, 29 (1976).

9 B. Rodgers, *Cloak of Charity: Studies in Eighteenth-Century Philanthropy* (London, Methuen, 1949).

10 D. Owen, *English Philanthropy 1660–1960* (Cambridge, Yale University Press, 1964).

11 Examples which range from tangential studies to those deeply implicated in marginal survival strategies include J. Styles, 'Clothing the North: the supply of non-elite clothing in the eighteenth-century north of England', *Textile History*, 25 (1994); T. Henderson, *Disorderly Women in Eighteenth-Century London* (London, Longman, 1999); L. Shaw-Taylor, 'Labourers, cows, common rights and parliamentary enclosure: the evidence of contemporary comment, c. 1760–1810', *Past and Present*, 171 (2001).

12 G. Boyer, *An Economic History of the English Poor Law, 1750–1850* (Cambridge, Cambridge University Press, 1990), particularly ch. 5, which maintains that income supplements did indeed have a role in the rising birth rate.

13 K. Williams, *From Pauperism to Poverty* (London, Routledge and Kegan Paul, 1981) see ch. 1 and especially p. 39; of course comprehensive, state-funded welfare, and other sweeping, structural measures such as a minimum wage, had been debated and been the subject of failed legislation before the 1940s, but without the critical momentum of political and popular support.

14 G. A. Oxley, *Poor Relief in England and Wales 1601–1834* (Newton Abbot, David and Charles, 1974).

15 K. D. M. Snell, *Annals of the Labouring Poor: Social Change and Agrarian England 1660–1900* (Cambridge, Cambridge University Press, 1985).

16 P. Slack, *Poverty and Policy in Tudor and Stuart England* (London, Longman, 1988).

17 P. Slack, *From Reformation to Improvement: Public Welfare in Early Modern England* (Oxford, Clarendon, 1999).

18 P. Solar, 'Poor relief and English economic development before the Industrial Revolution', *Economic History Review*, 48 (1995).

19 T. Wales, 'Poverty, poor relief and life-cycle: some evidence from seventeenth century Norfolk', in R. M. Smith (ed.), *Land, Kinship and Life Cycle* (Cambridge, Cambridge University Press, 1984), p. 356.

20 A. Tomkins, 'The experience of urban poverty – a comparison of Oxford and Shrewsbury 1740 to 1770' (unpublished DPhil, Oxford University, 1994); ch. 4 suggests that 'medical' relief, broadly defined, was not typically distributed to dependent parish paupers.

21 B. Stapleton, 'Inherited poverty and life-cycle poverty: Odiham, Hampshire', *Social History*, 18 (1993).

22 M. McIntosh, 'Networks of care in Elizabethan English towns: the example of Hadleigh, Suffolk', in P. Horden and R. M. Smith (eds), *The Locus of Care: Families, Communities, Institutions and the Provision of Welfare Since Antiquity* (London, Routledge, 1998).

23 P. Sharpe, 'Poor children as apprentices in Colyton 1798–1830', *Continuity and Change*, 6 (1991); *idem*, 'Survival strategies and stories: poor widows and widowers in early industrial England', in S. Cavallo and L. Warner (eds), *Widowhood in Medieval and Early Modern Europe* (London, Longman, 1999).

24 R. M. Smith, 'Ageing and well being in early modern England: pension trends and gender preferences under the English old poor law 1650–1800', in P. Johnson and P. Thane (eds), *Old Age from Antiquity to Post-Modernity* (London, Routledge, 1998); Cavallo and Warner, *Widowhood*; L. Botelho and P. Thane (eds), *Women and Ageing in British Society Since 1500* (Harlow, Longman, 2001); P. Thane, *Old Age in English History: Past Experiences, Present Issues* (Oxford, Oxford University Press, 2000).

25 Thane, *Old Age*, pp. 153–5.

26 S. Ottaway and S. Williams, 'Reconstructing the life-cycle experience of poverty in the time of the old poor law', *Archives*, 23 (1998).

27 Snell, *Annals*, particularly ch. 1.

28 P. Sharpe, 'The bowels of compation: a labouring family and the law c. 1790–1834', in T. Hitchcock, P. King and P. Sharpe (eds), *Chronicling Poverty: The Voices and Strategies of the English Poor 1640–1840* (Basingstoke, Macmillan, 1997).

29 T. Sokoll, 'Old age in poverty: the record of Essex pauper letters 1780–1834', in Hitchcock, King and Sharpe, *Chronicling Poverty*.

30 J. S. Taylor, 'Voices in the crowd: the Kirby Lonsdale township letters, 1809–36', in Hitchcock, King and Sharpe, *Chronicling Poverty*, pp. 111–12.

31 Taylor, 'Voices', p. 114, for example, holds that writers may have coloured their stories but did not deviate too far from their own perception of their circumstances because they were subject to scrutiny by their overseer or the overseer of their adopted township or parish. Also D. Valenze, *The First Industrial Woman* (Oxford, Oxford University Press, 1995), p. 22, who suggests that the evidence of settlement exams supports the idea that women might lack knowledge about the settlement, without acknowledging that women might have concealed their knowledge in order to manipulate their legal settlement. For a more sophisticated analysis of pauper letters see T. Sokoll, *Essex Pauper Letters, 1731–1837* (Oxford, Oxford University Press, 2001).

32 A. Tomkins, 'Poverty, kinship support and the case of Ellen Parker, 1818–1827', in S. King and R. M. Smith (eds), *The British Experience of Welfare* (forthcoming). See also T. Sokoll, 'Negotiating a living: Essex pauper letters from London, 1800–1834', in L. Fontaine and J. Schlumbohm (eds), *Household Strategies for Survival 1600–2000: Fission, Faction and Cooperation* (Cambridge, Cambridge University Press, 2000).

33 L. Hollen-Lees, *The Solidarities of Strangers: The English Poor Laws*

and the People, 1700–1948 (Cambridge, Cambridge University Press, 1998).

34 E. P. Thompson, *Customs in Common* (London, Penguin, 1993); D. Eastwood, 'History, politics and reputation: E. P. Thompson reconsidered', *History*, 85 (2000), p. 650.

35 Eastwood, 'History', p. 652.

36 N. Landau, 'The regulation of immigration, economic structures and definitions of the poor in eighteenth century England', *Historical Journal*, 33 (1990).

37 Hollen-Lees, *Solidarities*.

38 R. M. Smith, 'Charity, self-interest and welfare: reflections from demographic and family history', in M. Daunton (ed.), *Charity, Self-Interest and Welfare in the English Past* (London, UCL Press, 1996), p. 38, which both endorses and puts a different perspective on earlier work, such as D. Thompson, '"I am not my father's keeper": families and the elderly in nineteenth-century England', *Law and History Review*, 2 (1984).

39 Valenze, *The First*, p. 182; Smith, 'Charity, self-interest', p. 39, finds the value of parish pensions stagnating and declining in real terms after 1750.

40 J. Innes, 'The "mixed economy of welfare" in early modern England: assessments of the options from Hale to Malthus', in Daunton, *Charity*.

41 See amongst other work S. King, *Poverty and Welfare in England 1700–1850. A Regional Perspective* (Manchester, Manchester University Press, 2000), particularly ch. 7.

42 F. K. Prochaska, *Women and Philanthropy in Nineteenth-Century England* (Oxford, Clarendon, 1980); D. Andrew, *Philanthropy and Police: Charity in Eighteenth-Century London* (Oxford, Princeton University Press, 1989).

43 See for instance M. Gorsky, *Patterns of Philanthropy: Charity and Society in Nineteenth-Century Bristol* (Woodbridge, Boydell, 1999).

44 J. Broad, 'Parish economies of welfare, 1650–1834', *Historical Journal*, 42 (1999).

45 *Ibid.*, pp. 1002–3.

46 Williams, *From Pauperism*, p. 39.

47 O. Hufton, *Bayeux in the Late Eighteenth Century: A Social Study* (Oxford, Oxford University Press, 1967), pp. 90–1.

48 R. Jutte, *Poverty and Deviance in Early Modern Europe* (Cambridge, Cambridge University Press, 1994), p. 114.

49 Hufton, *The Poor*; the delineation of these categories was not innovative in itself, but drew on much older work by, among others, Le Roy Ladurie.

50 *Ibid.*, p. 70.

51 *Ibid.*, p. 71.

52 *Ibid.*, p. 127.

53 *Ibid.*, p. 76.

54 *Ibid.*, p. 79.

55 Clearly there was regional movement in search of work associated with particular localities, such as between Kent and London for example, but there was nothing within the confines of England on the scale of the French experience.

56 Refinements have also been offered in the continental literature. Most recently, Fontaine and Schlumbohm have employed the phrase '*Household* Survival Strategies' in order to recognise implicitly that 'getting by' was a function of the deployment of household labour/effort on the supply side and household negotiation on the demand side, with both processes played out against the backdrop of the constraints of society, economy and culture. See L. Fontaine and J. Schlumbohm, 'Household strategies for survival: an introduction', in *idem*, *Household Strategies*.

57 Hufton, *The Poor*, p. 367.

58 Valenze, *The First*; R. W. Malcolmson, 'Ways of getting a living in eighteenth century England', in R. E. Pahl (ed.), *On Work* (Oxford, Oxford University Press, 1988).

59 R. Wall, 'Work, welfare and the family: an illustration of the adaptive family economy', in L. Bonfield, R. Smith and K. Wrightson (eds), *The World We Have Gained* (Oxford, Oxford University Press, 1986).

60 I. Zangwill, *Children of the Ghetto: A Study of a Peculiar People* (London, J. M. Dent and Sons Ltd, 1909), p. 81.

61 S. Cavallo, 'Family obligations and inequalities in access to care in northern Italy, seventeenth to eighteenth centuries', in Horden and Smith, *The Locus*.

62 We have lagged substantially behind European scholars in the creation of a methodological and analytical framework. For three important early contributions to the European historiography see C. Fairchilds, *Poverty and Charity in Aix-en-Provence, 1640–1789* (Baltimore, Johns Hopkins University Press, 1976), who argued that institutional charity, begging and crime lay at the heart of any economy of makeshifts; S. Woolf, *The Poor in Western Europe in the Eighteenth and Nineteenth Centuries* (London, Methuen, 1986), who demonstrates how work, begging, charity and variation of family structure could be fitted together to generate an overall coping strategy; most importantly, see C. Lis, *Social Change and the Labouring Poor, Antwerp 1770–1860* (New Haven, Yale University Press, 1986), pp. 115–62, who tries to quantify and integrate the different strands of the economy of makeshifts in Antwerp, concluding that work, relief/charity, self-help, kinship and demographic expedients such as child abandonment were the key strategies for the urban poor whatever the explicit life-cycle stage. For the most recent attempts to conceptualise and quantify European makeshift economies, see contributions to Fontaine and Schlumbohm, *Household Strategies*.

63 In the seventeenth century, formal petitions were submitted to magistrates to change the decisions made by subordinate overseers or vestries; in the eighteenth century, approaches were more likely to be made in person or via informal letters: see Sokoll, *Essex Pauper Letters*.

64 Lancashire Record Office DDX 326/3, 'Garstang Vestry Minutes'. See also the chapter by Margaret Hanly in this volume. Vestries were not obliged by law to keep minutes until 1819: Eastwood, *Government*, p. 42.

65 Taylor, 'Voices', pp. 112–14; D. T. Andrew, 'To the charitable and humane: appeals for assistance in the eighteenth-century London press', in H. Cunningham and J. Innes (eds), *Charity, Philanthropy and Reform* (Basingstoke, Macmillan, 1998), pp. 91–3; Sokoll, *Essex Pauper Letters*, pp. 67–70.

66 L. Van Voss, 'Introduction', *International Review of Social History*, 46 (2001), p. 9.

67 P. Carter, 'Early nineteenth century criminal petitions: an introduction for local historians', *The Local Historian*, 31 (2001), pp. 143–4; it was in the nature of all petitions to encompass some description of the author's everyday life, see Voss, 'Introduction', p. 9.

68 P. Mandler, 'Poverty and charity in the nineteenth-century metropolis: an introduction', in *idem* (ed.), *The Uses of Charity* (Princeton, Princeton University Press, 1989), p. 15.

69 N. Z. Davis, *Fiction in the Archives* (Oxford and Cambridge, Polity, 1987), p. 3.

70 Mandler, 'Poverty', p. 1.

71 The Public Record Office's 'Access to Archives' project has catalogued the contents of various quarter sessions papers, giving easy access to multiple references to pawnbrokers and their involvement in court business; see www.a2a.pro.gov.uk.

72 L. Shaw-Taylor, 'Labourers, cows, common rights and parliamentary enclosure: the evidence of contemporary comment c. 1760–1810', *Past and Present*, 171 (2001).

73 L. MacKay, 'Why they stole: women in the Old Bailey, 1779–1789', *Journal of Social History*, 32 (1999).

74 C. Chinn, *Poverty Amidst Prosperity: The Urban Poor in England, 1834–1914* (Manchester, Manchester University Press, 1995); E. Roberts, 'Women's strategies, 1890–1940', in J. Lewis (ed.), *Labour and Love: Women's Experiences of Home and Family, 1850–1940* (Oxford, Oxford University Press, 1986); E. Ross, 'Survival networks: women's neighbourhood sharing in London before World War I', *History Workshop Journal*, 15 (1983).

75 J. Boulton, *Neighbourhood and Society: A London Suburb in the Seventeenth Century* (Cambridge, Cambridge University Press, 1987).

76 See, for instance, P. Dunkley, *The Crisis of the Old Poor Law in England 1795–1834: An Interpretive Essay* (New York, Garland, 1982).

77 Snell, *Annals*.
78 S. Horrell and J. Humphries, 'Old questions, new data and alternative perspectives: families' living standards in the Industrial Revolution', *Journal of Economic History*, 52 (1992).
79 Snell, *Annals*; Smith, 'Charity, self-interest and welfare'.
80 F. M. Eden, *The State of the Poor: A History of the Labouring Classes in England With Parochial Reports* (reprint, London, Augustus Kelley, 1963).
81 See S. Caunce, 'Twentieth-century farm servants: the horselads of the East Riding of Yorkshire', *Agricultural History Review*, 39 (1991).
82 J. S. Taylor, 'A different'.
83 This is true also of King, *Poverty and Welfare*.
84 For a review of this literature, see Innes, 'The "mixed economy of welfare"'.
85 R. Smith, 'Relief of urban poverty outside the poor law, 1800–1850: a study of Nottingham', *Midland History*, 4 (1974).
86 J. Robin, 'The relief of poverty in nineteenth century Colyton', *Rural History*, 1 (1990) and *idem, From Childhood to Middle Age: Cohort Analysis in Colyton 1851–1891* (Cambridge, Cambridge Group, n.d.).
87 J. Broad, 'The smallholder and cottager after disafforestation – a legacy of poverty', in J. Broad and R. Hoyle (eds), *Bernwood: The Life and Afterlife of a Forest* (Preston, University of Central Lancashire, 1997).
88 K. Wrightson and D. Levine, *The Making of an Industrial Society: Whickham 1560–1765* (Oxford, Oxford University Press, 1991).
89 In line with the value of common land and common rights set down by Neeson or Humphries. See J. M. Neeson, *Commoners: Common Right, Enclosure and Social Change in England, 1700–1820* (Cambridge, Cambridge University Press, 1996), and J. Humphries, 'Enclosure, common rights and women: the proletarianization of families in the late eighteenth and early nineteenth centuries', *Journal of Economic History*, 50 (1990).
90 B. Reay, *Microhistories: Demography, Society and Culture in Rural England, 1800–1930* (Cambridge, Cambridge University Press, 1996).
91 P. Hudson and S. King, 'A sense of place: industrialising townships in eighteenth century Yorkshire', in R. Leboutte (ed.), *Proto-Industrialization: Recent Research and New Perspectives* (Geneva, Droz, 1996).
92 M. Freeman, 'Plebs or predators? Deer stealing in Whichwood forest, Oxfordshire in the eighteenth and nineteenth centuries', *Social History*, 21 (1996). See also the discussion of the enclosure of the Otmoor wetland in S. King and J. G. Timmins, *Making Sense of the Industrial Revolution* (Manchester, Manchester University Press, 2001).
93 There is a considerable literature on these issues. For two examples, see J. Rule, 'Against innovation? Custom and resistance in the workplace, 1700–1850', in T. Harris (ed.), *Popular Culture in England*

1500–1850 (Basingstoke, Macmillan, 1995), and J. Bohstedt, *Riots and Community Politics in England and Wales, 1790–1810* (Cambridge Mass., Harvard University Press, 1983).

94 W. Coster, *Family and Kinship in England, 1450–1800* (Harlow, Longman, 2001).

95 R. Wall, 'Some implications of the earnings, income and expenditure patterns of married women in populations in the past', in J. Henderson and R. Wall (eds), *Poor Women and Children in the European Past* (London, Routledge, 1994).

96 R. Watson, 'Poverty in north east Lancashire in 1843: evidence from Quaker charity records', *Local Population Studies*, 55 (1995).

97 Valenze, *The First*.

98 P. Lane, 'Work on the margins: poor women and the informal economy of eighteenth and early nineteenth century Leicestershire', *Midland History*, 22 (1997).

2

'Not by bread only'?
Common right, parish relief
and endowed charity in
a forest economy,
c. 1600–1800

Steve Hindle

Overview

On 21 June 1607, Robert Wilkinson preached a sermon before
commissioners assembled at Northampton to try the participants
in the Midland Rising, a series of anti-enclosure protests involving
as many as one thousand participants, which had spread throughout Leicestershire, Northamptonshire and Warwickshire during
the spring and summer of that year. The rising had culminated
on 8 June in a bloody pitched battle at the village of Newton in
Geddington Woods, part of Rockingham Forest in Northamptonshire, in which some forty or fifty rebels were massacred by a
gentry force under Sir Edward Montagu.[1] For Wilkinson, the rising
was symptomatic of 'tempestuous and troublesome times' during
which the 'excessive covetousnesse of some' had 'caused extreme
want to other, and that want, not well digested, hath riotted to
the hazard of all'. Depopulating enclosure had deprived the poor
of their living, Wilkinson noted, and 'in case of extreme hunger
men will not be perswaded but they will have bread'.[2]

As might be expected of a court preacher speaking in the
presence of judges and law-officers of the crown, Wilkinson emphasised his horror that 'mechanicall men are come to beard
magistrates'. 'It is horrible indeed', he argued, that '*even the vile* ...

39

presume against the honourable'. Wilkinson was nonetheless surprisingly equivocal in his analysis of the causes of the rising,
condemning not only 'the rebellion of the many' but also 'the oppression of the mighty'. On the one hand, he reminded 'the many'
that 'man liveth not by bread only', urging them to 'be thankful
for those good things we have, & waite with patience for those
which yet wee have not'. This was to condemn the 'poverty without
patience' which had tempted the 'mad and rebellious multitude'
to use unlawful means to seek redress for their grievances. On
the other hand, however, he admonished 'the mighty' that 'man
liveth by bread', thereby exhorting the propertied to exercise their
traditional obligations of charity and paternalism. In doing so, he
actively promoted 'the cause and complaints of the expelled,
half-pined and distressed poore' who had been driven to rebellion
by the covetousness of the rich. 'Let it be a lesson for all states
generally', Wilkinson insisted, *'not to grind the faces of the poore'*.[3]
The commissioners themselves, however, were evidently rather
less even-handed in their interpretation of the causes of the rising,
and the convicted rioters were subjected to the full rigours of the
penalties stipulated by the treason statutes, their quarters bloodily
exhibited both at Northampton and at the neighbouring towns
of Kettering, Oundle, and Thrapston.

If the propertyless cottagers of this forest economy were not,
therefore, to live 'by bread only', how else were they to live?
Wilkinson's answer was, inevitably, scriptural, in the form of a
quotation from Matthew 4. iv: 'man shall not live by bread onely
but by every word that procedeth out of the mouth of God'.[4] The
modern historian's answer to Wilkinson's question is, of course,
rather less likely to turn on theological issues. Any understanding
of the survival strategies of the poor of Rockingham Forest necessi-
tates the analysis of the matrix of economic resources and welfare
provision which pervaded the economy of Geddington Woods
(known as Geddington Chase after disafforestation in 1676) for
two centuries after Wilkinson's sermon was preached and the
savage punishment of the Northampton trials meted out.[5]

Historians of early modern English welfare provision have gradually come to realise that although public bodies or officers –
churchwardens and overseers of the poor – gained control of some
relief funds (and indeed of the right to tax) from the late sixteenth
century, 'they did not achieve a monopoly of relief, but rather
joined the ranks of other official, collective and individual donors'.

Consequently, argues Joanna Innes, 'a "mixed economy of welfare" has persisted from that era to this, with, of course, changes both in the nature of constituent agencies and practices and in the balance between them'.[6] This interweaving of national and parochial, and of formal and informal, networks of care created a complex pattern of resources upon which the indigent might draw in different combinations at different stages of the life-cycle. As Innes's magisterial survey reveals, contemporaries from Matthew Hale to Thomas Malthus seem either to have been resigned to, or positively appreciative of, such diversity. For historians of English *thinking* about the poor, Innes's 'mixed economy of welfare' is likely to become as solid a piece of intellectual furniture as has Olwen Hufton's 'economy of makeshifts' for the historian of the *experience* of poverty.[7] Both concepts imply that 'legal charity' or formal welfare provided by the parish, which the historiography of poor relief has long emphasised almost by default, is uncharacteristic of the 'locus of care' as it has generally been experienced by the poorer sort of people in the English past.[8] Each concept, moreover, invites reconstruction of the alternative survival strategies through which the poor themselves might put together a living.

As Paul Slack has demonstrated, however, such reconstructions are particularly problematic.[9] The differing shape, size and texture of the planks in the makeshift economy of the poor render difficult any assessment of the precarious balance between them. Historians have gradually come to realise that, in shifting for themselves, the poor might combine any number of expedients: kin support and complex patterns of co-residence; gentry hospitality and communal charity; migration and mendicancy; petty theft and the embezzlement of perquisites.[10] All of these, it should be emphasised, are notoriously difficult to measure. In particular, there are few reliable means of calculating the value of casual charity, the 'alms given to the poor in the yard of an inn or at a man's door'.[11] Although it is probably true that, by the eighteenth century at least, the recipients of such spontaneous 'hospitality' were far more likely to have been strangers than known neighbours, they were apparently numerous enough to provoke contemporary concern. Furthermore, other types of assistance to the needy are equally invisible in the historical record: foremost amongst these is kin support. Although it has recently been argued that the 'attenuated nature of the early modern English kinship system' meant that protection had to be sought 'from within the collectivity rather than from the extended family or kin', we must nonetheless remain sensitive to the possibility that the spontaneous gift by both kin and neighbours, perhaps offered on the tacit expectation of reciprocity, played an important role in the survival strategies of the poor.[12]

These caveats borne in mind, this paper seeks to investigate the relationship between the various sources of income – common right, parish relief and endowed charity – upon which the rural poor of a seventeenth- and eighteenth-century forest economy might draw. Inevitably, the focus must be intensely local, partly because of the mysteries of source survival, partly because access to these resources was, by definition, regulated by social, economic and even moral imperatives which might vary significantly from community to community. Manorial custom, as *lex loci*, governed access to common right.[13] Both before and after the 1662 settlement laws, the effective operation of the Elizabethan poor relief statutes presupposed that parishes would be well-defended from the threat of exploitative in-migration.[14] Charitable endowments strictly regulated eligibility according to the terms set by individual testators.[15] While the highly localised nature of these resources has gradually become recognised, the precise nature of their inter relationship has seldom been investigated in the local context. Furthermore, although the enclosure of the common fields and wastes undoubtedly exerted a direct or indirect influence over all three resources, its role in shaping the 'mixed economy of welfare' has generally been assumed rather than analysed in the literature. Enclosure looms large in the rural history of the particular *locale* at issue here, for Northamptonshire was *the* county of parliamentary enclosure, and the parishes of Rockingham Forest were at the heart of resistance not only to enclosure by parliamentary act but also to the less formal enclosure-agreements, however arbitrary they might actually have been in practice, which had been undertaken in the area for the preceding two centuries. The following discussion therefore has two inter-related purposes. In the first place, it is intended as a case study of Innes's 'mixed economy of welfare', and as a reconstruction (albeit impressionistic) of the 'hierarchy of resort' that existed within it.[16] In the second place, however, its principal argument is that the *measurement* of provision for the poor raises far more fundamental and significant questions about the politics of *meaning* within the social economy. Accordingly, then, this chapter aims to provide a qualitative assessment

Table 2.1 Population and hearth tax exemption in three
Northamptonshire parishes, 1524–1801

Parish	Population estimates			Estimated number of families		Hearth tax exemption rate (%)
	1524	*c. 1670*	*1801*	*c. 1720*	*1801*	*c. 1670*
Brigstock	536	872	903	160	201	42.2
Geddington	272	496	663	135	154	40.3
Stanion	228	252	248	56	61	54.0
Total	1036	1620	1814	351	416	45.5

Source: Petit, *Royal Forests*, p. 144.

of the changing significance of common right, parish relief and
endowed charity in one particular local context (three parishes
which intercommoned on Geddington Chase in Northamptonshire) over a long period (the two centuries after which their
inhabitants had witnessed the Midland Rising and the retribution
that came in its wake).

A forest economy

The economy of the three parishes central to this study, Brigstock,
Geddington and Stanion, was dominated by what had originally
been Crown woodland in two walks, Farming Woods, 1,100 acres
north and east of Brigstock, and Geddington Woods some 1,400
acres to the west of Brigstock. The three 'core' parishes intercommoned on Geddington Chase, but the experience of the
neighbouring parishes of Weldon and Oakley also illuminates this
shady forest economy.[17] As Table 2.1 shows, two of the three 'core'
parishes experienced considerable population growth in the early
part of the period: from a combined Geddington Chase population
of approximately 1,000 in 1524, there was an increase of 60 per
cent to approximately 1,600 in 1670. This was succeeded by a
period of relatively slight demographic pressure over the long
eighteenth century, with the aggregate rising only by a further 20
per cent to a little over 1800 in 1801. In the 1720s, it was estimated
that the three parishes contained 351 'families or houses'; the
census enumerators' calculation of 416 'families' suggests that only

a further fifty households had been added by 1801. Furthermore, these aggregate figures conceal the stagnation of Stanion, which was probably less densely populated in 1801 than in 1720. As we shall see, the chronology of social change in this part of North-amptonshire owed rather more to secular trends in prices than it did to demographic pressure *per se*. The various attempts to enclose Geddington Chase in the 1600s, 1630s, 1720s and 1790s did not necessarily have common roots. They nonetheless provoked both intense resentment and widespread resistance.

As might be expected, the social and occupational structure of the region is rather more difficult to reconstruct. It has been estimated that while husbandmen and middle-sized farmers made up only 21 per cent of the early sixteenth-century population of Rockingham Forest as a whole, there was a large class, perhaps as many as 77 per cent of the total, of 'small cottagers, wage labourers and poor persons'.[18] If perhaps 30 per cent of Rock-ingham Forest households were too poor to be taxed in 1524, almost half as many again, some 43 per cent of the population, were exempt from the hearth taxes of the late 1660s and early 1670s, a figure almost ten percentage points higher than that for non-forest villages in Northamptonshire, and substantially higher than that for most rural non-industrial parishes in England as a whole.[19] Again, two of our three core parishes were typical of this pattern. Of the three, Stanion appears to have been the poorest. While 42.2 per cent of the households in Brigstock, and 40.3 per cent of those in Geddington were exempt, 54 per cent of the families in Stanion were 'poor' on this definition. Both population growth and hearth tax exemption rates are explained by the fact that whilst Stanion was the smallest of the three villages, and lacked any pasture of its own, virtually all its dwellings were ancient commonable cottages: there was, quite literally, no room for 'off-comers'. The survival of a fine series of militia lists for Northamptonshire makes analysis of the occupational structure rather easier for the mid-eighteenth century.[20] Of the 188 adult males listed for the three parishes in 1777, only eleven (6 per cent) were farmers. Forty-one (22 per cent) were labourers. There were, interestingly, significant differences between the three par-ishes: taken together the seventeen weavers and eight tailors in Geddington suggest that cloth-working accounted for over 30 per cent of the 'working population' of that particular parish at a time when the occupation went almost unrecorded in either of its neighbours. Brigstock and Geddington each had a full complement of local craftsmen: masons, carpenters and joiners, wheelwrights, butchers, tanners and cobblers.

The three parishes were long associated if not with extreme poverty, then with substantially polarised wealth. In 1610, George Sharp, the vicar of Brigstock, felt obliged to remind the 'rich and mighty men of the town' of the presence of 'others to be pitied for their very beggarly estates'. By 1643, 128 (61 per cent) of the 210 householders in the parish were poor enough to be eligible for the Earl of Salisbury's Christmas dole.[21] The existence of a substantial numbers of indigent residents haunted landlords well into the eighteenth century. Mr Edmunds, the Duke of Montagu's estate agent, contrasted the villages of Geddington Chase unfavourably with the Duke's own purlieu woods, bemoaning not only 'the depredations', 'ravages' and 'destructive havoc' wrought by the devouring jaws of a herd of hungry cattle, but also the 'inability of the occupier of an open-field farm to procure a sufficiency of food for their support in the winter season'. The resulting 'daily diminution in the growth of the underwood' rendered the cattle vulnerable to contagious maladies, which in turn prevented their owners from 'deriving any advantage from the commonage that year, and probably for many years to come'.[22] For Edmunds, then, rural immiseration was the inevitable inconvenience which must accrue where property was 'held under a mixture of interests', especially interests 'so extremely inimical to one another as those of the commoner and the proprietor of the timber'. And the consequence of rural immiseration was desperation and disorder.[23] Most seventeenth-century observers were convinced that forests in particular were a 'nursery for the county gaols'. Thus, John Norden, writing in the early seventeenth century in a language that was to be reappropriated for similar rhetorical purposes as late as the 1780s, argued that the forests were

> so ugly a monster as of necessity will breed ... more and more idleness, beggary and atheism, and consequently disobedience to God and the King ... wherein infinite poor, yet most idle inhabitants have thrust themselves, living covertly without law or religion, *rudes et refractori* by nature, among whom are nourished and bred infinite idle fry, that coming ripe grow vagabonds, and infect the Commonwealth with most dangerous leprosies.[24]

Such fears were undoubtedly fuelled by the long campaign fought by the commoners of Geddington Chase to protect their common rights, a campaign in which the Midland Rising was only the most violent engagement.

Common right

Although historians have recently come to emphasise the central role of customary right in the mixed economy of welfare, the study of forest rights in particular remains at a relatively preliminary stage.[25] Any discussion of common rights in the forest villages of Northamptonshire is indebted to Jeanette Neeson's remarkable study of the uses and management of waste, and of the richness of the economic equilibrium to which they contributed.[26] In Neeson's analysis, the forest economy offered not only pasture for cattle and swine on the forest commons, but also casual labour and reserves of nuts, berries, honey and game. The most significant resource of all, however, was fuel. Besides wood, forest fuel might include peat, turf, dried dung, gorse and heather. All of these might be used directly to warm a cottage, but each might equally be sold or traded for grain or other produce.

Neeson, moreover, argues against what she regards as historically uninformed models of the inevitable 'tragedy of the commons', in which poor regulation led inexorably to the exhaustion of natural resources, and seeks to demonstrate the fair and effective administration of use-rights by manorial courts.[27] This insight has recently been confirmed by more general surveys of the control of valuable communal resources. Donald Woodward, for instance, cites very widespread evidence of seventeenth-century by-laws identifying those who had the right to share in communal resources; stipulating the amounts which each individual could carry away and whether such material could be sold to outsiders; and determining the seasonality of the legitimate collection of materials. 'Without such regulations', he insists, 'many of the commons and wastes of early modern England would have been quickly denuded.'[28] The effect of these regulations, however, remains ambiguous. On the one hand, Neeson suggests that communal regulation favoured poorer rather than more affluent commoners. The management of waste fostered a fundamental social cohesion based on the ideology of custom, in which, she insists, 'the defence of common rights required the protection of lesser rights as well as greater'.[29] On the other, regulation was by definition an act of exclusion which prevented not only outsiders but also the occupants of non-commonable cottages from enjoying the uses of waste.[30]

While the evidence for the regulation of common right in our three core parishes is not overwhelming, it is nonetheless strong. In all Crown woodland, the gathering of wood for fuel was supposedly carried out only under licence from the forest officers and it is likely that the ancient settled poor of the parish would be the principal beneficiaries of such discretion: 'such only and so many of the poor persons as the verderers and woodward think meet' were to be 'admitted to gather sticks on Mondays and Thursdays only in every week'.[31] This practice was evidently observed in Geddington and Newton, where exchequer depositions of 1608 refer to the custom that 'divers poor ... had taken thorns and bushes to burn'.[32] Licensed sticking was, however, one thing, illicit 'gathering [of] sets and breaking of hedges' quite another. A crime characteristically associated with poverty, the casual pilfering of wood for fuel was a matter of national concern from the late sixteenth century, and its policing and punishment was entrusted variously to manorial juries, parish officers and the summary jurisdiction of magistrates.[33] In Geddington Chase, hedge-breaking was a matter of acute concern from as early as 1577, when more stringent restrictions on the admission of poor stick gatherers were proposed. The late Elizabethan records of the forest courts reveal an annual average number of fifty-six prosecutions for cutting greenwood or breaking hedges in the three parishes.[34] The very fact of poverty therefore ensured that 'there was a very fine line between the exercise of legitimate use rights and theft'.[35]

Wood was one of the main comforts of life, and both competition over, and control of access to, this valuable resource was accordingly intense. The pasturing of cattle, sheep and swine in the open fields and forest commons required similarly strict regulation. The regulation of pasture rights in the open fields of Geddington stretches back to the late fourteenth century. In Brigstock, the seventeenth-century common rights included the driving of sheep through forest ridings to the wastes of Benefield, for which a fee of a shilling a year was paid to the ranger; the daily and overnight pasturing of sheep on the wastes in the summer; and the folding of them in the winter.[36] The management of the forest commons was largely carried out through forest drifts or searches for illegally depastured animals. There were repeated complaints about the infrequency and inefficiency of these enquiries. The whole of Geddington Chase lacked a pinfold in 1598. The verderers stressed the need for one in 1602, yet a few years later it was again reported that the pound was 'very ruinous and wholly decayed. By reason whereof foreigners' cattle trespassing in the said office cannot be impounded as they should, neither yet the same driven in the time of year as it ought'.[37] The result of unregulated pasture was overstocking of the commons. Early eighteenth-century drift books reveal that an annual average of 217 cows and ninety-three horses were at pasture on the chase. After the 400-odd deer are taken into account, these some seven hundred animals were competing for a little over 320 acres of grazing.[38] Neeson's claims to the contrary notwithstanding, the resources of the forest were almost certainly approaching exhaustion.

The delicate social and economic balance of the forest commons is further revealed in a fragmentary series of manorial orders which survive for Geddington in the 1730s.[39] At first sight, the presentment and fining of five individuals in 1730 for 'unlawful encroachment on the commons' implies that resources were being tightly regulated; the fact that these same five, three of them widows, and all of them in receipt of parish charity, were presented and fined again for the same offence in 1731, 1732, 1734, 1735 and 1738 suggests that these were not marginal individuals, whose presence in the community was merely tolerated, but that these were the ancient poor of the parish whose precarious exploitation of the waste was reluctantly condoned, the fines amounting to little more than permission to retain with a rent. The trouble, of course, was that over several generations, the forest economy had come to absorb countless settlers of this kind. Squatters and other migrants were, in this sense, agents in the fabrication of their own economy of makeshifts: inventing traditions where there were none, claiming rights by virtue only of residence, manipulating custom in their own interest. Settlement at the margins of a forest economy was not, therefore, a survival *strategy* legitimately played out in the context of widely recognised ethical rules, but a survival *tactic* which ingeniously exploited the 'unstopped cracks in the wainscoting of power'.[40]

Early seventeenth-century population growth, especially through immigration, undoubtedly contributed to these difficulties. Squatting and the illegal erection of cottages were, as in other forest areas, notorious in Geddington Chase. The taking of inmates was complained of as early as 1577, several years before the statute that outlawed it. The three parishes saw the erection of at least twenty-three illegal cottages in the thirty years prior to 1637.[41] The leading ratepayers of Brigstock complained in 1623 that the burden of taxes was increasing because of the multitude of poor people, 'which have and do increase daily by reason of the continual erecting of new cottages and taking in of new inmates, being at least four score families more ... in these few years than in any ancient time'.[42] Some indication of the scale of illegal pasturing and wood-gathering is revealed by the papers relating to enclosure negotiations in 1721: the Duke of Montagu's steward drew up a list of the 116 houses in Brigstock that now claim right of common in Geddington Chase but noted that 'many of 'em examined into will be found to be tenements only, for none but ancient cottagers can be commonable'. He subsequently noted that only fifty-nine (51 per cent) of the houses could be certified as ancient commonable cottages when 'impartial' referees were invited to adjudicate the claims.[43]

All of which brings us to the vexed question of who actually was *entitled* to common right.[44] In the early seventeenth century, at a time when there were perhaps 170 households in the parish, Brigstock possessed fifty-three suit-houses, two half, and nine quarter suit-houses, whose tenants were allowed housebote (the right to take timber for house repairs) by order of the forest courts. This amounted to the taking of about fifty trees *per annum*, and was supplemented by an annual allowance of sixty-two loads of 'suit-thorns' at concessional rates out of the ridings of Geddington Chase. Similar provisions applied in both Stanion and Geddington, though the ratio of 'suit-houses' to all residents is rather more difficult to calculate until the early eighteenth century. The papers concerning the proposed enclosure of 1720 demonstrate that the proportion of common-right cottages varied even between these three adjacent parishes intercommoning together. The proportion of legally commonable cottages to all forest dwellings ranged from 84 per cent in Stanion (47 of 56), to 36 per cent in Brigstock (58 of 160) and 34 per cent in Geddington (46 of 135). Overall, therefore, only 43 per cent (151 of 351) of the households formally enjoyed common right in Geddington Chase. As we have seen, however, virtually all residents claimed common right in practice.[45] It is therefore unsurprising that the tenants of the ancient commonable cottages resented the poor migrants who claimed customary right simply on the basis of residence: they 'have no means to relieve themselves, there being little work to set them on, but by flocks go roving up and down the forest, parks and inclosed grounds near unto them to the great hindrance of all who have cattle and woods'.[46] For the poor migrant to the forest, therefore, custom came to be regarded not as *cohesive* but rather as a *restrictive* ideology, one of the structural constraints within, and around, which survival tactics were perforce developed.

What is especially striking about this complex economic equilibrium is the sheer endurance of the forest itself. Despite a long-running series of attempts to enclose this part of the Northamptonshire forest, the piecemeal extinction of common right was resisted at every stage. The projected mid-sixteenth-century enclosure of Benefield in Brigstock, was, it was recalled some 160 years later, 'staved off' both 'by the prudent but chargeable methods of law' employed by the Dukes of Montagu and by the levelling of trenches by the commoners. On this occasion, the commoners' interests were apparently protected by an alliance of aristocracy and gentry.[47] By the 1590s, however, the gentry had defected from this alliance, and Sir Thomas Tresham of Newton was amongst those eleven landlords prosecuted by Attorney-General Coke for enclosure and engrossing in the reaction against depopulation after the Oxfordshire rising.[48] His long-standing abuses in this respect almost certainly explain why Geddington Chase should be the epicentre of the Midland Rising of 1607.

The Northamptonshire disturbances of that year were, as we have seen, focused on the Tresham estates in and around Newton and Geddington. By Michaelmas 1607, 143 rebels had sued for pardon: seventy-eight (55 per cent) of them came from Rockingham Forest, the vast majority of those from Geddington Chase. The character of the rising can be assessed on the basis of the social profile of those pardoned: while 43 per cent were described as labourers; and a further 38 per cent were artisans, only 15 per cent were husbandmen.[49] Essentially, it seems, this was a rising of 'propertyless cottagers from forest communities'.[50] This contention is confirmed by the content of a seditious libel, protesting against the injustice of enclosure, which was wrapped round a ball of wax, thrown into the choir of Castor church and subsequently sent to the Earl of Rutland. Entitled the 'Poor Man's Joy and the

Gentleman's Plague', it began 'yow gentlemen that rack your rents, and trow downe land for corne, the tyme wyll com that som will sigh, that ever they were borne'. Protesting that 'living the poor doth want and living they shall have', it threatened the 'bloody enterprise' of pulling down those 'haughty minds' who oppressed the commons.[51] Copied in the hand of the Earl's household steward Thomas Screven, the libel almost certainly passed through the hands of his Grace's private secretary Robert Dallington, an individual of very substantial significance in the subsequent history of Geddington Chase.

Less than twelve months after the suppression of the rising, however, the commoners of Geddington sued Tresham in the exchequer for enclosing the Brand, a common disputed between the two parishes of Newton and Geddington. As late as 1610, Tresham had failed to comply with the orders of the Commissioners for Depopulation to restore some four hundred acres of land to nine 'depopulated' cottages in Newton.[52] The recalcitrance of the rich and mighty was similarly demonstrated by the behaviour of another Northamptonshire landlord, Thomas Lord Brudenell, when he was prosecuted for the depopulation of Hougham in 1636. Brudenell indignantly defended his 'benign and charitable' intentions, and claimed that he owned 'not a mannor house without a familie, nor a messuage, less than he was left, nor a farmer without his auntient quantitie or sufficient support, nor a cottager without livelyhood and worke, nor an impotent man without reliefe'. Nevertheless, the commoners convinced Archbishop Laud and the Commissioners for Depopulation that Brudenell had 'devoured the people with a sheapheard and a dog', a complaint that was to resonate through Rockingham Forest in general, and Geddington Chase in particular, over the next two centuries.[53]

The most significant eighteenth-century engagement in the attritional conflict over enclosure and common right was that fought between the commoners and 'Planter' John, 2nd Duke of Montagu, in 1721–23.[54] As part of very complex negotiations with the Earl of Cardigan, Montagu sent an open letter to the commoners of Geddington Chase, justifying his enclosure proposals on the grounds that ineffective management of the forest commons had led directly to increased poor rates: 'It is very well known that all Forest towns who have some privileges in the forest are thereby made the poorer and any gentleman's estate there must

be so much the worse in being charged with burthensome levies.'
Furthermore, he argued

> The pretence of some small privilege, as of gathering of dead wood
> in a forest and the like, are only cloakes for the greatest villainies in
> destroying the wood and the game. The children are brought up in
> this manner & instead of being inured to labour are accustomed to
> laziness which must intail poverty upon their posterity and charge
> upon an estate. It is therefore the interest of every person concerned
> to endeavour to stop the growth of such an evil not by depriving the
> poor of any privilege which they enjoy but by putting them into a
> better capacity to get their livelihood by providing of proper worke
> for them & take care that they be brought up to industry, & qualified
> to get their liveing anywhere and not to be confined to a forrest &
> earn their bread by pilfering and stealing.[55]

The details of the proposal need not detain us here: suffice to
say that common rights in the enclosed cow commons suggested
by Montagu would be restricted only to those with legally commonable cottages, which (as we have seen) constituted less than
half the dwellings in the three parishes. The evidence suggests
that these legal commoners were, initially at least, entirely persuaded by the plan: in Brigstock, only four of the eighty-two
proprietors and tenants who were consulted actually refused.[56]
Nonetheless, even though a parliamentary bill was drawn up to
confirm the extinction of common rights, all negotiations appear
to have broken down by the mid-1720s. Patterns of persuasion,
in turn creating complex loops of association among the inhabitants, apparently frustrated the plan.[57] None of this, unfortunately,
is visible in the archival record: Montagu's agent could only
blame 'the prejudices of some, the personal views of others, and
the ignorance, mistake and unreasonableness of the rest'.[58] This
was not only a narrow reading of the nature of opposition, it was
also a gross underestimate of its strength. Extensive proceedings
in the court of King's Bench reveal that violent protest had
broken out over the proposals by the end of 1724. The riots were
inspired by William Good, rector of neighbouring Weldon, who
had urged his parishioners to turn their annual perambulation,
the corporate manifestation of the village community which both
reflected and constituted a sense of belonging, into a protest
against the enclosure.[59]

Good's exhortations to resistance provide an important link
between the successful anti-enclosure campaign of the 1720s, and

its futile successor of the 1790s. In 1744, Good published an open letter to the commoners in Rockingham Forest. He intended not only to prove the rights of common to which *all* tenants in the commonable woods were entitled, but also to propose a strategy for the preservation of those rights 'at a very easy expense if they will unanimously pursue it'. Common right, he argued, was granted not by the favour of the landlord, but was inherited by all residents: 'all tenants in the commonable woods in the forest have as long as they shall continue tenants there an equal right of common with those that have houses and lands of their own, and as good a right by custom, and the laws of the land, as the owners of the woods have to the timber and underwoods'. Good argued that the mutual defence of these rights between the farmers and cottagers of inter-commoning parishes could best be provided by pooling financial resources: if the two hundred cottagers gave 2s. 6d. each, and the three hundred farmers 5d. each, the sum of £100 could be invested and the issue tried at law. Furthermore, he argued, he had taken legal advice and was now convinced that such proceedings would not be liable to the statutes of champerty, maintenance and combination. Good's open disavowal of all riotous and tumultuous proceedings was no doubt expected of him: rather more surprising is his advice that 'every parish that has any right of common in the forest of Rockingham to lay up two of these letters in the parish chest, which may be a means of instructing their children and their children's children how to preserve their right in the forest for ages to come'. The advice was undoubtedly heeded, for the 'letter' was republished in the context of the enclosure protests of the 1790s.[60] The economy of makeshifts was not therefore simply subject to an ongoing piecemeal process of *practical* redefinition by squatters and migrants who exploited the interstices of local custom; it was also periodically reinvented in a *cultural* sense by propagandists who actively sought to legitimate its redefinition in the wider interest of the forest community.

The issue of entitlement to the uses of waste was finally forced by the Duke of Buccleuch in the early 1790s. In the winter of 1792, eighteen 'small proprietors of land and cottages' in Brigstock delivered the first of several petitions to the Duke, urging him to reconsider his proposals for the enclosure of Geddington Chase. 'It is with no small concern', they pleaded (in an echo of the complaint of the commoners of Caroline Hougham), 'that we see whole lordships managed by a sheepheard or two and their dogs which in an open field state gave employ to a number of industrious families'. However much the proprietor may benefit, they insisted, enclosures

> never fail to increase the price of provisions and depopulate the country by forcing the laborious peasant and his family from his peaceful home to seek a precarious living in the capital already overgrown.[61]

His Grace, it seems, 'did not condescend to give [the] petitioners an answer'. Instead, and only after he was provoked by a further petition to his wife, he found it expedient to donate a cash sum to the overseers and churchwardens of the Geddington Chase parishes. The parish officers of Geddington 'humbly begged leave to return [their] sincere thanks to [his] grace for [his] gracious benefaction of ten pounds which has proved a very reasonable relief to the poor during this inclement winter', declaring that they had 'the honour to subscribe [themselves] [his] graces much obliged and very humble servants'.[62] Nevertheless, the Duke's belief that rights of common upon the chase were 'injurious' to his own interests encouraged him to draw upon his aristocratic neighbours to force through the necessary legislation. The parliamentary enclosure of Brigstock, Geddington and Stanion therefore proceeded in 1795, and proved to be one of only nine occasions when expectations of opposition provoked the House into permitting interested MPs to vote.[63] The avowed objective, 'to make these commons more useful to ye claimants and the woods more serviceable to himself' was rather undermined by the fact that compensation would not extend even to the Duke's own tenants. As a result, only thirty allotments were allocated to the commoners of Geddington, at a time when the parish population exceeded 660. The preamble to the Act insisted that it would be 'expedient' to make compensation 'convenient in situation and adequate in value' to the rights extinguished. The Duke appears to have been only too aware of how restricted those rights were in strictly legal terms.[64]

Opposition to enclosure in the eighteenth century was entirely characteristic of forest towns like Geddington, whose economy was dominated by forest trades, some cloth and lace-making and large forest commons.[65] Diffuse rather than consolidated in their landownership, usually combining agricultural and manufacturing activity rather than being dependent solely on agriculture, such villages were renowned for their spirited independence and their tradition of truculence. Those who lived there were by definition peculiarly dependent upon their own ingenuity in assembling a diversified economy of makeshifts. These were, after all, impoverished communities in which the marginal were more than usually vulnerable to indigence.

Parish relief

As to the operation of institutional poor relief in the region, the evidence is rather more formal but, sadly, only slightly less fragmentary. Although very little work has been done on the early history of the poor law in Northamptonshire, it seems that the decisive set of orders was made by the county bench only in 1625.[66] Surviving only in the churchwardens' accounts of Great Houghton, the orders stipulate the speedy execution of various statutes including '43 Eliz.', and the acts of 1607 against tippling and of 1624 against swearing, insisting on presentments of offenders to the magistrates in each hundred every three weeks.[67] Of the thirty-one surviving sets of seventeenth-century overseers' accounts from Northamptonshire, moreover, only seven date from before 1650.[68] For our three Geddington Chase parishes, overseers' accounts survive only in interrupted series for the mid-eighteenth century, and are particularly deficient for the period immediately preceding parliamentary enclosure in the 1790s.[69] As Figure 2.1 suggests, however, they do provide some impressionistic evidence of the scale of the burden of poverty, and of the remarkable increase in poor relief expenditure during and immediately after the enclosures were carried out: the open fields of Brigstock and Stanion were enclosed at the same time as Geddington Chase in 1795, the fields of Geddington itself only in 1807.

These figures must, of course, be interpreted as indices rather of *pauperism* than of *indigence*: they ignore the substantial numbers of poor people who were in need and not on regular relief. The size of this group is notoriously difficult to reconstruct, although Lee Beier estimates that they made up between 8 and 17 per cent of the populations of early seventeenth-century rural communities in Norfolk and North Yorkshire.[70] The task is made rather easier, at least for the early eighteenth century, by a series of marginal comments made by John Barton, minister of Geddington, in the

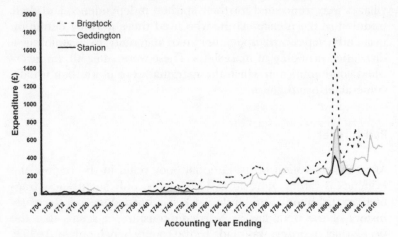

Figure 2.1 Annual poor relief expenditure in three Geddington Chase parishes, c. 1704–1817

parish register for the year 1701–2. Barton noted that while fifteen of those he baptised that year were 'poor', only one of them 'receiveth almes'.[71] Despite the fact that 'the poore' was a notoriously elastic (perhaps even a 'gentry-made') term amongst contemporaries, the distinction was a nice one, in that the overseers' accounts suggest that only a very tiny proportion of the needy regularly received parish relief.[72] In 1723, at a time when there were probably 135 households in Geddington, there were only seven regular pensioners, receiving a total of 10s. 3d. per week between them. By the 1740s, there were still only eleven pensioners, receiving a weekly total of 11s. 7d.[73] A similar situation prevailed in Brigstock, where a large constituency of those who received casual relief from the overseers supplemented the relatively small number of parish pensioners. In the period 1741–68, casual disbursements accounted for over 39 per cent of poor relief expenditure in Brigstock, though in one year (1743) they outweighed even regular payments, amounting to 55 per cent of the total.[74]

That eighteenth-century poor relief expenditure could be kept so relatively low in a *pays* renowned for the wretchedness of its poverty might, of course, be explained by the rigour and severity of the decision-making process amongst ratepayers and parish officers, who sought to restrict entitlement in order to prevent what they regarded as the unnecessary inflation of welfare costs.[75] But the possibility must also be considered that either the availability of common right or, less plausibly, the plenitude of charitable provision insulated the poor from a culture of dependency. One particular parish charity, founded in Geddington in 1636, is of particular interest in this respect, not least because it was endowed to provide the very commodity that had inspired Robert Wilkinson's sermon in 1607: bread.

Endowed charity

Robert Dallington was born in Geddington in 1561 'of humble yeoman stock'. A Cambridge graduate, he served as a schoolmaster in Norfolk before becoming 'travelling tutor' and 'secretary' to the Earl of Rutland, in whose service the seditious libel 'the poor man's joy and the gentleman's plague' had passed through his hands in 1607. He subsequently became an intimate member of the Godly circle surrounding Henry, Prince of Wales, and was appointed to the lucrative mastership of Charterhouse in 1624. He built a free school in Geddington in 1635, and by his will in 1636 endowed a charity with £300 'for the distribution of twenty-four three-penny loaves everie Sunday to twenty-four of the poor of the parish'.[76] The mechanics of the charity, like those of many such endowments, were intricate: the capital sum was used to purchase two closes, thirty-one acres in total, in the nearby parish of Loddington. The annual rents payable on these properties grew from £15 in the 1630s, to £19 in the 1670s, to £23 in the 1730s and £31 in the 1770s. After payment of land tax and tithe, and the provision of an annual dinner for the tenants, the bread was distributed weekly (at an annual cost of almost £16), and any remaining sums were divided amongst the twenty-four in cash at Easter: in 1745 this Easter dole amounted to £6.[77] This pattern was entirely typical of the 'charitable imperative' as it found expression in thousands of endowments across rural England.[78]

The terms for entitlement to the charity set by Dallington and his trustees, publicly declared in their 'directions for the choosing and well governing of the poor', were, however, quite extraordinary.[79] Their rigour might partly be explained by Dallington's own religious commitment or by his previous experience of administering discretionary charity at Charterhouse.[80] Local knowledge, however, almost certainly played its part. Dallington was doubtless aware of the long-standing concerns about immigration and law-lessness in this part of Northamptonshire. This was an exclusive charity in every sense of the word: its compassion had a hard edge. 'Deserving' persons were to be selected by the trustees, 'and then to draw lots till they have [the bread]'. The three basic requirements for eligibility range from the all-too-predictable to the very sur-prising: it is little wonder that 'the honest number of twenty four shall not contain any who has made himself poor by idleness, drunkenness or disorder', or that a discriminating attitude should be applied to incomers and strangers. Such provisions echo those of many a rural charity.[81] Dallington's criteria of residence were, however, extreme: recipients must be either born in Geddington 'or have dwelt in the town in good behaviour at least fourteen years before'. This extended time period is significant because it excludes servants, apprentices and young married couples. The third, and most surprising, clause states that 'if any have consumed their estates by giving away their estates to their children or by buying or building houses they shall not be partakers of this charity'. The attempt to prevent the elderly from receiving charity after they have passed property to their children implies that those very children should maintain their parents. The willingness of the trustees to locate charitable relief in the context of the transmission of property in the parish is among the more far-reaching provi-sions of any endowment in this period, and supports the recent claim that 'in providing welfare payments and services, seventeenth- and eighteenth-century overseers of the poor and charity trustees were not undermining inter-generational support within the family but in certain key respects were attempting to preserve or foster it'.[82]

Preliminary eligibility was, however, only the tip of an iceberg of other stipulations, which amounted to an extensive system of penalties and forfeitures. Recipients of the dole might have their loaf indefinitely withheld if they allowed 'married folk ... strangers or children' into their houses, or if they 'let part of their houses whereby the poor are increased and the town overcharged'. One week's provision would be forfeited by any of the twenty-four 'found begging, either at home or abroad', by any heard 'lying, scolding or slandering', and by any failing to attend church on Sunday morning. A whole month's entitlement would be withheld if any of the twenty-four or their families indulged in hedge-breaking, fence- and gate-smashing or unauthorised gleaning, a provision whose severity explicitly reflects the immediacy of memories of the 1607 rising. Perhaps most significantly, concern with youth unemployment and overpopulation was manifested in the most draconian of the terms: any of the twenty-four could be (permanently) 'displaced and another put in their room' if they 'kept more children at home than is needful for their use'. As in other forest economies, the authorities aimed 'to prevent young people staying at home (where they had to be supported from the poor rates) and to force them to find work, preferably elsewhere'.[83] The Geddington case anticipates by some seventy years the drastic order of the Buckinghamshire justices that the poor parents of those children in the forest parish of Brill in Bernwood who refuse 'to go out and hire at service' should have their parish relief or collection withheld until they forced their children into service.[84] Indeed, such orders became increasingly common throughout rural England, especially after the ambiguous apprenticeship clauses of the Elizabethan poor laws had been clarified by a statute of 1697.[85] The demeanour of recipients was also powerfully insisted upon by the trustees: no bread was to be received at all 'if any of the twenty-four do proudly or stubbornly refuse their penalty and do not meekly make their submission for their offence until that be done'.[86]

Painted on the charity board on the chancel wall at Geddington, the 'orders and directions' both symbolised the social discipline exercised by the trustees and advertised the ethical norms to which recipients of the charity were expected to conform. The discriminatory terms of the charity were not, however, simply symbolic. The regulations imply very active networks of policing and information into which both chief inhabitants and prospective applicants would be drawn. The absence of the early administrative records of the charity regrettably renders problematic the extent to which the rhetoric of the regulations was actually carried through to rigorous enforcement. The fragmentary surviving eighteenth-century trustees' orders suggest a *sporadic* pattern of social discipline imposed for *exemplary* purposes.[87] There were, inevitably, individual exclusions, both threatened and actual. Jonathan How, for instance, was to 'have no more benefit from the charity till he put his family into better order'. John Chapman Jr and John Clipshoe were, furthermore, 'admonished about attending church and if it be not reformed that they be excluded' from the twenty-four. There were also general trustees' orders which actually modified the terms on which bread was to be allocated. From the 1770s, 'younger persons' were denied access to the charity 'when they have constant collection of the parish'. The trustees were also required to maximise the revenue from the endowment: investigating whether the leases to their present tenants were binding; temporarily suspending the allocation of a half-guinea for the tenants' dinner 'considering the hardness of the times'; and enquiring whether they could sell wood from the Loddington closes without injury to the farm. The fact that these restrictive orders date from the late eighteenth century in general, and from the 1790s in particular, when the parish officers were struggling to cope with rising relief expenditure, is hardly coincidental.

By definition, the economic significance of the charity is extremely difficult to reconstruct. From the point of view of the trustees, overseers and ratepayers, the relative yield of the endowment was certainly diminishing over time. Although there is no basis for calculating poor relief expenditure in Geddington at the time the charity was endowed, it is likely that the £15 yielded annually in the 1630s looked very generous in the context of the burden of parish relief. By the 1770s, however, when the endowment was yielding about £31 annually, about *six times* that sum was annually being expended on the poor by parish overseers. It seems likely that the symbolic significance of the charity had declined accordingly. The calculation of the contribution of a weekly loaf in the budgets of the rural poor is beyond the scope of this analysis. In terms of its sheer longevity, however, the charity certainly came to form a central and robust plank in the social and political structure of the village: it survives to this day, and the church still contains a shelf for Dallington's loaves. The profile of its recipients is revealed by a list of the 'twenty-four' surviving in the parish register for 29 September 1735: twenty of the twenty-four were female, sixteen of them widows.[88] At first sight, then, the life-cycle seems to have been as decisive in the practicalities of entitlement to charity as it was to poor relief itself.[89] This assessment ought to be at least slightly qualified in the light of the existence of a further list of twelve individuals, including only two widows and ten adult males, who were considered deserving under the terms of the charity but were awaiting admission to the twenty-four. There seems, however, to have been considerable overlap between those in receipt of a parish pension and those who partook of Dallington's bread: eight of the eleven regular pensioners in 1743 had been among the twenty-four in 1735.[90] Impressionistic though it is, this is exactly the sort of analysis that must be conducted if historians are ever to understand the mechanics of the economy of makeshifts at the individual level.

The foundation of a second, and less well-documented, Geddington parish charity coincided with both the relatively high levels of relief expenditure in the late 1710s and early 1720s and with Duke of Montagu's enclosure proposals. In anticipation that Montagu's project would succeed, Samuel Lee endowed a trust with £100, intending that the proceeds be distributed to the poor of Geddington every Christmas day. As his Grace's Ranger on Geddington Chase, Lee was well familiar with the appalling levels of poverty in the parish. The charity was targeted 'on every such poor inhabitant of the parish as by age and infirmities should be reduced to want and necessity'. The trustees, then, were expected to give preference 'to poor widows and aged and infirm persons'. In practice, however, sums ranging from one to three shillings were distributed among 'all the poor persons belonging to the parish except such as partake of Dallington's charity'. The reference to the prior endowment, confirming that Lee's bequest was residual, emphasises the symbolic and practical significance of its predecessor. It is also a cogent reminder that, from the perspective of the propertied, if not of the poor, the planks of the economy of care should ideally *interlock* rather than *overlap*.

Conclusion

What, then, does the experience of the Geddington Chase parishes tell us about the hierarchy that existed within the 'mixed economy of welfare' in a seventeenth- and eighteenth-century forest environment? Three sets of conclusions suggest themselves: the first relates to the changing material significance, and in turn to the social and political meanings, of each of our three components, and especially of the Dallington charity, over time; the second to the relationship between enclosure and endowed charity; and the third to the characterisation of the 'mixed' economy as 'makeshift'. The following discussion will explore each of these issues in turn.

In the early seventeenth century, the value of Dallington's bread must have been relatively substantial in both material and symbolic terms. Over time, however, the very limited scope of the charity, hemmed in as it was with conditions and demands, must surely have become more apparent. Such charitable provision appeared token and conditional, resonant of that 'public theatre' of paternalism described by Edward Thompson.[91] While charity bread might be ranked ahead of, or (at the very least) alongside, the parish dole – though both were undoubtedly less significant than common right – at the beginning of our period, therefore, their relative importance had almost certainly been reversed by its end. Relative to the burden of the parish rate, twenty-four loaves did not represent a substantial cost by the late eighteenth century, but then they did not, by that time, buy much deference either. All of this suggests that common rights were the fundamental element in the matrix of resources, that the poor themselves recognised this fact, and that their long battle to defend them was justified. These suspicions are confirmed by the very substantial increase in poor relief expenditure in the years after enclosure took place.

As well as measuring the economic dimensions of this matrix of resources, historians might also usefully reconstruct its social and political significance. If there was a politics to the poor rate, to endowed charity, or to common right, it was 'a politics of meaning'.[92] To those who enjoyed it, of course, common right was symbolic of independence. But to those who were denied legitimate access, customary rights might be just one more example of the politics of exclusion through which the local hierarchy of belonging was constructed. There is a very real sense in which Robert Powell's famous condemnation of the depopulating enclosures of the 1630s holds true for the piecemeal regulation of rights throughout the seventeenth and eighteenth centuries as a whole: these were, indeed, 'stinted times' during which the poor were not only *hedged* out of the local community by enclosure, but *stinted* out of the customary economy by the increasingly aggressive regulation of rights.[93] The parish pension was itself a product of a culture of dependence and exclusion, often awarded only after protracted negotiations between the prospective pauper, the parish officers and the magistracy, during the course of which the poor were frequently reminded that they were not entitled to relief.[94] These exclusionary processes were in some sense mutually reinforcing: the regulation of common right and the allocation of parish pensions, for instance, might interact to encourage many parishes to export young people in order to prevent them from becoming a burden to the local community.

Endowed charities were also by their very nature exclusive. In this sense, Robert Dallington's church loaves had a 'value' far in excess of their nutritional contribution to the bellies of the Geddington poor. To the trustees of the charity, the recipients were 'bread people', a designation of dependency as well as of diet. Whether or not the poor read the 'orders and directions' in the same way is open to question. Robert Dallington's charity may well be a classic example of an endowment designed to ensure social conformity to new canons of respectability. As recent studies of the popular mentalities of subordination suggest, however, the deferential imperative might well have been a matter of public performance rather than of private conviction.[95] Was the deference and respectability expected of the 'bread people' always as forthcoming as the trustees expected?

Part of the answer to that question may well lie in the ability of the poor of Geddington Chase to supplement their income with the use-rights of the forest. Up until enclosure, common right might insulate the poor from the monopolistic pretensions of the trustees and parish officers. This tendency is neatly encapsulated in the objection of the vestrymen of Coton, Cambridgeshire, to the magistrates' decision in 1662 that they pay a pension to an ancient resident, complaining that he abused the officers, that he never came to church, that he spent any money he had in the alehouse, and that he did not need the money anyway as he had a cow and a calf.[96] After enclosure had removed the grazing rights for the cow and the calf, the bleak vision of 'nuclear family hardship', in which tiny households were saved from extinction only by overseers of the poor and the trustees of endowed charity, seems all the more compelling.[97] To this extent it is particularly unfortunate that Neeson's marvellous study of the impact of parliamentary enclosure in Northamptonshire paid so little attention to poor law materials, a *lacuna* which this essay is intended, at least in part, to fill.[98]

The second implication of the foregoing discussion relates to the relationship between endowed charity and enclosure. As Buchanan Sharp has noted, 'it was axiomatic among statesmen and social commentators that unimproved waste and pasture fostered a population of idle, disorderly and beggarly poor'.[99] This belief was used to justify enclosure that aimed to extend tillage, and in the process not only eliminated disorder and idleness but also reformed the manners and behaviour of the poor who obtained allotments of land as compensation for loss of access to the commons. The deployment of this instrument of reformation is perhaps most clearly seen in those instances of enclosure where the compensation for the poor commoners, directly or otherwise, took the form of the endowment of town and parochial charities managed by the better sort of the community.[100] At first sight, the experience of Geddington Chase seems to confirm Sharp's assessment, with Dallington's bread charity stipulating some of the most severe restrictions on eligibility yet discovered by historians of rural paternalism. Yet it must be remembered that Dallington's charity, endowed as early as 1636, *predated* the enclosure of Geddington Chase by over 150 years. Indeed, it is an extraordinary testament to the 'fierce and upstanding forest folk' (as the Reverend J. E. Linnell called them) that enclosure was staved off for so long.[101] In its own way, however, Dallington's charity actually sought to reinforce legalistic definitions of common right, for its establishment helped close the parish to those outsiders who might have been inclined to exploit the commonable resources of the Chase. In imposing order – 'in the choosing and well governing of the poor' – Dallington both sought to settle memories queasy at the carnage of 1607 and to stabilise population levels in a region notorious for its in-migration.

Finally, what does the experience of Geddington Chase tell us about the place of common right within the mixed economy of welfare? Modern historians, despite some fascinating experiments, have found it no easier than contemporaries to put a realistic value on rights lost at enclosure. They have been most successful with respect to grazing rights: Shaw-Taylor has estimated that cows kept on common land by poor people in the late eighteenth century could produce dairy products worth £7–10 per annum, perhaps as much as 40 per cent of an agricultural labourer's annual income.[102] But the value of forest rights is much more difficult to calculate, partly because of the extraordinarily diverse resources available in a forest economy. Even so, it has been estimated that fuel-rights in the late eighteenth century could have been worth between £2–5 per annum or 10–20 per cent of the earnings of an agricultural labourer.[103]

It is, accordingly, tempting to include common right in the

'economy of makeshifts', that series of sources of income – day labour, by-employment and casual jobs, charitable doles, neighbourly and/or kin support, loans and begging – on which the poor could draw to support themselves. To regard the exploitation of common right as a 'makeshift' strategy is, however, to misunderstand the highly diversified economies of those parts of England which failed to conform to the arable regime of sheep-corn country which has become the standard point of reference in most discussions of poverty. The drawing of one's livelihood from many different natural sources was far from 'precarious and uncertain', whatever the Duke of Buccleuch's estate agent might argue to the contrary, and had considerable merits, many of which might (in certain economic conditions) be far superior to wage labour, let alone to the parish pension.[104] From this perspective, the 'economy of makeshifts' is perhaps better described as an 'economy of diversified resources', an economy whose products arrived just as regularly and seasonally, if less visibly in the historical record, as corn, sheep and cattle.[105]

The economy of diversified resources practised on Geddington Chase was therefore a matrix of overlapping – though sometimes mutually exclusive – expedients, governed by a complex pattern of rights and obligations, claims and counter-claims. To understand it requires detailed consideration not only of the management of common right, but also of the operation of the poor law, and of the administration of endowed charity. In turn, it seems essential to take a long view of the significance of customary practice, for the battles to defend common right were often protracted, prolonged by the plebeian desire to preserve custom for posterity. The artificial periodisation – in Keith Wrightson's terms, the enclosure of English social history – has done us no favours in this regard: studies of opposition to enclosure in eighteenth-century Northamptonshire seem to have been written in ignorance of the long tradition of resistance to depopulation in the forest parishes discussed here. Furthermore, the disentangling of the validity of common right is a project which the commoners of the 1720s found essential and modern historians are at long last beginning to take seriously.[106] Finally, to attempt to study the dynamics of provision for the poor, either through parish pensions or endowed charities, in the absence of any consideration of common right seems fundamentally misguided. Robert Wilkinson was, in a sense which he failed to recognise, speaking the truth:

man does not live 'by bread only'. In practice, it seems clear that the survival of the indigent and their families owed rather less to faith, charity and hope, or even to their deferential deportment to win a weekly hand-out from overseer and trustee, and rather more to the tenaciously-defended uses (and, inevitably, the abuses) of waste. In Geddington Chase, wood rather than bread proved to be the staff of life.

Notes

1 For the Midland Rising, see E. F. Gay, 'The midland revolt and the inquisitions of depopulation of 1607', *Transactions of the Royal Historical Society*, new ser., 18 (1905); J. E. Martin, *Feudalism to Capitalism: Peasant and Landlord in English Agrarian Development* (London, Macmillan, 1983), pp. 159–215; and R. B. Manning, *Village Revolts: Social Protest and Popular Disturbances in England 1509–1640* (Oxford, Clarendon, 1988), pp. 229–46. For Montagu's role, see E. S. Cope, *The Life of a Public Man: Edward, First Baron Montagu of Boughton, 1562–1644* (Philadelphia, Philadelphia University Press, 1981), pp. 50–4.

2 Robert Wilkinson, *A Sermon Preached at North-Hampton the 21 of June Last Past Before the Lord Lieutenant of the County and the Rest of the Commissioners There Assembled Upon Occasion of the Late Rebellion and Riots in Those Parts Committed* (London, J. Flasket, 1607), sigs. A3–3v, D3. For Wilkinson himself, see J. A. Venn, *Alumni Cantabrigienses: A Biographical List of All Known Students, Graduates and Holders of Office at the University of Cambridge from the Earliest Times to 1900, Part I: From the Earliest Times to 1751*, 4 vols (Cambridge, Cambridge University Press, 1922–27), IV, p. 411. For the commissioners at the 1607 trials, who included several Northamptonshire landlords notorious for their enclosing activities, see Public Record Office (hereafter PRO) C181/2, fol. 32v.

3 Wilkinson, *A Sermon*, quotations at sigs. A4, B1v, B2, C4v, D2, F4 (emphasis in original).

4 *Ibid.*, sig. B1. For other examples of clerical insistence on patience and forbearance even in the face of oppression, see J. Walter and K. Wrightson, 'Dearth and the social order in early modern England', *Past and Present*, 71 (1976).

5 For clarity and convenience, Geddington Woods will be referred to as Geddington Chase throughout the remainder of this chapter.

6 J. Innes, 'The "mixed economy of welfare" in early modern England: assessments of the options from Hale to Malthus (c. 1683–1803)', in M. Daunton (ed.), *Charity, Self-Interest and Welfare in the English Past* (London, UCL Press, 1996).

7 O. Hufton, *The Poor of Eighteenth-Century France* (Oxford, Clarendon, 1974), pp. 25–68.

8 For this formulation, see P. Horden and R. Smith, 'Introduction', in P. Horden and R. Smith (eds), *The Locus of Care: Families, Communities, Institutions and the Provision of Welfare Since Antiquity* (London, Routledge, 1998), p. 1.

9 P. Slack, *Poverty and Policy in Tudor and Stuart England* (London, Longman, 1988), pp. 163–72.

10 The most important discussions of the resort to these expedients during the seventeenth century are I. Krausman Ben-Amos, '"Good works" and social ties: helping the migrant poor in early modern England', in M. C. McClendon, J. P. Ward and M. MacDonald (eds), *Protestant Identities: Religion, Society and Self-Fashioning in Post-Reformation England* (Stanford, Stanford University Press, 1999), pp. 125–40; I. Krausman Ben-Amos, 'Gifts and favors: informal support in early modern England', *Journal of Modern History*, 72 (2000); J. Boulton, '"It is extreme necessity that makes me do this": some survival strategies of pauper households in London's west end during the early eighteenth century', in L. Fontaine and J. Schlumbohm (eds), *Household Strategies for Survival, 1600–2000: Fission, Faction and Cooperation* (Cambridge, Cambridge University Press, 2001); J. Walter, 'The social economy of dearth in early modern England', in J. Walter and R. Schofield (eds), *Famine, Disease and the Social Order in Early Modern Society* (Cambridge, Cambridge University Press, 1989), pp. 75–128; J. Walter, 'Subsistence strategies, social economy and the politics of subsistence in early modern England', in A. Hakkinen (ed.), *Just a Sack of Potatoes? Crisis Experiences in European Societies, Past and Present* (Helsinki, Studia Historica 44, 1992), pp. 53–85; P. G. Lawson, 'Property crime and hard times in England, 1559–1624', *Law and History Review*, 4 (1986); J. Styles, 'Embezzlement, industry and the law in England, 1500–1800', in M. Berg, P. Hudson and M. Sonnenscher (eds), *Manufacture in Town and Countryside Before the Factory* (Cambridge, Cambridge University Press, 1983), pp. 173–210.

11 For an attempt, see S. Hindle, 'Dearth, fasting and alms: the campaign for general hospitality in late Elizabethan England', *Past and Present*, 172 (2001).

12 D. Cressy, 'Kinship and kin interaction in early modern England', *Past and Present*, 113 (1986), p. 69; Walter, 'The social economy', p. 82. For two early and very influential statements of the relationship between kinship networks and welfare systems, see P. Laslett, 'The family and the collectivity', *Sociology and Social Research*, 63 (1979) and P. Laslett, 'Family, kinship and collectivity as systems of support in pre-industrial Europe: a consideration of the "nuclear-hardship" hypothesis', *Continuity and Change*, 3 (1988).

13 For the early modern period, see A. Wood, 'The place of custom in

plebeian political culture: England, 1550–1800', *Social History*, 22 (1997). For the eighteenth century, see J. M. Neeson, *Commoners: Common Right, Enclosure and Social Change in England, 1700–1820* (Cambridge, Cambridge University Press, 1993), pp. 110–57. Also Leigh Shaw-Taylor, 'The management of commons in the lowlands of southern England, c. 1500–1850' (unpublished paper, 2001). I am grateful to Leigh Shaw-Taylor for a sight of this paper in advance of publication.

14 For regulation before 1662, see P. Styles, 'The evolution of the laws of settlement', *University of Birmingham Historical Journal*, 9 (1963) and S. Hindle, 'Exclusion crises: poverty, migration and parochial responsibility in English rural communities, c. 1560–1660', *Rural History*, 7 (1996). The post-1662 situation remains controversial amongst historians who disagree over the relationship between settlement and welfare legislation. For the view that settlement was regulated irrespective of potential liability, see N. Landau, 'The laws of settlement and the surveillance of immigration in eighteenth-century Kent', *Continuity and Change*, 3 (1988); N. Landau, 'The regulation of immigration, economic structures and definitions of the poor in eighteenth-century England', *Historical Journal*, 33 (1990); N. Landau, 'Who was subjected to the laws of settlement? Procedure under the settlement laws in eighteenth-century England', *Agricultural History Review*, 43 (1995). For the contrary position, see K. D. M. Snell, 'Pauper settlement and the right to poor relief in England and Wales', *Continuity and Change*, 6 (1991) and K. D. M. Snell, 'Settlement, poor law and the rural historian: new approaches and opportunities', *Rural History*, 3 (1992).

15 W. K. Jordan, *The Charities of Rural England, 1480–1660: The Aspirations and the Achievements of the Rural Society* (London, Allen and Unwin, 1961).

16 Quoting P. Horden, 'Household care and informal networks: comparisons and continuities from antiquity to the present', in Horden and Smith, *The Locus of Care*, p. 27; also the recent comparative discussion of three case studies provided in J. Broad, 'Parish economies of welfare, 1650–1834', *Historical Journal*, 42 (1999).

17 For the local economic context, see P. A. J. Pettit, *The Royal Forests of Northamptonshire: A Study in Their Economy, 1558–1714* (Gateshead, Northamptonshire Record Society 23, 1968), pp. 141–82; B. Bellamy, *Geddington Chase: The History of a Wood* (Irthlingborough, privately published, 1986); Neeson, *Commoners*; R. Moore-Colyer, 'Woods and woodland management: the bailiwick of Rockingham, Northamptonshire, c. 1700–1840', *Northamptonshire Past and Present*, 9 (1996–97); R. Moore-Colyer, 'Land and people in Northamptonshire: Great Oakley, 1750–1850', *Agricultural History Review*, 45 (1997); and *idem*, 'The small land occupier in east Northamptonshire, ca. 1650–1850', *Midland History*, 23 (1998).

18 PRO E179/155/160, analysed in Pettit, *Royal Forests*, p. 143.
19 See the findings of Tom Arkell reported in D. Levine and K. Wright-son, *The Making of an Industrial Society: Whickham, 1560–1765* (Oxford, Clarendon, 1991), p. 157, in which the exemption rates in rural (i.e. as opposed to either 'urban' or 'industrial') areas appear to be far lower than those in Rockingham Forest, ranging between 19.0 and 38.6 per cent. The dangers of using the hearth tax as an index of poverty *in isolation from other sources* are emphasised in T. Arkell, 'The incidence of poverty in England in the later seventeenth century', *Social History*, 12 (1987).
20 The following analysis is based upon V. A. Hatley (ed.), *Northamptonshire Militia Lists, 1777* (Gateshead, Northampton Record Society 25, 1973), pp. 17–18, 21–2, 26.
21 Pettit, *Royal Forests*, p. 175 n. 2.
22 The report of Mr Edmunds of Boughton House is printed in J. Donaldson, *A General View of the Agriculture of the County of Northampton* (Edinburgh, 1794), pp. 37–42.
23 The classic study of forest disorder in the early modern period remains B. Sharp, *In Contempt of All Authority: Rural Artisans and Riot in the West of England, 1586–1660* (Los Angeles, University of California Press, 1980). But now see also C. Harrison, 'Fire on the Chase: rural riots in sixteenth-century Staffordshire', in P. Morgan and A. D. M. Philips (eds), *Staffordshire Histories: Essays in Honour of Michael Greenslade* (Keele, Staffordshire Record Society, 19, 1999), pp. 97–126.
24 Norden's 'Proiect touching th' Improving of Wasts, Coppising & Inclosing of some common Fields in Forests' probably dates from c. 1609 and survives in a bound compilation of writings concerning the King's woods and forests sent to and/or collected by Sir Julius Caesar: PRO LR2/194, fols 304–7v (quotation at fol. 304). It was transcribed and published as John St John, *Observations on the Land Revenues of the Crown* (London, J. Debrett, 1787), p. 168, appendix II. For the context, see R. W. Hoyle, 'Disafforestation and drainage: the crown as entrepreneur?', in *idem* (ed.), *The Estates of the English Crown, 1558–1640* (Cambridge, Cambridge University Press, 1992), p. 359, n. 32. There is an invaluable brief discussion of 'ungovernable multitudes' in Northamptonshire forest villages in Pettit, *Royal Forests*, pp. 162–3.
25 J. Humphries, 'Enclosures, common rights, and women: the prole-tarianisation of families in the late eighteenth and early nineteenth centuries', *Journal of Economic History*, 50 (1990); P. King, 'Customary rights and women's earnings: the importance of gleaning to the rural labouring poor, 1750–1850', *Economic History Review*, 44 (1991); S. Horrell and J. Humphries, 'Old questions, new data, and alternative perspectives: families' living standards in the Industrial Revolution', *Journal of Economic History*, 52 (1992); and

L. Shaw-Taylor, 'Labourers, cows, common rights and parliamentary enclosure: the evidence of contemporary comment, c. 1760–1810', *Past and Present*, 171 (2001). The prominence of forest and woodland resources in the provision of fuel is nicely emphasised in D. Woodward, 'Straw, bracken and the Wicklow Whale: the exploitation of natural resources in England since 1500', *Past and Present*, 159 (1998).

26 Neeson, *Commoners*, pp. 158–84.
27 G. Hardin, 'The tragedy of the commons', *Science*, 162 (1968). For an interesting theoretical critique, see B. J. McCay and J. M. Acheson, 'Human ecology of the commons', in *idem* (eds), *The Question of the Commons: The Culture and Ecology of Communal Resources* (Tucson, University of Arizona Press, 1987).
28 Woodward, 'Straw', pp. 54–5.
29 J. M. Neeson, 'The opponents of enclosure in eighteenth-century Northamptonshire', *Past and Present*, 105 (1985), p. 138. Also the analyses of the social and cultural significance of custom in E. Thompson, *Customs in Common* (London, Penguin, 1991), pp. 1–15, 97–184; and in R. W. Bushaway, 'Rite, legitimation and community in southern England, 1700–1850: the ideology of custom', in B. Stapleton (ed.), *Conflict and Community in Southern England: Essays in the History of Rural and Urban Labour From Medieval to Modern Times* (Gloucester, Sutton, 1992), pp. 110–34.
30 Steve Hindle, 'A sense of place? Becoming and belonging in the rural parish, 1550–1650', in A. Shepard and P. Withington (eds), *Communities in Early Modern England* (Manchester, Manchester University Press, 2000), pp. 103–5.
31 Pettit, *Royal Forests*, pp. 162, 193, appendix III, clause 10.
32 Northamptonshire Record Office (hereafter NRO) Montagu (B) 10.24 (Brand Depositions).
33 For manorial jurisdiction over hedge-breaking, see M. K. McIntosh, *Controlling Misbehaviour in England, 1370–1600* (Cambridge, Cambridge University Press, 1998), pp. 84–8; for the discretionary power of overseers of the poor, see S. Hindle, 'Exhortation and entitlement: negotiating inequality in English rural communities, 1550–1650', in M. Braddick and J. Walter (eds), *Negotiating Power in Early Modern Society: Order, Hierarchy and Subordination in Britain and Ireland* (Cambridge, Cambridge University Press, 2001), pp. 112–13; and for the summary jurisdiction of magistrates, see J. A. Sharpe, *Crime in Seventeenth-Century England: A County Study* (Cambridge, Cambridge University Press, 1983), pp. 170–1. For the later history, emphasising the significance of the statute 15 Charles II, c. 2, see R. W. Bushaway, 'From custom to crime: wood gathering in eighteenth- and early nineteenth-century England: a focus for conflict in Hampshire, Wiltshire and the south', in J. Rule (ed.), *Outside the Law: Studies in Crime and Order, 1650–1850* (Exeter, Exeter University Press, 1982),

pp. 65–101. Also the discussion in R. W. Bushaway, *By Rite: Custom, Ceremony and Community in England, 1700–1800* (London, Junction, 1982), pp. 207–37.

34 Pettit, *Royal Forests*, p. 162.

35 Woodward, 'Straw', pp. 55.

36 D. Hall, *The Open Fields of Northamptonshire* (Gateshead, Northamptonshire Record Society 38, 1995), pp. 9–14, 214–15.

37 Pettit, *Royal Forests*, p. 155.

38 Bellamy, *Geddington Chase*, p. 48.

39 The following analysis is based upon NRO x7523 Montagu (B) 43 Geddington (5 Books) x. 1330 (court rolls 1730, unfol.; 1731, fos 6–7; 1732, fo. 6; 1734, fo. 5; 1735, fo. 5; 1738, fo. 29).

40 K. Wrightson, 'The politics of the parish in early modern England', in P. Griffiths, A. Fox and S. Hindle (eds), *The Experience of Authority in Early Modern England* (London, Macmillan, 1996), p. 35.

41 Pettit, *Royal Forests*, pp. 143, 145. On the statute of 1589 and its implications, see Styles, 'The evolution'; and Hindle, 'Exclusion crises'.

42 Pettit, *Royal Forests*, pp. 170–1. This formulation, even down to the (possibly formulaic?) number of poor immigrants, is intriguingly almost identical to that used in the Hertfordshire parish of Layston in 1636: Hindle, 'Exclusion crises', pp. 133.

43 NRO Brudenell MS I, vi, 60.

44 For the optimistic reading, emphasising widespread access, see Neeson, *Commoners*, pp. 55–80; for the pessimistic reading, based on a highly legalistic interpretation, see Shaw-Taylor, 'Labourers'.

45 NRO Montagu (B) Box 10.26 (An Estimate of the Chase); Neeson, *Commoners*, p. 62, n. 23.

46 PRO C3/332/42.

47 NRO Montagu (B) Box W28 (Barton to Montagu, Nov. 1710).

48 PRO STAC5/A13/36; J. Walter, 'A "rising of the people"? The Oxfordshire rising of 1596', *Past and Present*, 107 (1985).

49 NRO Montagu of Boughton (Buccleuch and Queensberry) MSS, vol. XIII, fos 17, 18a–c.

50 Manning, *Village Revolts*, p. 242.

51 Belvoir Castle, Muniment Rooms, Room I, Case 3, vol. XV, fols 40–1.

52 NRO Montagu (B) Box 10.22 (Brand Depositions in the Exchequer); PRO E163/17/8. For another example of Tresham's hard dealing, see PRO C2/James I/s24/55 (June 1618).

53 M. E. Finch, *The Wealth of Five Northamptonshire Families, 1540–1640* (Oxford, Northamptonshire Record Society 19, 1956), pp. 162–3. For other uses of this idiom, see Wilkinson, *A Sermon*, sig. C4v; and R. Powell, *Depopulation Arraigned, Convicted and Condemned By the Laws of God and Man* (London, 1636), pp. 54–5.

54 Described in some detail by Bellamy, *Geddington Chase*, pp. 45–9.

Supplementary material is in NRO Montagu (B) 10.26; and NRO Brudenell MS I, vi, 1–75.

55 NRO Brudenell MS I, vi, 59 (Some Reasons Offered to Such Persons as Have Common Right in Geddington Chase, c. 1721).

56 NRO Montagu (B) Box 10.25 (A Particular of the Persons Who Have Been Acquainted With His Grace's Proposals).

57 S. Hindle, 'Persuasion and protest in the Caddington Common enclosure dispute, 1635–39', *Past and Present*, 158 (1998); S. Hipkin, '"Sitting on his penny rent": conflict and right of common in Faversham Blean, 1595–1610', *Rural History*, 11 (2000).

58 NRO Montagu (B) Box 10.25 (J. B. to the Earl of Cardigan, 27 November 1721).

59 Thompson, *Customs*, pp. 98–9; Hindle, 'A sense of place?', p. 108.

60 The following quotations are drawn from the copy in the Bodleian Library, Oxford (Northamptonshire Gough 10): *A Letter to the Commoners in Rockingham Forest Wherein is Briefly and Plainly Shewn the Right of Common They Are Intitled to in the Forrest and a Method Propos'd By Which They May Preserve Their Rights at a Very Easy Expense If They Will Unanimously Pursue It By a Commoner* [Ms: 'i.e. the reverend Mr Good of Weldon'] (Stamford, printed by F. Howgrave, 1744) [price three pence] pp. 4, 12–13, 18.

61 NRO Montagu (B) 10.26 (Petition of the Inhabitants of Brigstock, 30 November 1792). Cf text at note 53, p. 51.

62 NRO Montagu (B) 10.26 (The Small Proprietors of Brigstock, Stanion and Geddington to the Duchess of Buccleuch, July 1794); 10.26 (Churchwardens and Overseers of Geddington to the Duke of Buccleuch, 26 July 1795).

63 Neeson, *Commoners*, p. 273, n. 44.

64 Shaw-Taylor, 'Labourers'.

65 Neeson, *Commoners*, p. 281.

66 For recent pessimism about the speed with which the Elizabethan legislation was introduced in the parishes, see P. Slack, *From Reformation to Improvement: Public Welfare in Early Modern England* (Oxford, Clarendon, 1998), p. 67, n. 55. For the more optimistic reading see S. Hindle, *The Birthpangs of Welfare: Poor Relief and Parish Governance in Seventeenth-Century Warwickshire* (Warwick, Dugdale Society Occasional Papers 40, 2000), pp. 9, 22.

67 NRO 175p (Great Houghton Parish Papers)/28 (Churchwardens's Account Book, c. 1634–98), unfol.

68 Based on an analysis of the parish papers held in the NRO.

69 This discussion and Figure 2.1 are based on an analysis of the overseers' account books of Brigstock: NRO 48p/34 (1738–50), 65 (1751–56), 36 (1764–70), 38 (1770–80), 39 (1790–1800), 55 (1800), 40 (1800–1), 32 (1803–7), 37 (1807–10); of Geddington: NRO 133p/80 (1715–23), 82 (1743–51), 83 (1752–65), 84 (1765–74), 86 (1774–83), 91 (1783–87), 93 (1794–98), 95 (1800–8), 97 (1808–13),

99 (1813–17); and of Stanion: NRO 298p/25 (overseers' and church-wardens' accounts, 1701–20), 34 (overseers' and churchwardens' accounts, 1736–54), 30 (overseers' and churchwardens' accounts, 1784–95), 28 (1795–1801), 35 (1801–5).

70 A. L. Beier, 'Poverty and progress in early modern England', in A. L. Beier, D. Cannadine and J. Rosenheim (eds), *The First Modern Society: Essays in English History in Honour of Lawrence Stone* (Cambridge, Cambridge University Press, 1989), p. 207. Also Hindle, *The Birthpangs*, p. 16.

71 NRO 133p/2(1) (Parish Register 1700–45), unfol.

72 For the loose use of the term in the eighteenth century, see F. M. Eden, *The State of the Poor*, 3 vols (London, 1797). For 'the poore' as a 'gentry-made' term, see Thompson, *Customs in Common*, p. 17.

73 NRO 133p/80 (unfol.), 82 (unfol.).

74 NRO 48p/34 (unfol.), 65 (unfol.), 36 (unfol.). In early seventeenth-century Warwickshire, casual relief accounted for less than 10 per cent of expenditure on the poor: Hindle, *The Birthpangs of Welfare*, p. 16.

75 This was, of course, one of the avowed intentions of the Elizabethan poor laws: Hindle, 'Exhortation and entitlement', p. 110.

76 For Dallington himself, see Karl-Josef Holtgen, 'Sir Robert Dallington (1561–1637): author, traveller, and pioneer of taste', *Huntingdon Library Quarterly*, 47 (1984); *idem*, 'The English reformation and some Jacobean writers on art', in U. Broich, T. Stemmler and G. Stratmann (eds), *Functions of Literature: Essays Presented to Erwin Wolff on his Sixtieth Birthday* (Tubingen, Niemeyer, 1984), pp. 119–46; R. Strong, *Henry Prince of Wales and England's Lost Renaissance* (London, Thames and Hudson, 1986), pp. 30–1; and S. Porter, 'Order and disorder in the early modern almshouse: the Charterhouse example', *London Journal*, 23 (1998). Copies of Dallington's will, dated 20 April 1636, survive as PRO PROB 11/176; NRO 133p/158–9, 166–68.

77 These details on the mechanics of the charity are drawn from NRO 133p/160–64.

78 Quoting C. Jones, *The Charitable Imperative: Hospitals and Nursing in Ancien Regime and Revolutionary France* (London, Routledge, 1989), p. 1. Despite its notorious limitations as a source for the *scale* of philanthropy, Jordan, *The Charities*, remains invaluable as a study of the *texture* of endowed charity.

79 All quotations from the charity regulations in this and the subsequent paragraphs are taken from NRO MISC Photostat 1610.

80 Porter, 'Order', pp. 8–9.

81 For striking examples of discriminatory endowed charities, see K. Wrightson and D. Levine, *Poverty and Piety in an English Village: Terling, 1525–1700* (2nd edn, Oxford, Clarendon, 1995), p. 179

(Henry Smith in Terling, Essex, in 1612); and H. M. Wood (ed.), *Wills and Inventories from the Registry at Durham, Part IV* (Newcastle, Surtees Society 142, 1929), pp. 18–19 (Gilbert Spence in Tynemouth, Durham, in 1607).

82 Horden and Smith, 'Introduction', p. 6.

83 J. Broad, 'The smallholder and cottager after disafforestation – a legacy of poverty?', in J. Broad and R. Hoyle (eds), *Bernwood: The Life and Afterlife of a Forest* (Preston, University of Central Lancashire, 1997), p. 102.

84 W. Le Hardy and G. L. Reckitt (eds), *County of Buckingham: Calendar to the Session Records*, 7 vols (Aylesbury, 1933–80), II, 398.

85 8&9 Will III c. 30 (1697). See S. Hindle, '"A troublesome and difficult business": pauper apprenticeship under the Elizabethan poor laws, c. 1598–1700', in P. Lane, N. Raven and K. Snell (eds), *'Much Toil and Little Hope'?: Work, Gender and Wages in England, c. 1600–1830* (Woodbridge, forthcoming, 2003).

86 For a similarly bald statement (intriguingly, in another forest economy) of the 'deferential imperative' through which subordination was organised, see S. Hindle, 'Hierarchy and community in the Elizabethan parish: the Swallowfield Articles of 1596', *Historical Journal*, 42 (1999), p. 850.

87 The following discussion is based upon NRO 133p/179 (Account Book of Receipts and Expenditure of Dallington Charity, 1744–1847), unfol.

88 NRO 133/P2(1) (Parish Register, 1700–45), unfol.

89 T. Wales, 'Poverty, poor relief and the life-cycle: some evidence from seventeenth-century Norfolk', and W. Newman-Brown, 'The receipt of poor relief and family situation: Aldenham, Hertfordshire 1630–90', both in R. M. Smith (ed.), *Land, Kinship and Life-Cycle* (Cambridge, Cambridge University Press, 1984); L. Botelho, 'Aged and impotent: parish relief of the aged poor in early modern Suffolk', in Daunton, *Charity*; and R. M. Smith, 'Ageing and well-being in early modern England: pension trends and gender preferences under the English Old Poor Law, c. 1650–1800', in P. Johnson and P. Thane (eds), *Old Age From Antiquity to Post-Modernity* (London, Routledge, 1998); also B. Stapleton, 'Inherited poverty and life-cycle poverty: Odiham, Hampshire, 1650–1850', *Social History*, 18 (1993).

90 Levine and Wrightson, *The Making of an Industrial Society*, p. 355, found that only thirteen (10 per cent) of the 126 parish pensioners in Whickham were in receipt of funds from the endowed parish charities in 1743.

91 Thompson, *Customs in Common*, pp. 42–9, especially p. 45.

92 Wrightson, 'The politics', pp. 31–7; also C. Geertz, *The Interpretation of Cultures: Selected Essays* (London, Basic, 1973), pp. 311–26.

93 Quoting Powell, *Depopulation Arraigned*, pp. 50, 77. These ideas are developed at greater length in Hindle, 'A sense', pp. 96–114. For

the view that stints were more effective than hedges in the politics of exclusion, see Shaw-Taylor, 'Labourers', p. 126.

94 For recent pessimism over the extent to which the poor were entitled to relief, especially in the seventeenth century, see Hindle, 'Exhortation and entitlement', p. 113.

95 For an assessment of the usefulness of the distinction between the 'public' and the 'hidden transcript' of social relations, see J. Walter, 'Public transcripts, popular agency and the politics of subsistence in early modern England', in Braddick and Walter, *Negotiating Power*. For the distinction itself, see J. C. Scott, *Domination and the Arts of Resistance: Hidden Transcripts* (New Haven, Yale University Press, 1990).

96 W. M. Palmer, 'The reformation of the Cambridge Corporation, July 1662', *Proceedings of the Cambridge Antiquarian Society*, new ser. II (1913), p. 92.

97 Laslett, 'Family'.

98 A criticism made forcefully by Roger Wells in his review of *Commoners*. See *Southern History*, 16 (1994) pp. 202–4.

99 B. Sharp, 'Common rights, charities and the disorderly poor', in G. Eley and W. Hunt (eds), *Reviving the English Revolution* (London, Verso, 1988), p. 108.

100 Broad, 'The smallholder'.

101 J. E. Linnell, *The Old Oak* (London, Constable, 1932).

102 Shaw-Taylor, 'Labourers'.

103 Humphries, 'Enclosures', pp. 53; Neeson, *Commoners*, p. 165.

104 Woodward, 'Straw'.

105 For a classic example, which demonstrates the enduring capacity of such a lifestyle to support individuals and families, see E. H. Whetham, 'The waygoing', in E. H. Whetham, *The Agrarian History of England and Wales, Volume VIII: 1914–39* (Cambridge, Cambridge University Press, 1978), pp. 321–2.

106 Shaw-Taylor, 'Labourers'.

3
The economy of makeshifts and the role of the poor law: a game of chance?

Margaret Hanly

Overview

> Ann Wilson hath this day behaved very insolent at the meeting in
> Tottington Chapel Vestry – July 10th 1817 [1]

Ann Wilson was a weaver of Tottington Lower End aged 37 years who earned 3s. per week. She is one of the poor who appear in the pages of the Survey of the Poor taken in Tottington Lower End parish in Lancashire in 1817. Her life was not without colour, for she is shown as a woman without a husband and having three illegitimate children. The eldest, a boy of ten, worked in a local colliery and earned as much as his mother at 3s. per week; there were also two daughters, aged seven and a half and two and a half respectively, the youngest being noted as 'a bastard by her sister's husband'. Her possessions consisted of two pairs of looms and one bedstead and bedding; she was employed by Wm Holt, owed £2 11s. in rent and by 1819 the poor relief records reveal that she was in receipt of 3s. per week from her community. Such details, sparse as they are, begin to give a very vivid picture of the economic circumstances of one particular person, and they also open a window into the economy of makeshifts that so many of her Lancashire contemporaries had to exploit in order to survive.[2]

For Ann Wilson, an application for relief to the vestry under the terms of the old poor law was clearly part of her conception of the economy of makeshifts. So was work for both herself and her children, going into arrears with rent and, perhaps, bearing an illegitimate child.[3] Wilson was not alone in regarding the poor law as an important part of the makeshift economy. While welfare historians have come to appreciate that there were marked regional differences in the number of paupers recognised by the poor law and the level and form of relief given to them, what is clear is that the number relieved by the poor law increased considerably across the country after 1760, as did the cost of relieving them.[4] If we add in those who felt poor enough to apply to vestries for relief but were turned down, then it is clear that more and more people saw a role for the poor law in the economy of makeshifts as the eighteenth century progressed and that more and more communities recognised this role too. The important question for welfare historians has been: how extensive was that role? Was the poor law an integral part of the economy of makeshifts or did it figure merely as one of the possibilities depending on the pauper rather than on their poverty? And how exactly did relief payments relate to other payments in the family economy of makeshifts?

As Alannah Tomkins and Steven King suggest in the introduction to this volume, historians disagree on these questions. Such disagreement is not surprising. Certain categories of poor people were likely to be more dependent on the parish than others at all times whereas for many it became a relevant factor at a particular phase of their lives. The family with several young children, some too young to work, those affected by illness or lack of work, those faced with low wages or who had poor skills could easily find themselves in a spiral of poverty which reduced them to pauperism. Others would escape from this when the children were old enough to work and contribute to the family economy only to find their circumstances reduced again when they reached old age. For those families where both parents and some of the older children at least could work their economy of makeshifts would be constructed largely from this source. For those with a sick or absent parent or for a deserted wife or widow with children the application for relief from the parish had a greater urgency. Understanding the role and character of poor relief in the welfare process is thus at least partly a function of reconstructing life-cycles of need, as Steven King and Alannah Tomkins suggest in their conclusion.

Even before this, however, it is necessary to try and uncover the *sentiment* of the old poor law if one is to locate it in general terms in the wider economy of makeshifts. Again, historians disagree on this matter, but for the purposes of this chapter, which concentrates on the economy of makeshifts in Lancashire, it is appropriate to characterise the poor law as *defensive*. Despite recent attempts to rethink the powerlessness of the poor, in Lancashire power and authority very clearly lay with the officials who were charged with the obligation of both collecting the poor rate and of dispensing the amount of this allotted to the poor.[5] Apart from the statutory duty to relieve, these officials laid down their own tacit criteria for determining what they deemed to be poverty and who was worthy to be helped from the resources available. Their responsibility lay both to the ratepayers, to whom they had to give an annual account, and to the needy, whose survival they had to be seen to ensure. The vestry or overseer therefore had to consider the legal requirements and for this reason it was necessary to ensure whether applicants for relief were the responsibility of the parish and if not whether they could be removed elsewhere. If they could establish a valid settlement the pauper had to prove need. This would include confirming to the satisfaction of the overseer that all other avenues of help had been explored. These would cover work and this would mean also their wife and children, applying for charity, selling or pawning their possessions, relying on kin, taking in lodgers and even considering emigration. Even the aged were not immune from these strictures and many worked into extreme old age, as Pat Thane has recently shown.[6]

The parish officers would, if the pauper were deemed worthy of relief, grant whatever amount and in whatever manner they chose. This did not mean that the request of the pauper was honoured; in many instances cash was not given or in small amounts and instead goods in the form of coal, cloth, clogs, or foodstuffs were provided. These often represented what the vestry could acquire at the lowest price. It does not escape attention that many members of Lancashire vestries or other prominent ratepayers were often the local manufacturers or merchants whose goods would be made available for sale to the vestry for this purpose.[7] In practice, even the briefest survey of Lancashire poor law records reveals that parish officers faced a constant tension between thinking long-term and reacting to short-term local influences on the supply of or demand for relief. Thus the presence of vagrants in the Lancashire market town of Garstang posed a persistent problem for the vestry, resulting in stringent vestry rules as an attempt to control their numbers and to persuade them to move on. In the meantime, the vestry took its eyes off the rising value of pensions and had to periodically cut back. In Rossendale, the existence of a factory or mill often proved to be the impetus to direct the parish relief towards apprenticeship for pauper children, or a reason to deny relief to a pauper reluctant to accept (or simply unable to survive on) a less than basic wage. This short-term pragmatism did little to address the clear over-supply of labour in the area. Meanwhile, at particular times of crisis or as the numbers of the poor simply increased many Lancashire parishes adopted a policy of judging applicants for relief by standards of morality and gave the appearance of being more concerned with the character and disposition of a pauper than with the fact that the person was in need. In such circumstances, as will be seen below, the parish was adroit in marrying its requirements to keep the poor rate at a minimum level and meeting the needs of the poor by effectively making the poor look after their fellow paupers.

These observations could be made about most counties at some point in time, but rarely do they apply so completely or for so long as in Lancashire. Not surprisingly – another of the general points raised by Alannah Tomkins and Steven King in their introduction – it was rare for the Lancashire poor law to provide relief at a level, or with a constancy that was sufficient to guarantee subsistence. More than the poor elsewhere, those in Lancashire had a particular need for recourse to the economy of makeshifts. The broad outlines of this economy of makeshifts are set out else-where in this volume, but a brief recap is useful for this chapter. Thus, as well as work, what must be borne in mind are the un-written and unspoken factors which figured largely in the economic lives of many: the help from kin and neighbours, the reliance on credit both social and fiscal, the place of crime in the survival of many at the very edges of destitution, and the charitable grant which eased the burden of those not only without regular work but also those with low or intermittent wages. In all Lancashire communities that I have studied, certain basic expectations prevailed. These were that the poor would work if work was available unless prevented by age (and this would mean extreme old age), youth or sickness. They would have a minimum of possessions which they would be expected to sell or pawn in times of difficulty. Some would be members of, and could draw benefit from, sick clubs or friendly societies. They would look to, and in turn give support to, their 'kin' or network of friends, family and associates often living close by and who provided a raft of help and care in times of difficulty.[8] *Lastly*, a fact that we can see from the very sparse inventories periodically taken of pauper goods, the poor would turn to the township or parish for relief. Even then, as I have suggested, paupers would sometimes be offered relief in a form which they did not want or which was simply of little use or was insufficient. Those who were granted some relief from the parish were undoubtedly still poor in the Lancashire context.

This chapter will begin to explore the economy of makeshifts generally, and the relationship between that economy of makeshifts and the character of the poor law in particular, for one of England's most neglected counties, Lancashire. It utilises rich documentation drawn from a variety of Lancashire communities located in Figure 3.1: the Select Vestry and Overseers' accounts from Garstang, including the Survey of the Poor in 1818,[9] the Survey of Poor Families in 1817 from Tottington,[10] the Census of the Poor from Great and Little Marsden in 1826,[11] the View of the Poor taken by Richard Eastwood of the same townships in 1829,[12] the Census of the Poor for Ashton and Haydock in 1815[13] and the names of the sick and poor of Barrowford.[14] While poverty and welfare in growing urban centres such as Liverpool and Manchester have been dealt with by others,[15] poverty, welfare and the economy of makeshifts in rural and rural industrial areas like these have more rarely been considered for the north of England generally and Lancashire in particular.

Places and sources

The townships of Haydock and Ashton-in-Makerfield were both part of the larger parish of Winwick. The main features of Haydock, described at a later period, were undulating and flat, having features typical of a colliery country, and in the east were fields and plantations in which oats, wheat and vegetables were grown. Coal was found in the eighteenth century and mining became the central industry of the place, though it did not dominate the occupational structure at any point.[16] The adjacent township of

Figure 3.1 Map of Lancashire

Ashton-in-Makerfield was similarly described as being mostly flat, with cultivation of root and grain crops. Baines's Lancashire Directory of 1825 further described Ashton as 'a large and populous village the centre of a brisk manufacturing district where the poor are industrious and their employers prosperous'.[17] Collieries were also beginning to form part of the local economy by the early nineteenth century, as was small-scale metal working. In contrast Garstang, located on the main road from Preston to Lancaster, had a mainly agricultural structure with the land predominantly turned over to pasture and some wheat and oats grown. The main industry, which was situated to the south of the town at Catterall, was a calico printing works that failed in 1830. The town had an 1801 population of some 731 and was the focus of a great deal of passing traffic both in the form of goods and vagrants. The townships of Great and Little Marsden, meanwhile, were subdivisions of the parish of Marsden and both were to be absorbed at the end of the nineteenth century into the towns of Brierfield, Nelson and Colne. The agricultural land was poor in quality and used almost entirely for pasture. Industry consisted of some small-scale coal mining and cotton manufacturing and quarrying on the moorland areas. Common features can be found between these townships and that of Tottington Lower End. This place which, together with Tottington Higher End, originally formed all the northern part of the parish of Bury, was a rural area which became industrialised within one eighteenth-century generation and bore all the hallmarks by the early nineteenth century of a society in the process of very radical change. Initial industrialisation came via cotton manufacturing, and the later establishment of mill and factory sites brought with them an increasing population persistently faced with the vagaries of the trade cycle. The development trajectory of Barrowford (then known as Barrowford Booth) was slightly different. Located near the border with Yorkshire it was in hilly country with little arable land and chiefly grassland used for pasture. Cotton mills were established here but they were late in coming and transient in their existence.[18]

The pattern in all of the above areas between the late eighteenth and early nineteenth centuries is one reflecting rapid social change as both agriculture and industry experienced some of the most intensive developments in their regional history. In Lancashire in particular, areas enjoying natural sources of energy such as water power felt the impact of early industrial development by the late eighteenth century. However, such development was not always consistent as co-requisites for long-term prosperity, such as development in communications and marketing, often failed to materialise. Speculative ventures of the sort that we see in all of these communities often failed. For the poor these conditions produced a great time of uncertainty in which the means of drawing together a livelihood ostensibly became one of increasing difficulty. Their economy of makeshifts had in many ways lost the certainties enjoyed by previous generations. The place of work in a fixed locality had gone and the support of kin and neighbours had for many to be re-established as they migrated to find work. The poor law remained, but its role had on the face of it been altered by industrialisation. Throughout industrial Lancashire, the tension between a potentially unlimited demand for welfare but a limited willingness to supply resources for the poor law through a local rate had become keen by the late eighteenth century, and nowhere more so than in the communities described above.

The corollary of such tension, however, is that the Lancashire poor law during this period becomes extraordinarily well documented. In particular overseers, vestries, charities and philanthropists became keen to take regular censuses of the poor and the potentially poor, their family circumstances, their economic position and, when we look carefully at the sources, the implicit economy of makeshifts in which poor people were engaged. Such censuses of the poor form the empirical bedrock of this chapter. Before use is made of such sources, however, it is necessary to examine them quite closely. Although all of the census documents that I will be using contain fairly detailed information about the poor listed, it is important to appreciate the reason why they were compiled and from whose point of view.

Thus an increasing amount of legislation was passed during the eighteenth and early nineteenth centuries in an attempt to enforce, clarify and control the earlier poor law measures, necessitating better record keeping. Parliament had already made provision for general records to be kept, and presented at certain intervals to magistrates, showing how much had been raised in each parish by way of the rate and how this was spent, which included the provision made for the poor.[19] From the 1770s, and more keenly in the nineteenth century, the government sought to improve record keeping further, requiring periodic returns to parliament. Its efforts to bolster the number of vestries and select vestries also led to better record keeping at local level. Others also had an interest in keeping comprehensive records. As we have seen, local overseers and vestries faced with a tension of supply and demand were likely to have wanted better records, whatever directions were coming from the government. Their efforts in this area were bolstered by those who kept records as a precursor to the distribution of charitable funds and religious advice or who needed to know the potential supply of labour in a locality.

Such diverse reasons for recording and retaining information about the Lancashire poor mean that we must be careful in our interpretation. There is a danger, for instance, that a survey of 'the poor' undertaken by the overseer on behalf of a vestry will record only those being paid by the parish rather than also including 'the poor' whose applications for relief had been refused. Even if this were not the case, a census of the poor would be taken at a fixed point in time or over a short period and thus can yield only a snapshot of conditions at that moment. The nature of the questions asked can also introduce bias, both in the sense that we often do not know *exactly* what was asked, nor the agenda behind the questions. Manufacturers and industrialists were anxious to know the extent of the possible labour force. The overseer or vestry needed to have some assessment of the numbers being relieved at a particular time but might also have been trying to quantify the extent of their liabilities. Other groups such as the Quakers, who had a social brief to assess the extent of the numbers of the sick and their needs through their questions obtained details as to the amount of earnings and parish relief received by the sick and poor and from this information the subscription raised by the charity was allotted. In other words, different sorts of information was collected in different surveys and a different spin was placed upon this information depending upon the circumstances. The censuses employed here demonstrate the full range of these motivations, and it is as well to describe their contents at the outset.

The first from which data as to the economy of makeshifts will be used and conclusions drawn is the 'Survey of the poor of Ashton and Haydock' taken in 1817. This would have been taken by the overseer at the request of the relief committee and details shown cover the name of the pauper, with his or her infirmities, employment and money already coming in, normally from his or her work, and any allowance made. By contrast the survey of the 'State of the poor of Garstang', reported on to the vestry in January 1818, contains details of the poor relieved with comment as to their age, income from both earnings and the parish and information on the general condition of the pauper. Particulars are given of their possessions and details of the family size can be gathered from the comments made, as can family networks and relationships. The 'Survey of poor families' taken on 29 May 1817 in Tottington Lower End also gives details of the pauper and family, trade or other skills if any and the employer. In addition, the survey records the household goods owned and general remarks made by the officer taking the survey. These include references to the pauper's health and general situation, allowing a relatively clear picture of the generalised economy of makeshifts to appear.

Other surveys were taken with a charitable motivation in mind, and one of the major contributors in this area were the Quakers who raised funds for distribution to the poor normally through the offices of local committees. Although generous, the Quaker families who contributed to such relief efforts were nonetheless people of business and they were methodical in their recording of what conditions they found and what they felt was due in any particular situation. Questions were asked of the poor requiring details such as the numbers of children in any household, the number of looms, the weekly earnings of the household and the amount of relief from the parish. The implication is strongly given that the donors felt that the poor were unable to live on even a combination of wages and relief at the amounts earned or received from these sources and were in need of added assistance, usually in the form of clothing. For this reason details are also given of grants made by the relief committee in the form of both cash and kind, something which gives an insight into the wider economy of makeshifts. The account of 'A subscription raised for the poor' and of its distribution in 1819 to the poor within the township of Great and Little Marsden is one such source. This subscription was raised by the personal application of Susanna and Ann Eckroyd. The poor were no doubt selected both for their circumstances as well as their needs but the way in which their conditions are described helps to provide details of how their livelihood was made. The motivation of those who prepared the details of the poor and their circumstances was charitable, but they were acutely aware that they had to account to those who subscribed so the details shown are precise and methodical. They would no doubt have checked on the veracity of the replies they received in so far as wages and parish relief were concerned. This said, it must be appreciated that those poor who were included in these surveys were those who were deemed to be in need and the number and situation of those who were excluded is not known. Neither are the criteria for assessing need given, something which is applicable to all of the sources used here.

Meanwhile, there were other reasons for listing the poor than merely establishing whether they were managing to put together a basic living. Manufacturers and industrialists had a need, as I have already suggested, for establishing the availability of labour, particularly those with skills. Such surveys were records taken over a few days of the poor who were employed giving an indication of those who were working, their income composed of wages and allowances from the parish and other sources if any, together with a note of those able to work but without current employment. A survey of the 'Manufacturing and other labouring poor' in the township of Marsden, taken between 24 and 27 March 1829 by John Eastwood, was just such a listing.[20] The information collected gives a shaft of light on the circumstances of the poor caught at a time when poverty was increasing both as a result of the numbers moving into the developing towns and the greater demand on resources. It also gives an indication of how control of their economies of makeshifts was slipping away from the poor as vestry and manufacturer were often drawn from the same group of people and probably colluded in so far as wage and relief levels were concerned. Not only are such details given in this survey but the numbers of weavers and winders are shown and also those who were deemed able to work but had no employment. The survey was comprehensive; 301 families were visited containing some 1,850 persons. The census of 1821 had shown the population as 2,052.

The sick poor were also occasionally listed separately from other groups, usually by charitable groups. The early nineteenth-century pauper listing for Barrowford is just such a survey. It follows the model of other charitable surveys in that the emphasis is laid on the needs of the poor in so far as their possessions are concerned. Their present situation and their wants are shown, together with a note of what the committee had chosen to give. Also shown is a description of the present situation of the pauper and whether or not they are considered to be industrious. This document, like others of its time, concentrates on the character and worthiness of the paupers and not primarily on their poverty.

Each of the above sources may be said to give a different perspective on the poor and how they managed to put together a livelihood. It will be necessary to see how this worked in practice by looking at the basic components of a typical economy of makeshifts as seen in these records.

The lessons of the surveys of the poor

The central plank of any Lancashire economy of makeshifts for those who had the ability to undertake it (and often even for those who physically did not!) was work. In an objective sense, the role of work in the economy of makeshifts depended upon the amount of work available, the health and level of skills of household members, the exact composition of the household, the life-cycle stage of the underlying family and, crucially, the buoyancy of wages, which were in turn dependent upon markets, trade cycles, costs of raw materials and the transaction costs of finding work for those who were self-employed. In these senses, workers in Lancashire are often seen to have had significant advantages over their counterparts elsewhere, with wage levels higher, transaction costs lower and labour markets more open even than the neighbouring industrial county of West Yorkshire.[21] Not surprisingly, then, the censuses of the Lancashire poor in the early nineteenth century have a considerable focus on work opportunities and remuneration both as a reason for granting help and as a source of alternative income.[22]

The survey of the poor of Ashton and Haydock is a useful starting point. The majority of those listed comprised the life-cycle poor – the aged, children, overburdened young families and the sick – and almost all of them were doing some form of paid work. Some were employees, others were self-employed earners and the rest worked in the twilight zone where they worked for the parish as part and parcel of the relief process, for instance in providing a home for 'tablers' for whom the parish paid a rent and board. While the employment may have been diverse, the common factor was limited remuneration. The majority of those who were employees or self-employed were spinners or weavers working in a domestic context and earning on average just 5s. per week. This was low even by the standards of agricultural wages in the south at the same juncture. Even worse was the plight of those who were feltmakers, tailors or who carried out metal working on a small scale by making needles and pins. Wages for the former were on average 4s. per week and for the latter, often a 'female' occupation, they could be as low as 6d. Low pay was thus both a reason for people to appear in the census of the poor *and* a central part of the economy of makeshifts in the township. Even the aged and sick worked here. Simultaneously, bolstering the work component of the economy of makeshifts was seen by the vestry as part of the solution to poverty. On several occasions, for instance, the response of the vestry to the survey was to buy a 'card and wool' for hard-pressed paupers. The parish also repaired looms and on two occasions even purchased the finished cloth from the paupers. Ultimately, though, the poor law drew an implicit connection between the work and community welfare angles of the economy of makeshifts. Thus Margaret Longworth, aged 83, described as 'crazie', earned 6d. per week from spinning and the parish paid her rent and gave her a cash allowance of 3s. per week. Peter Morrison, aged 60, had a lame wife of 55. He earned 3s. per week for haymaking and other casual or seasonal work opportunities, while the parish paid an allowance of 1s. 6d. At the other end of the age scale, George Crompton and his wife were both aged 35 and had five young children under 9 years of age. Their joint earnings were 4s. per week, with the parish paying the rent for the family and a cash allowance of 2s. 6d. Even children were caught up in this work–poor relief contract, with Benjamin Wright, an orphan aged 12, earning 6d. per week and getting a further 2s. from the parish. Such observations should not perhaps surprise us – King has recently argued for a work–welfare nexus in seventeenth-century Bolton [23] – but they do imply that the remuneration from work was part of the economy of makeshift mindset of both paupers and officials in nineteenth-century Lancashire.

We might make similar observations about both of the listings of the poor of Great and Little Marsden. While the terms of reference for these surveys were probably wider than those for Ashton and Haydock, it is clear that great importance was attached to work. Both surveys record the number of looms owned or rented by the family listed as poor, suggesting the ubiquity of low-paid weaving as a component in the Lancashire economy of makeshifts as late as the 1830s. [24] Moreover, the later listing (1829) details not only the wage levels of those poor and in work but also those able to work but who were unemployed or under-employed. Such was the case, for instance, with Ann Whitacker who headed a household with two children and was described as a weaver willing to work but unable to get it. As with Ashton and Haydock, then, work was a key variable in the economy of makeshifts. A further aspect of the Marsden surveys, however, is worth highlighting. Thus it is clear that in the eyes of contemporaries it was possible for even relatively high family wages to be outstripped by particular family circumstances. One family with four handlooms earned £1 7s. per week in 1829, while families working in mills generated 18s. per week. Notwithstanding these wages, such families are labelled as 'poor' in the survey, a sign that even deploying a family labour force could not make work the sole pillar of the economy of makeshifts. The case of Thomas Hartley, a dyer, illustrates the complex place of work in the makeshift economy. He had a family of nine, and although Hartley and four of his working children were able to put together an income of 18s. per week, four other household members were either unable to get work or were too infirm. The family was thus classed as poor by the census takers. Poor relief once again figures as an important boost to this sort of work-related remuneration. Some 34 per cent of the families in the 1829 listing combined work and poor relief payments, and the vestry clearly had an implicit notion of the income appropriate to certain family circumstances. Thus Henry Thornber was a weaver with a family of six. Thornber and three of his sons managed to scrape together a collective income of 5s. per week, while two of his other children working in the mills generated a further 7s. While the takers of the survey considered the family poor, no poor relief was apparently directed to support the family. Robert Rushton was also a weaver and had exactly the same family size. However, collectively the family income from work was 6s. 6d. per week and the parish supplemented this figure with weekly relief of 1s. 6d.

In Tottington Lower End the 'Survey of poor families' taken in May 1817 records 'poor' family units weaving fine quilts that could earn 14s. per week alongside weaving families having one or two looms and earning wages as low as 2s. per week. That work as a cornerstone of welfare was prominent in the psyche of these poor people can be seen by the listing of possessions that accompanies the survey. Thus Ashton Rothwell was a 43 year old carter who owned his own cart and horse. He earned 8s. per week, while his wife, a weaver, contributed a further 2s, per week. A family income of 10s. per week to support two adults and three young children would have been roughly adequate. However, the family also possessed three pairs of looms, with the clear implication that man and wife undertook domestic weaving on an ad hoc basis to supplement their income. John Holt, 30 years of age, was in a similar position. He earned 15s. per week as a collier and his total family income was 20s. per week. However, he still retained two pairs of looms, presumably as insurance against the seasonality and short-term nature of the mining industry. At the opposite end of the life-cycle, Thomas Booth, described as nearly blind, and his wife, who were aged 81 and 79 respectively, demonstrate even more powerfully the desire to make work a part of the makeshift economy. Despite their age, the couple still retained a pair of looms which it is stated 'he would not give up'! The parish allowed them 3s. 6d. per week in cash and paid their rent, testimony again to the link between work and poor relief that we have seen for the other townships considered above.

The survey of Garstang gives less detail about the work patterns of the poor who are listed, probably because it was taken with the prime purpose of monitoring allowances which were subsequently ordered to be cut. Those who appeared in it were predominantly old or infirm, and where income from work was noted it was because of special circumstances such as particularly poor wages or a very young family. The survey shows, for instance, that Martin Holmes aged 73 years earned the sum of 3s. per week, with the vestry supporting him in his bid for independence by allowing him his rent and 2s. relief each week. Paradoxically, it is the lack of information in this survey that confirms the centrality of work to the local economy of makeshifts. The vestry *presumed* work was available and it ensured that those who could work did so by offering very low levels of relief to any who thought otherwise. There was a presumption that work was available and the vestry were particularly keen to bolster a local work ethic by forcing the apprenticeship of older children in families that applied for relief. In a general sense, then, the story of Ann Wilson at the beginning of this chapter, in which her son aged ten earned as much as his mother through working in a colliery, gives an indication of how the economy of makeshifts was slanted for most of the Lancashire poor.

What becomes clear from the censuses of the poor, however, is

that work alone was often not a sufficient avenue to guarantee
subsistence in these rural Lancashire communities. Some families
certainly earned relatively high wages, while the connection between work and poor relief could also generate comfortable family
incomes. However, if we consider all of the census documents
side-by-side, it is clear that the majority of those listed did not
have a subsistence income either absolutely or compared to the
agricultural labourers of the rural south. The recorded income of
some childless couples from work and poor relief was lower than
3s. per week, while some widows with children were ostensibly
surviving on less than that. For families containing children income
levels were generally higher, but even in this context family
incomes of less than 5s. per week are apparently recorded in the
surveys. In other words, individuals and families *must* have had
access to other strands in the Lancashire economy of makeshifts.

One other potential source of support was kinship networks
and the benefits of social and fiscal credit which resulted from
their exploitation. This might be said to be a hidden factor in
the economy of makeshifts, one which depended greatly on the
individual circumstances of the pauper, the size and location of
the extended family and the community in which the pauper
lived.[25] Of course, others in this volume have pointed to the
difficulty of reconstructing kinship networks and measuring their
potential impact on welfare,[26] and in one sense this chapter is no
different from the rest in this difficulty. The censuses of the poor
used here do not conveniently record kinship details or the lending
and borrowing networks of which people would have found themselves part. However, if we make two very crude assumptions –
that the density of surnames correspondence in a community is
some indication of the density of kinship links in that community,
and that the ordering of paupers in the census of the poor bears
some resemblance to their residence patterns – then we *can* begin
to say something about the broad outlines of kinship support.
Two things are particularly striking. First, that there were wide
differences between communities in implied kinship density. The
survey of the poor for Ashton and Haydock suggests that some
40 per cent of paupers may have been related to each other when
we employ our crude assumptions. Moreover, since people sharing
the same surname often appear in sequence it is perhaps a
reasonable presumption that relatives lived proximate to each
other. Indeed, in this small and stable community it is perhaps

not surprising that dense kinship networks emerged. As Barrett suggests elsewhere in this volume, a symbiotic relationship existed between members of such communities, one which was weakened only as the economic basis altered. Such alteration was taking place in Tottington Lower End and Great and Little Marsden, where rural industrial development stimulated in-migration and diluted pre-existing kinship networks. While censuses of the poor in these places do provide evidence of shared surnames – in Great Marsden in 1829, for instance, one quarter of all people listed shared the surnames Hartley, Rushton, Greenwood and Varley – the overall numbers are small compared to say Ashton or Garstang. More importantly, those sharing surnames are generally recorded as living in many different districts rather than immediately proximate to each other, and this might be read as an indication of a looser and less functional kinship system.

Of course, this is largely speculation. However, for one Lanca-shire rural community – Garstang – we can link vestry records with the census of the poor to confirm that *apparently* dense kinship networks feed through to *real* kinship networks. In Garstang, then, 42 per cent of those who appear in the pauper survey of the town in 1817 can be shown to be related to each other using the vestry records to reconstruct kinship networks. This is only just more than the 34 per cent who would have been considered as 'kin' using my assumptions above. However, the Garstang records also allow us to go further, for they begin to show the functionality of kinship too. Children are shown as residing with grandparents and vestry evidence tells us clearly that the earnings of resident children contributed to the family economy of the older generation. Sometimes, the relationship was reversed. In 1816, John Leather-barrow attended before the vestry to say he *could not keep* his father for the 2s. per week that he had been granted previously by the vestry and asked for 3s. This was allowed and even by 1818 Edmund Leatherbarrow is still shown as receiving this amount.[27] In effect, the vestry had formed a partnership with the family of Leatherbarrow, to the advantage of all parties except perhaps Edmund Leatherbarrow himself. Sometimes the arrange-ments were more complicated. Ann Kitchen received 2s. 6d. per week and had her rent paid by the township. However, her relief was contingent on boarding Lawrence Dickinson (for whom she received an additional 2s. per week) and Grace Kay (an additional 1s. per week), both of whom were her in-laws. Once more, the vestry sought to bolster a primary kinship connection through imaginative use of small relief payments.

Such observations lead us back to the role of the poor law in the economy of makeshifts, an important topic little covered in the rest of this volume. With one exception, all of the surveys used in this chapter detail the amount of parish relief and its mode of payment, whether in cash or kind, something that we have seen in reviewing the connection between work and poor relief earlier. Not surprisingly given what we know about the tenor of relief policy in Lancashire, none of the surveys record generous allowances.[28] On average regular payments amounted to just 2–3s. per week, confirming the limited role for relief in the economy of makeshifts. However, such figures tell only part of the story. Relief often came with strings in the form of parish duties such as looking after the old or young who had no other support and who were labelled 'sojourners' or 'tablers' in the pauper censuses. This observation applies particularly to Ashton and Haydock, where some 15 per cent of those listed were ascribed as 'tablers'. Perhaps a more important drawback than the strings, however, was the apparent uncertainty of relief payments in some communities. The vestry in Garstang, for instance, kept a very tight control over expenditure, granting relief at a low level on a short-term basis even to the aged. Pensions were reviewed (and cut) regularly and little by way of changing circumstances escaped the gaze of the overseer. In Tottington Lower End, pensions were apparently more generous and more certain. However, since this survey also recorded the material condition of 'the poor' it is possible to highlight a further drawback to incorporating the Lancashire poor law as a main pillar of the makeshift economy. Widow Smith had four children aged between two and ten years and was described as a nurse. She earned 1s. 9d. per week and her 10 year old daughter earned a further 1s. Parish relief gave her 5s. each week, a generous allowance by poor law standards. However, her possessions at the time of the survey were described simply as 'neither bed nor bedding, only a little straw'. Thomas Nuttall, with a wife and three children all under seven years, earned 7s. 6d. as a weaver. He received no poor relief at the time of the survey but rent of £4.4s. was owed. A chest of drawers had been taken away by the landlord as partial settlement of the debt. John Howgate, a 27 year old weaver, is recorded as having lost his wife two weeks previously, and already his domestic environment had been denuded of every comfort. These are interesting cases, showing as they do that selling or pawning goods was another part of the makeshift economy, just as Alannah Tomkins suggests elsewhere in this volume. More generally, however, the Tottington survey highlights a general scarcity of household possessions, indicating that before the poor could even begin to think about the poor law as part of their makeshift economy, they would have to be in a severely distressed state. The contrast with Essex pauper inventories is substantial.[29] The final problem for those who might have wished to incorporate the poor law into their makeshift economies is illustrated by the surveys of Great and Little Marsden and Barrowford. In these places, substantial amounts of relief were given in kind rather than cash, introducing rigidity into the coping strategies of poor families, where flexibility was the valued prize. The poor law, then, was just a small part of the potential Lancashire economy of makeshifts.

Perhaps a more important component is evidenced by the taking of some of the pauper surveys in the first place. Thus, established religious groups such as the Quakers collected from their number on a countrywide basis to help the poor and the outcome of their work is seen in the surveys of Great and Little Marsden and, it is thought, Barrowford. From the listing of the sick and poor of Barrowford, details can be found of the residence of the poor together with the number in the family and the beds, looms and blankets that they had. Details were then recorded of the items requested by the poor, including petticoats and clogs. Before it is shown what they were given there is a comment as to their 'present situation'. Thus the residence of Ann Bury was described as 'very bad', as was the condition of her furniture. Her present situation was stated to be 'not well off' and she was recorded as 'not active'. Her family of three had only one bed and one blanket, and the Quaker relief committee awarded her the one blanket that she had requested. Such 'relief' illustrates clearly some of the major drawbacks facing those who wished to pursue charity as one element of an economy of makeshifts – charity was often intermittent, could come in a form that was not particularly useful, and was rarely generous. A further problem is that those who controlled charity – even the Quakers of Barrowford – often employed moral judgements in deciding who to relieve and what relief to give, a point raised by Sarah Lloyd elsewhere in this volume. James Hargreaves had a family of five and possessed three looms. He was described as 'middling well off and industrious' and received a blanket. Jude Robinson who had a family of six with two beds and blankets was described as being of 'bad character' and was only awarded one petticoat for a child. Others were presumably turned down altogether before they made it to the lists.

The 1819 survey of Great and Little Marsden, also taken as a record of the dispensation of Quaker charity, provides similar detail. The subscription raised was distributed between the poor chosen and details of their residence, number of children under eight years, the number of looms held, weekly earnings and parish relief were recorded. Mary Grimshaw of Heyhead was one recipient. She had six children, three being under 8 years and two under 6 years, and two looms and she earned 7s. 6d. per week. She received 4s. per month from the poor law and was granted a blanket and stockings to the value of 7s. 5d. The story of Mary Grimshaw, one of dozens that could be told, is both an indication of the diversity of the economy of makeshifts and confirmation of the value of charity in some cases. In money terms, this one charitable payment had provided almost as much as two month's worth of relief from the parish. If we in turn recognise that all of the places mentioned here supported several small charities giving relief in cash or kind, it will be apparent that charity might be a substantial element of the economy of makeshifts in rural Lancashire. This said, there were once again moral overtones covering the gateway to charity. John Edmundson, for instance, had three children, all under 8 years of age, and earned 13s. a week. He also kept two looms, presumably as a precaution against trade downturn. However, he was deemed 'not deserving', despite being on a lower income than others who were successful, and he got nothing. The economy of makeshifts was thus a complex maze of opportunities in which some planning and a lot of luck were necessary to generate a living income.

This discussion does not, of course, exhaust the information on the economy of makeshifts that can be gained from the pauper censuses. Thus in Ashton there is evidence that paupers were able to earn money from seasonal work such as haymaking, while in Tottington Lower End John Holt managed to keep two cows on the waste to bolster his income. Moreover, in all of the places mentioned here, illegitimate births were numerous, with Tottington Lower End registering a particularly high rate during the first two decades of the nineteenth century. Given that even Lancashire parishes would generally assume responsibility for an illegitimate child born within their boundary, allowing the mother also to claim and rely on poor relief whilst the child was young, it might be correct to style this 'demographic strategy' as part of the economy of makeshifts. Nor were families in these surveys averse to criminal activity. Again in the survey of poor families in Tottington Lower End it is noted that two paupers were transported, leaving their families to be assisted by the parish. Samuel Ogden was transported for stealing, leaving a wife, who was lame, and four children. The two elder children earned 7s. 4d. between them, their possessions were minimal and rent was in arrears. Such observations confirm once again that a diverse economy of makeshifts of the sort that we see in these communities did not in any sense guarantee subsistence.

Conclusion

The role of the poor law in the economy of makeshifts was an uncertain one for many. In the Lancashire context, its benefits were harsh and were not readily given without other avenues of support being tried and exhausted first. For many paupers the application to overseer or vestry must have been a sign of desperation, and even then the outcome of such application might be the granting of relief for a short period only or sometimes in a form not wanted such as a referral to the workhouse or, if settlement was uncertain, a removal to another parish. A policy of short-term measures, frequent reviews of relief, even of cash pensions for the old, and in general an approach that was mean and selective resulted in the role of the poor law being pushed to the margins of the economy of makeshifts for many in rural Lancashire. Including the poor law in a makeshift economy really was a game of chance and, for much longer than was the case elsewhere, a diverse economy of makeshifts had to be the mainstay of welfare for the majority of the Lancashire poor. Using rich pauper census material, I have begun to outline this economy of makeshifts. When properly contextualised with pauper letters, overseer accounts, vestry minutes, diaries and other material, these sources may eventually go some way to allowing us to fulfil the research objectives set out in the conclusion to this volume. In the Lancashire context, however, we must come back to the idea that while the number of strands to the economy of makeshifts may have been greater than was the case, for instance, in the rural south-east of England, effectively navigating within and between these strands was also more difficult. Nor should we forget that a relatively harsh and non-interventionist poor law, when viewed against the backdrop of substantial life-cycle and cyclical poverty, probably diluted the value of some of the strands of the economy of makeshifts by forcing larger numbers to pursue limited resources. Luck, chance and some forward planning were vital elements in successfully making do and a sensitive reading of pauper censuses of the sort available for early nineteenth-century Lancashire begins to show this very clearly indeed.

Notes

1 Manchester Central Library (hereafter MCL) L 21/3/12, 'Survey of poor families in Tottington, 1817'.

2 The literature on the economy of makeshifts has been dealt with in the introduction to this volume, and is not considered here for that reason. For details on the very substantial level of background poverty in Lancashire, see S. King, *Poverty and Welfare in England 1700–1850: a Regional Perspective* (Manchester, Manchester University Press, 2000).

3 In Lancashire, having an illegitimate child made getting relief more certain and keeping it more definite, though of course the poor law would have tried to recoup the cost of relief through a bastardy affiliation order.

4 For recent synthesis, see King, *Poverty and Welfare* and A. Brundage, *The English Poor Laws, 1700–1930* (Basingstoke, Palgrave, 2002).

5 On the power of the poor, see contributions to T. Hitchcock, P. King and P. Sharpe (eds), *Chronicling Poverty: The Voices and Strategies of the English Poor, 1640–1840* (Basingstoke, Macmillan, 1997). For the interesting view that 'the poor' were very likely at some point in their lives to have been involved in local political processes and thereby possessed implicit power, see T. Harris, 'Introduction', in *idem* (ed.), *The Politics of the Excluded, c. 1500–1850* (Basingstoke, Palgrave, 2001), pp. 11–13. Much of the rest of the discussion in this section is drawn from my Oxford Brookes PhD thesis 'Poverty and welfare in rural Lancashire, 1750–1834'.

6 P. Thane, *Old Age in English History: Past Experiences, Present Issues* (Oxford, Oxford University Press, 2000).

7 For more on this, see S. D. Chapman (ed.), *The Autobiography of David*

Whitehead of Rawtenstall (1790–1865) Cotton Spinner and Merchant (Helmshore, Helmshore Local History Society, 2000).

8 The physical location of the poor became of great importance in a rapidly expanding urban situation such as we find in Lancashire, where social and fiscal networks of kin were often not immediately available and had to be re-established.

9 Lancashire Record Office (hereafter LRO) DDX 386, 'Vestry minutes'.

10 MCL L21/3/12, 'Survey of poor families'.

11 MCL L1/2/24/1, 'Poor within the township of Great and Little Marsden, 1819'.

12 MCL L1/2/24/19, 'Statement'.

13 LRO DDKe 24/10/1, 'Survey of the poor'.

14 MCL L1/41/9, 'Names of the sick and poor of Barrowford'.

15 See for instance G. B. Hindle, *Provision for Relief of the Poor in Manchester, 1754–1826* (Manchester, Chetham Society, 1975).

16 E. Baines, *History, Directory and Gazetteer of the County Palatine of Lancaster, volumes 1 and 2* (reprint, Newton Abbot, David and Charles, 1969).

17 *Ibid.*, *volume 1*, p. 74.

18 For more on the general background of the development of the Lancashire economy, see J. G. Timmins, *Made in Lancashire* (Manchester, Manchester University Press, 1998); C. B. Phillips and J. H. Smith, *Lancashire and Cheshire from 1540AD* (London, Longman, 1994); C. Aspin, *Manchester and the Textile Districts in 1849* (Helmshore, Helmshore Local History Society, 1972).

19 It is important to note that the money raised by a notional 'poor rate' could actually be spent on a wide variety of things other than the poor, including meeting county rate obligations.

20 He was the clerk to the vestry, but the survey was made by direction of the Master manufacturers.

21 M. Huberman, *Escape From the Market: Negotiating Work in Lancashire* (Cambridge, Cambridge University Press, 1996).

22 Work patterns do not feature in the listing of the sick and poor of Barrowford. However, the charitable donations in the township were not given lightly and certainly not without there being evidence of need in terms of earnings forgone due to sickness.

23 S. King, 'Locating and characterising poor households in late seventeenth century Bolton: sources and interpretations', *Local Population Studies*, 68 (2002), 42–62.

24 On this, see J. G. Timmins, *The Last Shift* (Manchester, Manchester University Press, 1993).

25 A point made several times by Pat Thane in her discussion of the support mechanisms available to old people. See Thane, *Old Age*.

26 See chapters by Barrett, Tomkins and King.

27 DDX 386/3, 'Garstang vestry minutes'.

28 King, *Poverty and Welfare*.
29 P. King, 'Pauper inventories and the material lives of the poor in the eighteenth and early nineteenth centuries', in T. Hitchcock, P. King and P. Sharpe (eds), *Chronicling Poverty: The Words and Lives of the English Poor, 1640–1840* (Basingstoke, Macmillan, 1997).

4

'Agents in their own concerns'? Charity and the economy of makeshifts in eighteenth-century Britain

Sarah Lloyd

Introduction

In 1721, several 'Welsh gentlemen' complained to the governors of the Welsh Charity School in Clerkenwell, claiming that poor families were leaving Wales for London so that their children could benefit from the charity.[1] Consequently, they said, agricultural labour was in short supply, damaging the country. Their objections challenged the institution's patriotic and utilitarian credentials and adapted general criticisms – that charity schools took poor children away from husbandry, among other evils – to a recent and distinctive foundation, which targeted the Welsh for financial and political support.[2] What they understood by 'country' – was it Wales or Britain, for example? – was not stated in the school's minute books, and is one of a number of instances where institutional specificities cut across broader charitable discourse. The governors responded with a new rule, restricting admission to those children whose parents, friends or relations had lived in London or Westminster for at least three years.

Brief though the report is, the incident engages on a number of fronts with what historians have conceptualised as an economy of makeshifts. Although it would be difficult to confirm or deny the Welsh gentlemen's complaint without extensive reconstruction of parish records, the governors appeared to take it seriously. If this migration was indeed happening, it suggests complex networks about which we can only speculate through which information about metropolitan opportunities travelled as oral, written or printed report, circulating across considerable distances, spreading information to particular groups who might then act upon it. And all this within barely two years of the school's opening in 1718. The governors' ruling, extended to friends and relations, also suggests their recognition of patterns of assistance that went beyond immediate kin to fill gaps or maximise chances. Whatever the geographical and social details – and it would be useful to know whether the 'Welsh gentlemen' were directly engaged in farming and came from areas connected to London by droving – this episode reveals a series of differences around the meanings of migration and disagreements between various groups over the best means of dealing with poverty. First, decisions made by the poor themselves ran against what others thought socially beneficial and appropriate, not only where adaptation and opportunity were at issue, but even survival. What was a chance for poor parents was from their employers' perspective a dangerous means of desertion, and it seems plausible to assume that such differences shaped experience and behaviour on both sides. Second, the Welsh School incident produced disjunctions between forms of charity intended to relieve the worst manifestations of poverty (destitution, idleness and insubordination) and definitions of poverty as an enforced laboriousness, for which no amelioration was required or desirable. Employers and the charity school claimed to advance national economic interests, yet for a while their approaches seemed to be incompatible. What both sides shared, however, was an extremely narrow concept of lower-class autonomy, or capacity for independent action, which they regarded as behaviour that had to be contained. Arguably, the governors' new rule was not simply a gesture of appeasement but also an attempt to restrict mobility, as the school struggled in other contexts and ways to contain parental, and in some cases pupils', assertions of control over animate and inanimate things – teachers, pupils, clothing, apprenticeships and the children's time.

In this chapter I want to elaborate on the idea of an economy of makeshifts through examining the charitable context in which the poor Welsh parents, and hundreds of thousands like them, responded to various opportunities and attempted to turn them to a perceived advantage. What types of support did charity offer poor people; what did they value in it? How was charity constituted and experienced during the eighteenth century? As a survival strategy, the economy of makeshifts was not simply a set of economic resources, but was shaped by a network of meanings, rules, sanctions and conventions, which, in the case of charity, were the subject of intense, national scrutiny, and which in all cases generated complex power relations. Central to my argument is a conviction that, in at least this context, makeshifts operated as a form of cultural exchange. Charitable assistance could only flow through relations of uneven reciprocity, which constantly pushed the boundaries of knowledge, inclusion, expectation and endurance. While it is true that in discerning exactly how social relations worked the poor had much more at stake than the better-researched rich, it is also the case that conjecture and assumption, however ill-founded, permeated decisions about what, if anything, should be done about poverty.[3] I am therefore concerned here with the ways the beliefs and actions of the poor Welsh intersected with the frameworks within which the Welsh gentlemen, charity school trustees and thousands of others operated when they determined who should benefit from their benevolence and in what circumstances. What principles and assumptions shaped the actions of donors, officials, applicants, neighbours and recipients; to what extent and how did individuals and institutions recognise and respond to survival expedients as practised by the poor?

Detailed archival research has already gone some way in mapping local economic contours and types of support available under the poor law or from charities during the eighteenth century.[4] The sources I use in this chapter – petitions, minute books, accounts, sermons and local surveys – could be cross-referenced and incorporated into such studies. In this instance, however, I am not using them to reconstruct the experience of any social group, but selecting them instead for what they reveal about the social dynamics of charity. Running through charity records in particular are stories about the lives, behaviour and demeanour of the poor, and about their interactions with various officials. In essence, reports summarised initiatives taken to connect recipients of charity ('objects' as they were commonly termed) and their relations and friends, to the social objectives espoused by each fund (whether to ease suffering, reform morals or bring national prosperity). The following section focuses on schools, a specific form of charity. It examines various occasions when the actions, and sometimes the words, of charity applicants, recipients and officials were reported; it traces manoeuvres around access to material benefits and the creation of social relationships. While these stories were clearly enmeshed in wider contexts, they were frequently enigmatic, not least because they were told by officials rather than by the 'objects' themselves. The remainder of the essay locates this genre of evidence within a broad eighteenth-century discourse to suggest how charity's many meanings, relationships and resources were produced. What emerges are connections and discrepancies between various understandings of charity and lower-class survival. Such complexities mattered, I argue, because they shaped the experience of poverty in the most fundamental ways; they also suggest the extent to which the practice of eighteenth-century charity was a contested attempt to manage the terms of survival. Furthermore, the detail of such encounters between the poor and the charitable invites historians to look beyond food, clothing and other material resources to consider the cultural imperatives that diffused any economy of makeshifts.

Charity schools

The Welsh Charity School had been founded in 1718 by 'a few worthy public-spirited gentlemen, of the Principality of *Wales*' to educate, clothe and apprentice the sons of poor Welsh parents living in London and Westminster and without a settlement there.[5] The charity opened to girls in 1764, boarded children from 1768 and moved into purpose-built premises next to the Foundling Hospital in 1772; the move from Clerkenwell to Gray's Inn Road marked an expansion of the charity's pretensions and scale. Boys were instructed in the principles of the Church of England and learnt to read, write and cast accounts; girls also learnt writing and the 'four rules of arithmetic'.[6] Boarded boys were set to work winding worsted in 1776, some decades later than the general trend in charity schooling, to inure them to labour and early rising.

While religious instruction and economic utility were emphasised in most eighteenth-century charitable endeavours, other aspects were particular to the Welsh School.[7] Within a couple of years of its foundation the governors, who referred to themselves as 'the Directory', had managed to link their institution with the stewards for the British Feast (the Honourable Society of Ancient Britons), established in 1715 to celebrate loyal Welshness.[8] Every St David's Day, the children marched in the Ancient Britons' anniversary procession – an event advertised to a wide audience through the newspapers – and the collection taken after a sermon was donated to the school. This association with the socially elite Society of Ancient Britons was of the sort many charities desired, but failed to create, and it secured the school some hefty donations: from the late 1770s until the end of his life, the Prince of Wales gave one hundred guineas annually.[9] By the late eighteenth century, histories of the school emphasised its noble supporters, obscuring its much more modest and precarious origins in Clerkenwell: in 1719 the landlord had even shut out the boys and master to the 'Scandall of the Gentlemen Subscribers'.[10] The school's origins, connections and geographical range set it apart from the parochial charity schools encouraged by the Society for Promoting Christian Knowledge (SPCK), and it was not until the 1750s that the Welsh charity was included in the SPCK's published list of schools. Its pupils were not drawn from a particular parish; they constituted a specific community of the Welsh in London. But they were selected according to their families' neediness and the issues the governors struggled with – disciplining the children, maintaining the uniforms, controlling the parents – also bothered the SPCK. The Welsh school was thus both typical of the early eighteenth-century charity school movement and distinctive in its possibilities, limits and contingencies.

Charity schooling generally promised recipients and benefactors long-, rather than short-term benefits. If the trustees are taken at their word, the children learnt how to support themselves in useful trades in the future. In the meantime, their parents or 'friends' kept them, with occasional provision of food and some clothing to offset the expense. But it was not only a question of *what* the Welsh Charity School, or indeed other charities, supplied to the poor; as important is the matter of *how* this system of material benefits worked. What were the contexts in which all sorts of 'objects' circulated? In understanding this, makeshifts expand beyond scraps of food, cloth or cash into the social relations that contained and gave them additional meaning. And here I refer both to the internal dynamics of charitable relationships, and to their uneasy accommodation with other social expectations, evident, for example, whenever poor parents negotiated the intersection between charity, survival and their own care for a child. If the poor were to make the most of charity or any other resource – as a framework of makeshifts invites us to consider – they had to know something of how it was managed. This might be an 'outside' form of knowledge or compliance that amounted to little more than wearing leeks on St David's Day, but other circumstances required applicants to make quite complex assessments of how to present themselves and what to tolerate – a sort of 'inside' knowledge. Experience and word-of-mouth suggested some techniques; charity sermons spelt out the rules of giving and receiving to the poor as well as the rich. But the main point I want to reiterate here is that as the poor sought and acquired material things, they constantly engaged with – perhaps adapted or exploited – ideas and structures formed by other social groups in other contexts. Even in the matter of bread, and nothing is more symbolic of survival and of Christian charity in this period, it mattered whether it was white or brown, made of wheat or other flour. And in the battles over bread, and the meanings attached to the coarsest sort – fit only for animals, or proper for the labouring poor – survival and makeshifts were locked into broader cultural contests to which the poor were far from oblivious.[11] If charity and makeshifts were types of cultural exchange, what was happening the other side of the charitable relationship to shape the forms and conditions of benevolence? What exactly did charity mean in practice at the Welsh Charity School? What were the signs and how might they have been read?

The Directory of the Welsh School cultivated patrons, managed fund-raising, appointed and instructed the master, oversaw the school premises and determined the conditions under which children were accepted into and continued at the school. All aspects of their business exemplified the governors' understandings of charity: as a Christian duty, a means to salvation, social cohesion and national prosperity, and a mark of social differentiation. The contexts in which each of these activities took place – appeals to Welsh bishops, gifts to supporters, dinners and plays, ordering uniforms, plans for a new building, nominations and expulsions of pupils – interacted with unpredictable circumstances all of which expanded the practical and symbolic operations of charity. For many years, for example, Ynyr Lloyd, school trustee, treasurer and businessman, was paid by the charity to clothe the boys.[12] In 1759, his nephew, subsequently school treasurer, offered a portrait of his uncle to hang in the committee room, just one of the objects the school acquired from the mid-eighteenth century as expressions of institutional pride (others included a dial, names of donors on a board, black balls for balloting, the statue of a boy, a clock).[13] Instead of dismissing either the commercial or painted versions of Ynyr Lloyd as somehow extraneous to charity, they suggest how charitable activity created a series of relationships in which the boundaries between different sorts of social participation (charity, Welshness, business, pleasure, family, conviviality, discipline) are hard to define and probably should not be drawn. And if they cannot be drawn for the school governors, they also remained fluid for the children and their parents, whose experience of charity took a number of forms and was open to their own particular interpretation too. When the boys were set to copy out notices of meetings, a means of saving money while advertising skills acquired in the school, they gathered some sense of the school's operations and social networks.[14] While it is important not to overestimate this knowledge or its usefulness in gaining a subsistence, it would also be misleading to assume that the boys were merely copying machines dissociated from the governors' institutional manoeuvres. Similarly, interactions – sometimes conflicts – between parents, children, teachers and governors at the Welsh and other schools reveal the complexities in eighteenth-century charitable circulation, the influences that intruded into the committee room and school, the ways in which the poor might participate in a charity and utilise its resources. What the children and their kin saw in the entrance hall and committee room or on the school's facade imparted information about what charity meant and how it was applied. Names of donors in gilt letters proclaimed the school's status and reminded pupils of the names they should know, of deference, of difference. Statues of idealised charity children projected neatness and docility. Although they appeared to promise clothing and buckled shoes in return, we cannot assume that the poor – Welsh or not – saw these as rewards for virtue since the figures implied possibility and improbability equally; like and unlike simultaneously.[15] Heterogeneous interpretations and encounters, which must often be read between the governors' lines, constituted the operational detail of charity.

Charity schools explicitly offered three benefits: clothes, a basic education and the necessary premium to secure an apprentice-ship.[16] The charitable relationship in clothes, as in other benefits, was negotiated at two levels: by recipients, but also by officials, who did not form a static structure against which beneficiaries struggled, but were adaptive themselves. Clothing was a valuable benefit: it cost subscribers considerable sums to provide (estimated by the SPCK in 1717 as 17s. 11d. per boy[17]); as the example of Ynyr Lloyd suggests, its provision was also an important oppor-tunity for patronising supporters' businesses.[18] Uniforms were regarded by officials as a means to regulate pupils' and their parents' behaviour. Clothes were prized by their recipients for whom they represented a substantial annual cost,[19] making them a key item in the circulation of goods and services within the charity economy. But they were worth more than their material components, second-hand price or value as a pawn. Subscribers extracted considerable pride from clothing the objects of their beneficence; and although the evidence is more tenuous, recipients used uniforms for a variety of purposes, including an assertion of expectations, even rights, and an ingenuity in the arts of survival.

According to the Welsh Charity School rules, each boy (and from 1764, each girl), was to be 'clothed' annually on St David's Day. We do not know what happened to the remnants of the previous year's clothes: were they a perquisite, along the lines of a livery to be recycled within families or neighbourhoods or traded?[20] The governors recorded little interest in what happened once the clothes had served their purpose in the school, but while the uniforms remained under their eyes, they invested them with considerable symbolic weight. Thus in a special ceremony, attended by the directors, each boy received a hat, two shirts, two bands, a blue coat, breeches and a waistcoat of Welsh manufacture, and pairs of stockings, shoes, buckles and gloves.[21] Girls got new 'Bodies', upper petticoats, hats, 'Blew Cloaks' and presumably shoes and stockings.[22] The bestowal and acquisition of material benefits had performative components and prerequisites. The clothing ceremony, restricted to governors, pupils and master, enacted an idealised relationship between the charity and its beneficiaries, free of the complications introduced by publicity. The date asserted a shared Welsh connection and by adding details patrons could inscribe new messages and claims on the persons of the children: in 1777, a subscriber donated buttons with the

Prince of Wales feathers pressed upon them, advertising and consolidating the charity's claim on royal patronage.[23] Bestowing the clothes marked the children as belonging to the school – evident when they accompanied the socially exalted, and nominally Welsh, Society of Ancient Britons to dinner on that day; it declared that these were the objects of charity – with its complex attendant meanings; in reaching out across social distance, it created it. In buying and displaying clothing of Welsh manufacture, the school elaborated its patriotic claims, but like the Society of Ancient Britons, this was a decidedly metropolitan phenomenon which produced a version of Welshness for a London audience, national political figures with a Welsh power base, and an expatriate community. This last included the children, their friends and relations. Although there is no direct evidence from the Welsh charity, pupils of other London schools added unauthorised items to their uniforms on special occasions, suggesting that the children had their own sense of what it meant to belong to and celebrate a charity.[24] The means of economic survival might thus encompass ideas of solidarity and even pleasure. Beverley Lemire's assertion, that 'the selection of apparel was replete with personal, economic and cultural considerations' which worked within and across social groups, applies also to situations where individual choice was institutionally constrained.[25]

Clothes were a gift only in the sense that they entailed social obligations. On the governors' side, the meanings and responsibilities were quite clear. The children were to wear the full uniform on Sundays; if expelled for misbehaviour or absent, the clothes might be taken from them and given to another pupil. In 1741, a boy was readmitted to the school and allowed to wear his new outfit on 1 March, but was not allowed to have it again until he had demonstrated good behaviour.[26] Children and their parents might expect to keep the clothes when they left the school, but this was jeopardised by bad behaviour and expulsion. Nevertheless, the governors' uses of the clothes, and therefore the recipients' experiences of them, were more complex than simply a crude means of controlling children and their families. They were used to forge both sides of the work relationship, giving the poor an incentive to labour and employers an inducement to take children on: thus a boy expelled for non-attendance in 1774 was allowed to keep his clothes if a master could be found to take him to sea.[27] Sometimes clothes were at stake in a decision, the exact

reasons for which are impossible to discern from the extant
minutes. In 1775 John Harris was expelled from the Welsh School's
boarding house for running away too often; called before the
governors, his mother behaved with great insolence and contempt
(usually sufficient at this and other institutions to sever connections), yet the governors allowed Harris his 'learning' and clothes
as a day pupil if he attended constantly.[28] Here they seemed
prepared to overlook bad behaviour: was it because of Harris's
sponsor, or some unrecorded context for his disappearances, or
because they did not hold the son responsible for the mother; or
did the governors regard expulsion as a failure of the charity?
What one can say, is that uniforms were significant bargaining
tokens in a series of relationships the governors did not necessarily
dictate.[29]

Within the recipients' communities it appears that other certainties flourished. From various sources of evidence, clothes
emerge as an enabling commodity and they were well entrenched
as a form of eighteenth-century alternative currency. Servants
received liveries and their employers' cast-offs as part of their
wages; clothes could be exchanged or offered in partial payment
for something else (such as food or accommodation). They were
pawned or sold for cash. They might be worked up in the
household or semi-commercialised contexts to fit other wearers
or purposes. Second-hand clothes dealing was a substantial urban
trade with well-developed social networks of exchange. The circulation of clothes mapped neighbourhood economies, sociability
and dispute, and records of transactions that went wrong indicate
the complex conventions through which clothing was lent, borrowed and taken.[30] Little of this surfaces in the Welsh school
records. The governors may not have known or traced the circulation of clothes. Perhaps the resale or exchange opportunities
for charity clothing were limited in comparison with other garments, so that uniforms, like liveries, were only partially integrated
into these markets?[31] Whatever the case, hints about recipients'
uses of clothing appeared only in the governors' suspicions and
complaints, and details may have been less important to them
than the general prevention of misuse. In 1721, for example, the
committee resolved that parents must give a note promising to
return the clothing when required or pay 25s. as a forfeit.[32]
Although the Treasurer was to take every measure to recover
misappropriated clothes, the rules were reiterated in subsequent

years with various sureties attached.[33] From the Welsh charity's earliest days, governors worried that clothes were worn inappropriately and not cared for properly when they left the school premises. They tried to control access to the uniforms, and to this end ruled repeatedly and ineffectively that the parents were to provide clothes bags. In the 1720s, they tried a scheme whereby the Revd Williams kept the bags, giving them to the boys on Saturday ready for church and receiving them back on Monday.[34] Evidently the scheme failed: either the parents did not have the wherewithal to provide the requisite cloth bags, or they did not wish to divert resources that way, or they hoped to pawn the clothes between Monday and Saturday, or they wanted to keep them at home (presumably with the attendant risk of losing them to theft[35]). Eventually, in 1751, the governors gave up and instructed the school master to get thirty 'Baggs'.[36]

All this activity around uniforms, sureties and bags derived in part from the different, and sometimes contested, ways objects in the charitable economy 'belonged' to institutions and individuals. The evidence implies that school governors understood the charity to own the clothes absolutely until the child finished at the school and left for an apprenticeship. By threatening to prosecute, they claimed this as a legal right. However, their fears mapped the limits of the school's influence and power, which waned as children and things moved out of the charity's spatial and temporal control. To what extent, therefore, did parents and children consider that school clothes were theirs, that they owned them in some degree? For poor households, clothes were charitable benefits to be kept in the family: holding them seems to have afforded some sort of claim. In 1709 a mother petitioned the governors of another London charity school, St Saviour's, Southwark, to accept a different daughter 'she fitting the Clothes for her'.[37] Bags and the taking of measurements (for shoes at least[38]) meant that each child wore his or her 'own' clothes, that they were not part of an undifferentiated pool. By pawning, parents secured access to other goods and services; families did not necessarily claim an absolute right to clothes, but in the process of lodging or redeeming them did take possession to be at least a temporary and expedient form of ownership.[39]

Similarly, complaints about what the children were doing in their school uniforms represented a difference between benefactors and recipients over the purposes of charity. While the governors saw uniforms as ends in themselves (a sign of belonging to the charity, decent clothing), children and their parents were more likely to regard them as something to be put to use. In short, while the governors detached the imperatives of charity from the pressures of making ends meet, parents and children did not observe such distinctions. In 1721, the governors complained that several children 'have been detected of selling Nosegays running of Errands during Divine Service of a Sunday in their Charity Cloaths'.[40] Attending church was not immune from other pressures, and we might also wonder whether the charity uniform itself circulated in a broader economy of meanings as a reference, as a guarantee of being known and reliable, which could be put to use in earning some money. William Hogarth, who identified social abuse by reversing conventional values, certainly seems to suggest this: two gin-sippers in *Gin Lane* (1751) are uniformed charity school girls.[41]

On a more general level, the conflicting demands of survival and charity (a variant on the Welsh gentlemen's 1721 complaint to the school) emerge through problems of absenteeism. Children stayed away from the Welsh and other charity schools when some financial difficulty or low-skilled employment opportunity arose. In 1749 a boy was removed from the school as no one could feed him while his father was away.[42] In 1770, a mother thanked the governors for the education of her son, but asked that he be discharged: as she could no longer keep him in food, he had got a place as an errand boy.[43] Since the governors dismissed as ineligible children whose parents were deemed able to provide for them, such instances were hardly surprising.[44] It is significant that even in the case of the metropolitan Welsh School, rules were reiterated and boys expelled for absence most frequently in the months around harvest. Nevertheless, the governors attempted to enforce attendance. On occasion, when asked appropriately, they gave permission for a boy to go into 'the country' (probably not Wales, but outside London).[45] Permission made the difference between a boy being 'discharged' or absent, and in the latter case, the governors reasserted their authority by threatening expulsion. In an attempt to control unauthorised absences, parents were summoned to the school to explain and were threatened with forfeiting the clothes.[46] By introducing work to the curriculum in 1776 school governors attempted to institutionalise, contain and marginally profit from general – if not specific – activities some boys were already doing.[47] They may also have sought to extend existing employment opportunities, otherwise limited by season or restricted by age. Through these arrangements, the governors brought charity and 'getting by' into line, not least by enforcing the correct work discipline.

Contrary to school propaganda, therefore, charitable assistance and labour were frequently at odds in practice, a discrepancy which duplicated tensions over the purpose of a charity school and who should receive the education: the extremely poor, who drained resources, or the self-sufficient. But what made these problems greater were conflicts about who had authority over the children. These questions emerged at all charity schools and were made urgent by occasion and place. Thus complaints about the behaviour of children and their parents at the anniversary meeting of all the charity schools of London and Westminster risked those schools' relationship with the SPCK and disrupted the symbolic values they crafted. In daily business, the dynamic surfaced as a direct clash between parents and governors, or their proxy, the teacher. In several instances, the Welsh School governors claimed that an absent boy's mother had encouraged him to stay away. The governors of St Saviour's Girls Charity School (in a poorer part of town, with less prestigious supporters) also complained about absenteeism and parental indifference or connivance, battling to secure the children's presence and time: girls absconded to sleep in the warmth of the glass works in January 1710; mothers were ordered to appear before the trustees to explain why they kept their daughters at home.[48] Disputes between parents and charity officials over clothes, discipline and apprenticeships – three major elements of a charity education – were fuelled by differences about what behaviour was justified and what outcomes were desirable. In the process they revealed poor parents' attempts to make the charity suit their ends, both legitimately and fraudulently.

Discipline may not seem to fit within the conceptual framework of makeshifts. As exercised in charity schools it was not immediately linked to present survival; it did not hold body and soul together; it was not a direct equivalent to food, shoes or shelter. Nevertheless, the management and compromises of discipline exemplify the degree to which material opportunities were permeated by social negotiation. If power relations saturated makeshifts, as the history of clothes suggests, then discipline was a key field of operation for benefactors and recipients whose activities and knowledge ensured the production of charity and access to what it offered. Traffic around rules produced the contexts in which long- or short-term benefits were won or lost. Most frequently evidence concerns breaches, not observance, of the rules, responses indicative of alternative social strategies and the limits of what could be tolerated on either side. Misuse and disrespect tested officials' forbearance; conformity and deference stretched recipients' patience.

Disputes over discipline – both that exercised on the children, and their parents' lack of restraint – suggested how, contrary to the idealised social relations of school propaganda, the poor had limited but effective power to obstruct, constrain or redirect charitable intentions. In 1708, for example, the governors of St Saviour's Girls Charity School

> Order'd that Elenor Simpson be discharg'd ye School; her Mother having come and scolded ye [Mistress] and at [one of the trustees] for giving ye Child due Correction for coming late, and having also pawn'd her Child's Clothes, and slighted the Charity.[49]

By taking action the governors simultaneously asserted their authority and registered its loss. In the absence of lower-class gratitude, a sort of eighteenth-century institutional grease, the school committee comprehensively failed to control its reputation in the broader community and maintain discipline at the school. In response to many such incidents at St Saviour's, the governors made new rules which threatened expulsion if a child's parents or relations were rude or quarrelsome. Mothers were the most significant offenders, but fathers, aunts and 'friends' also participated, turning up to scold and abuse the schoolmistress, refusing to let their daughters 'Submitt to the orders of the School', showing 'sawciness' in correcting the mistress for her faults and behaving in a 'very rude and unhandsom mannor'. They were ordered before the trustees to explain themselves: some asked the mistress's pardon or made their 'submission'; others failed to turn up and their children were duly expelled. In one case the governors agreed that girls of good character were not responsible for their mother's 'passion and indiscretion': they were allowed to stay.[50]

Disputes over food, which carried complex social meanings of care, sociability and connection, indicate that incidents commonly represented by middling-class governors as plain proof of immorality or rudeness were moments when power relations within and outside an institution – when practices and expectations – became particularly entangled. London and Westminster charity school trustees tried to stop parents turning up at the anniversary service with food and drink for their children.[51] Was it the sign of disorder officials feared or a jab at the dignitaries who had kept the children walking or standing for hours without refreshment; was it an assertion of parental 'rights' or a moment of shared festivity? A late-century mother persisted after warnings in taking cakes and gingerbread to her daughter at the York Grey Coat School; eventually she was called before the Ladies Committee and proved 'troublesome' (tenacious of a prerogative to treat; critical of the charity's fare?). Threatened with her child's expulsion, however, she became 'very penitent'.[52] At the Welsh School, the governors noted ungrateful and insolent mothers, but the teacher did not complain of parental rudeness. This difference may be attributable to the social provenance of the Welsh school's pupils about whom we know little other than that their families survived without a settlement – a variant on the usual practice of offering charity education to those whose families were not currently on the parish.[53] Or perhaps St Saviour's regime of discipline (early on the governors ordered a wooden 'Ruffe' to punish those who misbehaved [54]) was especially contentious; or the difference may have arisen from the gender dynamics of a schoolmistress disciplining girls. Whatever the case, in all such incidents, mothers and others asserted their authority over and care of the child, and challenged those who claimed an authority derived from hierarchy (it is no coincidence that repentant mothers made a *submission*). In some circumstances, the authority the parents challenged was itself differentiated along lines shaped by tradition and degrees of ceremonial weight and publicity, as was the case at the York Grey Coat School where 'ladies' made the decisions, and 'gentlemen' decreed at their request. Some of those hauled before committees retracted their criticisms and accusations. A sufficient number refused to submit to the trustees to suggest that either the putative advantages of a charity education were insufficient to outweigh issues of control and direction, or their desire for that education had ceased, releasing them from the necessity of conforming to the governors' expectations.

Apprenticeship, secured with a fee, also brought parents and governors into negotiation and sometimes conflict. At issue were the time at which the governors released a child and the choice of trade. Since apprenticeship was a resource with cash value, charity school governors were generally concerned to assert control and detect any abuses. In the first half of the eighteenth century, Welsh School boys were apprenticed to surveyors, watermen, builders, blacksmiths, basket-makers, shoemakers and soap boilers, or sent to sea. Girls were put into domestic service and branches of the clothing trade. Parents who asked the governors to release their child took the appropriate action; those who took children out of school without 'acquainting' the trustees lost the benefit of the charity.[55] In matters of apprenticeship, mothers again emerge as key intermediaries both at the Welsh School and at St Saviour's, and not just in the absence of another parent, nor simply where their daughters were concerned.[56] In 1722, for example, the Welsh School governors ordered that a boy was to be put on any trade his mother thought proper.[57] In 1777, a mother brought a watch-case maker to the school to take her son apprentice.[58] Mothers, and less frequently fathers, turned up at the trustees' meetings to make their requests, and it is worth recalling that the other context in which they appeared was when called to answer for their own or children's breaches of discipline. They entered what the governors knew to be their own space, furnished with objects signifying power and possession: chairs upholstered with leather, a large round table, plans of the school, a list of subscribers, a steel stove and a lock and key to the committee room door.[59] The politics of trustees' meetings required the performance of appropriate behaviour and sentiment: solicitation, submission, gratitude. Were women particularly adept at or dependent on using this to secure specific objectives? Was their participation an aspect of familial and neighbourhood relations? Again, the evidence is indicative, but cannot be conclusive.

Since they valued appropriate display or performance, trustees sometimes worried that appearances were misleading and suspected that all was not as it seemed. In 1776, a father petitioned the Welsh School for the bounty money to be paid out to his son's master. The Vice-Treasurer, however, suspected a fraudulent combination between the father and master as the boy was still living with his father: it is unclear whether the information came fortuitously or was sought out.[60] Although this incident is unique in the eighteenth-century Welsh School minutes, it does suggest how informal or alternative arrangements might have penetrated the more formal dispositions charity officials wished to make and enforce. Apprenticeships – like uniforms – could be put to creative use in raising ready money (the bounty). The governors response – that for the boy's sake, they would pay if he were put out to a master of good character – demonstrates again that children were not necessarily punished for parental misdemeanour, and perhaps that the father's fraud was regarded in its informal rather than legal context, as connivance not theft. Mary Alexander, an orphan with no friends, was called before the Welsh School trustees in 1775 to explain that she had run away from her place because it was too hard; she was allowed to return to the school until another arrangement could be found for her.[61] In theory at least, dealings with orphans were more straightforward, uncomplicated by parental interference. Much of this discussion remains highly speculative and cannot be pushed too far: we know too little of how the governors judged individual characters, or what local information they had, to be able to discern their reasoning and priorities. But such material does demonstrate the sorts of relationship governors contemplated in their dealings with poor 'objects'. Thus despite the language of binaries through which charity was represented – the rich and the poor, donors and objects – charitable practice required that some account be taken of the social environment beyond institutional walls, beyond the rooms and spaces in which officials dispensed benevolence. And even in the most literal ways, these other worlds called: the Welsh School governors ran a losing battle to stop the boys disappearing on their own affairs, either when sent on errands, or when they purloined the key of the gate to let themselves out. Eventually the governors had the height of the school wall raised and the top set with broken bottles to stop the boys absconding.[62] Trustees might have preferred to represent charity children standing alone with only their benefactors to help, but in practice relations and friends frequently intruded to insist on their connections with the children and any material benefits they held.[63]

Taken together, these fragments of evidence suggest the resourcefulness of children and parents, who seized opportunities and chose between limited options. Thus pupils climbed walls, obeyed the teacher or stayed away; parents marched into the yard, faced the governors, or placed their children simultaneously in two different institutions.[64] Without knowing the specific reasons for their decisions, these episodes nevertheless invite us to re-examine the ways beneficiaries dealt with governors and teachers. Rudeness and sauciness were not necessarily mistakes of the sort that jeopardised the future in a Hogarthian moral tableau; they manifested a form of authority, marking the limit of what was acceptable, bearable or feasible in a social environment where resourcefulness and assertiveness were wielded and honed as survival skills. As we have seen, some parents later changed tactics. In much the same way, submission also had more than one meaning. It could be just what it seemed. But it could also be a form of camouflage, of assertion (witting or not) which operated strategically through conformity, denial or silence: economy with the truth during settlement examinations would be an obvious parallel.[65] Parents asked permission to take their children out of the school, preferring immediate employment opportunities to education. Some parental statements, accompanied by the appropriate gestures of thanks, conveyed the failure of charity: children had to starve or leave, a message the governors understood and debated as an impossible choice between usefulness (with starvation) and ruin (without an education).[66] Yet again, while benefactors and commentators generally insisted that charity ensured survival – a move that asserted their control by narrowing the gap between charity and quotidian struggles – poor parents often seemed much less convinced by the correspondence. In this sense charity institutions operated a compromise between philanthropic ambitions to regulate the lives of the poor and lower-class attempts to preserve maximum room for manoeuvre.

Charitable interactions, whether marked by conflict or agreement, extended in many different directions. In the case of the Welsh School, the charity created material opportunities for parents and children, for the trustees and their businesses, for all who sold their services to the school, and for prominent Welshmen, such as Sir Watkin Williams-Wynn. If charity is regarded as a form of circulation rather than a material thing, it tied all these groups into various relationships of application (whether of parents to trustees or governors to wealthy patrons) and it created uneven relationships of acquiescence and power. Here the connections with 'makeshifts' were most straightforward. But as other historians have pointed out, economic benefit alone cannot explain why poor children attended school.[67] Nor can the eighteenth-century virtue of benevolence be reduced to financial profit. And charity had other qualities too, creating spaces in which all sorts of association might be made. This particular charity was an institution through which questions of belonging were negotiated. The Society of Ancient Britons' sermon was preached in the 'British tongue' (Welsh), which the Prince of Wales would certainly not have understood, but meaner members of the congregation might have followed. It is unclear how many of the children, their teachers or the governors spoke Welsh; the strength of their individual connections with Wales, and through Wales with one another, would have varied. Welshness, like the uniforms of Welsh manufacture, cockades and leeks, operated most powerfully in public.[68] But before asking whether Welshness or any other form of cultural representation has a place in the framework of makeshifts, I need to discuss the Welsh School's broader context: what did eighteenth-century charity offer, how were its meanings constructed, and to what extent did it accommodate lower class social networks?

Charity

So far, I have argued that we need to complicate our approaches to makeshifts and charity, if we are to understand how the eighteenth-century poor survived. Charity was not equivalent to poaching as a way of getting by, and I would suggest that this was as obvious to the poor as it was self-evident to the rich. Charity was more than its material benefits, both in the meanings attached to alms and in the expectations of donors and recipients. While the system of charity and lower-class survival were deeply implicated, there was no direct or coterminous match; both had additional and different imperatives. In the most extreme cases, charity failed altogether; at other points it offered a guide to survival. For most of the century it had very little to say about how the poor might fend for themselves.

Failure, survival, neglect and charity were all evident in a 1763 case that was singled out by J. P. Malcolm for his *Anecdotes* of the eighteenth century (1810).[69] When two dead, naked women were discovered in an empty London house, several other women, including one Elizabeth Pattent, were found upstairs. The details can be read on a number of levels: as a mediated story of survival and as an explicit commentary on what charity should be, but in its difficulties and paradoxes, it becomes an account of charity's shortcomings, whether practised between peers or across social divisions. Pattent, an out-of-place servant, told how she had learnt at the Fleet Market that the house was empty. She worked for food at her late mistress's cookshop and had pawned her apron for 6d. to buy beef and plum pudding for the women downstairs. She also nursed a girl who had recently arrived in the house, but denied all knowledge of the dead women's clothing. The parish, organised charity and alms were strikingly absent from all but the girl's story: she had been wrongly denied relief under the poor law and the alms she received still left her 'emaciated beyond description'. The dead women, for whom Pattent could only supply the name 'Bet', were isolated and anonymous. Malcolm drew many lessons from this, all of which corresponded with conventional eighteenth-century morality. The dead women, who had starved rather than steal, 'met death ... supported by pure consciences' and deserved 'statues to their memory'. The virtuous Pattent worked every day for a miserable pittance and passed the night relieving the sick. Pattent's story also tells how care and information were shared among the poor; odd hints depict communities of market traders, single women and even petty patriots, who con-sumed that archetypal British food, beef and plum pudding. Pawnbrokers and ex-employers were a means to survival, but assistance was limited: Pattent stopped going downstairs when the women sickened. It would have spoilt Malcolm's account, and jeopardised Pattent, to suggest that she had stripped the bodies of the dead and returned to the pawnbroker's, so that detail and the possibility that Pattent knew more than the names she divulged was left hanging. Instead, Malcolm reflected on what charity should have meant:

> Is it not shocking to think on this catastrophe, when we reflect on how many would have contributed to the relief of this family of misery, had they known their wants, when advertisements for daily relief appeared from the distressed and were successful.

In emphasising the reactions of the newspaper reading classes, Malcolm closed questions about how those dead women might have signalled their needs and to whom. He downplayed the crucial issue of what measures were legitimate to take, which was particularly relevant when those without means helped those with even less, and he evaded the paradox that virtuous, uncom-plaining submission meant starvation. He shifted attention from co-operation among social equals to condescension and sentiment across social ranks, a distinction that underwrote both the material benefits and theoretical literature of charity. It is Malcolm's understanding of charity, not Pattent's experience of neighbourliness that dominates historical records and therefore shapes the following characterisation. But that characterisation also exemplifies the disjunctions – potential or real in the case of 'Bet' – between charity and survival, between assistance proffered vertically or horizontally.

Charity was an important source of assistance to the eighteenth-century poor, particularly to the young, sick and elderly, supplementing diet and income, providing shelter, clothing and basic education. The scale and duration of such benefits (how substantial the aid, whether it was a one-off payment or continued support) depended upon local social and economic resources and patterns of initiative, fashion, history and tradition which were also geographically specific. Claims on relief might be parochial, denominational, occupational or regional, and benefactors drew on their familial or personal histories to create patterns of memory and commemoration. The map of charity did not therefore correspond to a map of destitution, and formal charities required the poor, or their sponsors, to insert themselves into existing structures and meet admission criteria. The mixture of charitable forms shifted during the eighteenth century as, for example, metropolitan opportunities – especially schools and hospitals – expanded and long-established cash doles lost purchasing power. The balance between testamentary donation and lifetime charity also changed. Throughout the century, from whatever sources, substantial sums were disbursed: in the 1790s, Frederick Eden opined that 'more is expended annually on those objects, who are selected by the discretionary charity of individuals, than on the national Poor [the statutory relief system]'.[70] Given the amounts raised through donation, subscription and testamentary bequest, questions about how and why funds should be distributed loomed in discussions of the poor law, and shaped strategies for soliciting charity. New entrepreneurial institutions (including the Welsh School) adapted a long tradition of Protestant commentary to attract supporters, raise money and promote certain understandings of charity.[71] For both donors and recipients, the type of material assistance mattered, but so did the form and content of these exhortations to charity.

The rules of charitable giving were expounded in an extensive literature that was intricately bound up with individual charities' strategic purposes and thus determined to a significant extent what was available to the poor and how they might grasp it. From at least the early eighteenth century, published sermons and accounts were part of a charitable market embedded in the increasingly elaborate structures of urban and print culture, and formed through the politics and spaces of hearing and reading. Charity school sermons not only reached several audiences when first preached (governors, benefactors, teachers, the children), but constituted new audiences once printed. Issues and debates circulating in print shaped ideas about charity and mediated them to those practising benevolence in various contexts. The production of knowledge about charity was therefore enmeshed in broader cultural politics – whether concerning governance, pleasure or profit. Print became both a channel and a space for philanthropic action as charities used the press to gather supporters, convey expectations and demonstrate merit, particularly through advertisement. The Foundling Hospital, for example, in addition to advertising various fund-raising entertainments and religious occasions, also publicised the time at which a new set of children would be taken in. Ostensibly, this was directed at those with children to leave.[72] Did lower-class mothers burdened with children read the newspapers? Did other sources of information prompt them to search for this announcement? Or were these notices directed at their 'friends' and advisers, who perused papers in coffee houses, lodgings, above or below stairs? What negotiations of association, hierarchy and patronage did these advertisements open or exploit? Simultaneously, as a piece of administrative information, these notices reminded another reading public of the charity's work. The power relationships created in and maintained by print defined charity and created opportunities: directly in the case of the begging letters published as newspaper advertisements to which Malcolm alluded;[73] and proximately in relations between recipients, officials and donors. In short, the system of eighteenth-century charity was permeated by novelty and survival strategies were adaptive, incorporating new elements along with more familiar methods and gains.

'The nature and extent of charity'[74]

To whom should charity be given? Answers to this question determined access to charity and its points of intersection with

lower-class survival strategies. Clerics and moralists – the theore-
ticians of charity – included ties of family and friendship in its
orbit and supposed that even the poor were capable of exercising
it, but in practice they concentrated discussion on the destitute
and on those with ample means to relieve sufferings.[75] This was
significant in excluding charity circulating within lower-class networks and in suppressing knowledge of the uneasy relationship
between charity and making ends meet evident whenever the poor
Welsh manoeuvred for maximum benefits. As I shall argue, this
silence had at the very least the theoretical effect of constraining
lower-class autonomy. Towards the end of the eighteenth century,
William Paley acknowledged other meanings of charity, but concerned himself only with 'promoting the happiness of our
inferiors'.[76] Throughout the century, debate on this matter was
shaped both within the discourse of charity and through its
intersections with a parallel discussion of statutory relief (the poor
law) which also worked around the central categories of the
deserving and undeserving. A third definition spanned both charity
and parish relief: that of poverty, understood variously as the
mass at the bottom of the social heap, and as a much smaller
group who had fallen into destitution. Most secure in their claims
to material assistance during the century were those who faced
extraordinary difficulty through no apparent fault of their own:
either because afflicted by some disaster carrying no suspicion of
moral culpability, inability to work or because they were particularly
vulnerable. Impoverishment through the effects of bad weather
or fire was a well-established occasion for soliciting and receiving
charity, so was sickness. Pregnant (married) women, orphans and
elderly spinsters attracted attention because of their condition or
because they had no parent or child to turn to. Archbishop Secker
(1693–1768) thought age, infirmity and a large family had the
strongest claim on the charitable, a definition the Welsh School
governors also applied. Religious education targeted the spiritually
destitute, those in whom poverty had bred ignorance.[77] And finally,
the 'charity of due correction' was reserved for the idle, vicious
and vagrant poor.[78] Although commentators thought it important
to set out the principles of charitable giving, details concerning
how much should be donated, for example, were difficult to define
exactly: '[God] hath not indeed fixed the proportions of any
kind of charity: for circumstances vary so infinitely, that general
rules concerning such matters are impossible.'[79] Claims made by

particular charitable institutions and organisations were therefore important in applying, elaborating and modifying general rules. Hospital supporters asserted that those who had suffered crippling injury at work were worthy recipients of charity. More controversially, from the late 1750s the Magdalen Hospital proposed prostitutes as members of the deserving poor, qualified by penitence. The proliferation of specialised charities subdivided the deserving even further, targeting specific types of people or social groups, carving out fields of expertise from a broad, heterogeneous category of need. Thus in the early eighteenth century, the SPCK identified children as a means to national moral reformation. In the second half of the century, various societies, hospitals and dispensaries singled out the unvaccinated, lunatics, foundlings, sufferers from venereal disease, distressed musicians, the blind, unmarried but pregnant women, debtors, abandoned girls and sick children, devising forms of assistance outside traditions of almshouses, food hand-outs or cash.[80]

The poor law had long effected distinctions between those requiring assistance (the impotent) and those in greater need of employment or discipline than doles (including the able-bodied who refused to work). In practice, however, many parishes included able-bodied poor among their pensioners.[81] Charity worked in an opposite direction, from a principle of latitude towards more restricted application, to produce a similar pattern of discretion and variation. According to one extremely inclusive interpretation of Christian tradition, the poor were God's representatives on earth. Charity was therefore not something done simply to benefit the poor, or for immediate social gain, but as a sign of duty to God. Clerics emphasised that charity only worked if practised with an appropriate religious sense, elaborating on the meaning of charity for the donor (literally the difference between death and salvation).[82] From this perspective, the poor were a spiritual conduit or currency converters, a means to lay up 'Treasure in Heaven', a line of argument that deferred questions of the recipient's merit.[83] This principle was in decline during the first half of the eighteenth century. Discrimination was anyway extensively practised by individuals throughout the century – encouraged even by clerics who recommended the spiritual merits of expansive giving while simultaneously stressing the necessary prudence and regularity through which the truly Christian donor would easily discern the 'due limits and measures of charity'.[84] The new associational charities – including schools – emphasised their ability to channel assistance in the most socially efficacious directions. Competition for funds between various organisations intensified arguments about how money would be spent and the benefits of clubbing together: to discern the true circumstances of applicants and achieve more with amalgamated sums.[85]

As it became less interesting – or perhaps less convincing – to consider the poor as witnesses who would testify for the rich at the day of judgement, so the immediate effects of charity and the duty of bestowing it responsibly became more important to preachers. Such changes in rhetoric accompanied shifts in charitable practice and new management techniques that institutionalised applications for relief and located charity as an instrument of social, economic and national priorities.[86] But some remnants of those other traditions continued in the writings and practice of William Law and John Wesley, and in habits of casual almsgiving.[87] Although the scale of this last is impossible to quantify, its traces survive in account books and diaries – in small sums paid to beggars or ragged children encountered while travelling, for example.[88] The practice of answering begging letters – both personally addressed and published in the newspapers – bridges almsgiving tradition and new ways of communicating through print.[89] Overall, however, increasing and systematic attention was given to the effects of charity on recipients, a focus that borrowed from and consolidated a late seventeenth-century economic tradition which calculated the cost and value of the poor. Recipients were not necessarily more 'individual' or autonomous, but they were more firmly established as human actors, stripped of what now seemed simply a metaphoric role as Christ's representatives on earth.[90] But this, and complaints about indiscriminate charity along the lines advocated by Law, did not necessarily demonstrate a secular rationale for charity. For commentators writing at both the beginning and the end of the century, charity education was predominantly religious; work was a moral duty; throughout various national emergencies patriotism operated within a providential framework. Donors' behaviour and sentiments still mattered both in determining the value of a gift and the effect of giving on the donor; a spiritual dimension survived.

While discussions of charity focused on poverty and its relief, they had little to say about scraping a living. Why? First, failure to survive, not success, was the starting point for benevolent

intervention; second, the way the legitimising framework was constructed made questions of agency, which the concept of makeshifts
privileges, extremely problematic.

Assertion and rights

Charity operated within a framework of application and suppli-
cation. Petitioners did not assert a much-debated right to assistance
that emerged most clearly in relation to the poor law.[91] In contrast,
as supporters pointed out, charities were characterised by a regime
of voluntarism shaped by patronage, benevolence and gift. Nevertheless, matters were not quite so clear cut. In practice, as the
Welsh School evidence suggested, the management and control
of resources was a sensitive issue which raised issues of entitlement
and claim. Petitions for charity – standardised by institutions such
as the Magdalen Hospital, which printed blank forms for applicants
to fill in – coexisted with assertive political conventions in which
petitioners demanded redress, expressed grievances and claimed
a right to participate in government.[92] Nor were these complications simply an effect of practising charity. In theory the rich were
obliged to assist the poor, and distinctions between parochial
welfare and charity were only drawn in an argument secondary
to the broad principle. Matthew Hutton, Bishop of Bangor, told
supporters of the London Infirmary in 1746 that the poor had a
'natural right' to charity and compassion from their rich neighbours.[93] The concept of stewardship, according to which the rich
managed rather than possessed wealth absolutely, enforced this
obligation in the language of liberality and justice.[94] A convention
of designating illustrious patrons as 'stewards' of a charity's annual
meeting perpetuated at least a trace of this idea. While establishing
the duty of charity, understood in its widest sense as relief,
social commentators – including those who used the strongest
terms to characterise the obligation – limited the poor's scope to
enforce this claim. In withholding assistance, the rich man broke
his faith not with the starving and cold, but with the absolute
proprietor, God. For this reason, the poor's rights to charity were
unenforceable with no redress possible on contractual grounds.

  In a parallel move, social institutions, providentially arranged,
gave donors additional rights while further restricting the poor's
right to relief. In the 1770s, one subscriber to the Welsh charity

claimed that choosing children to attend the school was his 'property'.[95] Legal frameworks, in particular, were significant in shaping answers to questions about charity. In the 1730s, Joseph Roper asserted that by law and in respect to all except God, 'we' have an 'exclusive' property.[96] It was significant that Hutton designated the poor's a *natural* right, that is a right that existed outside of or prior to human institutions. Hutton declared that no laws or regimes of property should abridge the poor's rights to take what they needed to keep life and soul together.[97] But for much of the century the definition of that moment of absolute necessity was extremely narrow, hedged about with prudential considerations. Mary Astell asserted that 'it is better to suffer some real Wants than by invading a Neighbour's property, the Laws of Society and Good Government are broken'.[98] To compensate for these restrictions, preachers insisted that the rich should seek out the poor and hear the cries of the modest and downtrodden, a responsibility absorbed by institutional charities and hedged with suspicions. The unintended consequence of deserving, uncomplaining, docile poverty was, of course, that the poor might starve to death, like Elizabeth Pattent's neighbours.

If the foregoing discussion seems very broad compared with the details of charity schooling, this is because charity schooling operated in a field whose generalities preoccupied commentators, not least because the rules of charity were deemed universal, god-given, natural principles. The governors of the Welsh and other charity schools made their decisions in a context that included, but was not restricted to, questions of education and the circumstances of a particular group of children. Their actions had resonances in a general discourse they and others promoted, shaped and adapted. Thus the question of rights inflected their dealings with both the poor Welsh and affluent donors; it permeated their interpretation of lower-class behaviour; it was partially resolved through determinations in the minute books that asserted the rights of the Directory to propose and dispose. The Welsh School governors emphasised the duty of helping those with large families and their contribution to the nation; but their Welsh focus created a variant of mid-eighteenth-century patriotism and benevolence. They followed the standard recommendation of caring for neighbours, but gave it their own meaning – the Welsh in London – creating a particular sense of community, which was neither wholly geographical nor simply differentiated economically in its constitution. Other variants on community were less accept-able to the philanthropically minded. Elizabeth Pattent's world of markets, cook shops, squats and pawnbrokers may have been close to that of many charity school children, but for the rich it was conceptually very different.

Makeshifts and virtue

The qualities sought in and impressed upon the poor during the eighteenth century are well known: deference, submission, hu-mility, gratitude, contentment, social usefulness, piety, frugality, industriousness, honesty, obedience, loyalty, chastity;[99] and, less consistently, self-reliance and cleanliness (early in the century, the SPCK declared that parents should send their children to school 'clean washed and comb'd', but arrangements for washing were first discussed by the Welsh School trustees in 1773 [100]). Piety and obedience required and got much attention to bridge possible conflicts of virtue; self-reliance was a later contender in a long list of not necessarily compatible elements. Expressed in sermons and moral tracts, all of these qualities floated in general, idealised contexts; utilised by charity officials in their dealings with the poor and in their records of actions taken, they assumed specificity and context. Institutional charity regimes were organised around these 'duties'. Thus charity schools taught Christian doctrine, sought to prepare their charges for a life of useful toil, required obedience to school rules and so on. The Welsh School, in common with many lying-in hospitals, enforced Christian virtues – and new legal frameworks – by demanding to see marriage certificates.[101] Alms-house trustees evicted the drunken and quarrelsome. In shaping arrangements, virtues and duties therefore amplified the oppor-tunities and restrictions each institution presented to those wanting access to its resources, both the material and less tangible assets. While complicating charity, this material does little to disturb that apparently closed system of rich and poor, moral theory and practice.[102] Although evidence from charity minutes and parish records goes further in suggesting that these regimes operated within broader networks of social relations (especially neighbour-hood and kin) and economic openings (employment and the poor law) these other contexts were not widely recognised as a locus of virtue and social connection.[103]

One of the most explicit discussions of lower-class networks operating independently of other classes' charity appeared in Archbishop Secker's sermons. Preaching in 1754 before supporters of the 'London Hospital for the relief of sick and diseased persons, especially manufacturers, and seamen in merchant service', another cause justified by a national utility argument, Secker offered a generally negative view, but one which, interestingly, not only recognised social relations among the poor but also set them within a persistent pattern of debt:

> They follow, at random, the suggestions of neighbours, no wiser than themselves: or, after languishing long, and growing worse than they needed, have recourse for cure, often to ignorant, often to rapacious creatures; who, if they chance to recover, yet strip them of all, and load them with debts, that disquiet the rest of their days.

Secker described the Hospital's intended beneficiaries as lacking any economic leeway: 'many also, with the utmost diligence and parsimony, can but just live'.[104] Elsewhere he assumed that families had (and took) primary responsibility: hospitals' great charity was in giving the sick 'helps' their distressed families could not.[105] As a young man in London and Paris, Secker had studied physic and his professional expertise may have been important in shaping these insights.[106] In general, however, such perspectives did not permeate charity sermons, either because they were regarded as extraneous to the preacher's argument or because he lacked the necessary anecdotal evidence. What is certain, is that during the mid-eighteenth century lower-class survival networks and charity practised by the poor lacked two vital ingredients: it denied the rich an opportunity to demonstrate their benevolence and thus it also stifled the hierarchical dynamic thought so essential to social order and cohesion. Were the poor to stay at home, they would not only be at the mercy of unskilled advisers, but would be beyond the reach of 'vigilant Superintendence': religious instruction given in the wards.[107] Set in this context, general silence in sermons and commentaries about an economy of makeshifts speaks loud about its irrelevance to the theory of charity, even though access to charity was an important element in making ends meet and kindness among equals, however poor, fell within the general eighteenth-century definition of charity. Clerics and moralists regarded independent action, unmediated by social difference, much as the Welsh gentlemen saw it, as a disruptive influence.

Potentially different were new charitable initiatives of the last third of the eighteenth century: friendly societies and savings banks sponsored and directed by the benevolent, and those shifts in established charity institutions which Donna Andrew has traced, all of which made much of enabling the poor to fend for themselves.[108] In the same period, discourse on poverty revalued the quality of independence as something worthy of the labourer. As a commentary on matters agricultural suggested in 1810, the poor should be 'as much as possible the agents in their own concerns'.[109] The qualification is significant. I want to conclude by considering how a philanthropic interest in independence might shed light on those earlier awkward intersections of charity and survival; and reflect on what the evidence of charity can add to our understanding of makeshifts in eighteenth-century Britain.

Conclusions

The actions of the Welsh pupils and their parents were not simply self-reliance *avant la lettre*; at times their behaviour skirted perilously close to insubordination and theft. Crucially, their activities lacked the orderliness and supervision recommended in many late-century proposals. In a sense, therefore, the notion that the poor should be agents 'as much as possible' recognised the economic and moral restrictions on the practice of independence as promoted by commentators who formalised practices and contexts evident earlier. However, the process that legitimised making-do and now incorporated it into a discourse of charity worked to contain its creative and ingenious potential. It narrowed charitable opportunities for both the rich and the poor, limiting the latter to saving from wages and cheap cookery.[110] What distinguished relations at the Welsh School from late-century theories were their respective cultural exchanges, and it is these that emerge as crucial to understanding a whole area of social, economic and even political life historians now term 'makeshifts'.

Take charity uniforms, for example. As pieces of clothing, uniforms circulated, like other garments, within families and in exchange for goods and services. But the social circumstances through which uniforms were acquired differentiated them too. We diminish our historical understanding of the poor and of charity if we reduce them to a set of objects in search of objects:

ciphers like the buttons on which the Prince of Wales's emblem was pressed. The ceremonies in which the boys were clothed or walked with the Society of Ancient Britons made the uniforms part of a much more complex system of social relations in which the children participated, albeit on an unequal footing (and indeed inequality was the point). And the cultural exchanges that occurred, that gave encounters between governors, parents, pupils and teachers meaning, included salvation, 'friendship' (in the eighteenth-century sense of sponsorship), tradition and history. Broadly elaborated theories of charity, expressed and applied in different contexts and spaces, framed these encounters and provided a powerful set of general principles and injunctions. Interpretations emerged from different levels of exposure: snippets carried away from hearing a sermon or reading a newspaper; benevolent clichés of self-congratulatory after-dinner gossip; market conversation; systematic enquiry; visual memories; and experiences of alms and prayers. Sometimes parents and officials had explicitly different intentions and expectations of what charitable exchanges should be. At other times, the evidence of acquiescence leads to no certain conclusion, but could include a sense of belonging and ownership independent of that which clerics and shopkeepers, among others, enjoined. We should not be romantic about makeshifts, nor allow it to produce an over-determined concept of agency (a formula in which action equals autonomy and resistance). But if we examine charity as just one element in a network of makeshifts, we begin to discern the religious, material and cultural opportunities charity mediated and shaped, and so uncover the complexity of makeshifts itself.

Notes

I would particularly like to thank Gillian Russel, Alannah Tomkins amd Judith Pabian for their comments on an earlier draft of this chapter. I am also grateful for the financial support from the Australian National University through its Faculties Research Grant Scheme.

1 National Library of Wales, Welsh School Ashford, Minutes of the Board of Governors and Trustees: 22 February 172[1].
2 M. G. Jones, *The Charity School Movement: A Study of Eighteenth Century Puritanism in Action* (Cambridge, Cambridge University Press, 1938), pp. 68, 95–6.

3 P. Mandler, 'Poverty and charity in the nineteenth-century metropolis: an introduction', in P. Mandler (ed.), *The Uses of Charity: The Poor on Relief in the Nineteenth-Century Metropolis* (Philadelphia, University of Pennsylvania Press, 1990), pp. 1–37 (p. 1); S. Cavallo, 'Conceptions of poverty and poor-relief in Turin in the second half of the eighteenth century', in S. Woolf (ed.), *Domestic Strategies: Work and Family in France and Italy 1600–1800* (Cambridge, Cambridge University Press, 1991), pp. 148–99 (pp. 149–50).

4 A. Tomkins, 'The experience of urban poverty: a comparison of Oxford and Shrewsbury 1740–1770' (unpublished DPhil, University of Oxford, 1994).

5 *An Account of the Rise, Progress, and Present State of the Welsh Society, for supporting a Charity School, erected in Grey's Inn Road London* (London, E. & T. Williams, 1790). See also R. Leighton, *Rise and Progress: The Story of the Welsh Girls' School and of the Honourable and Loyal Society of Ancient Britons* (London, Governors of the Welsh Girls' School, 1950); P. Jenkins, *The Making of a Ruling Class: The Glamorgan Gentry 1640–1790* (Cambridge, Cambridge University Press, 1983), pp. 241–4.

6 Welsh School Minutes, 11 December 1718; 4 January 1773; C. Rose, 'Evangelical philanthropy and Anglican revival: the charity schools of Augustan London, 1698–1740', *London Journal*, 16 (1991), pp. 35–65.

7 Jones, *The Charity School Movement*; D. Andrew, *Philanthropy and Police: London Charity in the Eighteenth Century* (Princeton, Princeton University Press, 1989).

8 T. Jones, *The Rise and Progress of the Most Loyal and Honourable Society of Antient Britons* (London, W. Wilkins, 1717).

9 A. Aspinall (ed.), *The Correspondence of George, Prince of Wales 1770–1812* (London: Cassell, 1963–71), I, p. 305; IV, p. 162.

10 Welsh School Minutes, 12 February 171[9].

11 F. M. Eden, *The State of the Poor*, 3 vols (London, 1797), I, pp. 510–11, 533; J. Tucker, *The Causes of the Dearness of Provisions Assigned; With Effectual Methods for Reducing the Prices of Them* (Gloucester, R. Raikes, 1766), pp. 42–3.

12 Welsh School Minutes, 8 January 1729.

13 *Ibid.*, 3 September 1759.

14 *Ibid.*, 6 March 1775.

15 On double readings see R. Paulson, *Hogarth*, 3 vols (New Brunswick, Rutgers University Press, 1991–93), III, pp. 22–6.

16 For histories of charity schooling see Jones, *The Charity School Movement*; Rose, 'Evangelical philanthropy and Anglican revival'; A. Tomkins, 'Charity schools and the parish poor in Oxford, 1740–1770', *Midland History*, 22 (1997), pp. 51–70; W. M. Jacob, 'The eye of his master: children and charity schools', in D. Wood (ed.), *Studies in Church History: The Church and Childhood* (Oxford, Blackwell, 1994), pp. 363–77; R. W. Unwin, 'Charity schools and the defence

of Anglicanism: James Talbot, rector of Spofforth 1700–08', *Borthwick Papers*, 65 (1984); D. Simonton, 'Schooling the poor: gender and class in eighteenth-century England', *British Journal for Eighteenth-Century Studies*, 23 (2000), pp. 183–202.

17 *Methods Used for Erecting Charity Schools, with the rules and orders by which they are governed* (London, Joseph Downing, 1717), p. 35.

18 Not all establishments regarded this as a legitimate combination of charity and private benefit. The Marine Society explicitly prohibited any governor who derived profit from the society from serving on the committee: Marine Society, *A Short History of the Society together with the Act of Incorporation and the Bye-Laws* (12th edn, London, 1965), p. 66.

19 Eden, *State*, III, appendix 12, pp. cccxxxix–cccl: clothing 4 people in 1795 could cost over £5; in Hertfordshire, clothes for a child – excluding shoes – were said to be 10s.

20 B. Lemire, *Dress, Culture and Commerce: The English Clothing Trade Before the Factory 1660–1800* (Basingstoke, Macmillan, 1997), chapter 4.

21 Welsh School Minutes, 11 December 1718

22 *Ibid.*, 3 December 1770, 4 January 1773.

23 *Ibid.*, 1 December 1777.

24 S. Lloyd, 'Pleasing spectacles and elegant dinners: conviviality, benevolence and charity anniversaries in eighteenth-century London', *Journal of British Studies*, 41 (2002).

25 Lemire, *Dress*, p. 3.

26 Welsh School Minutes, 1 February 1741.

27 *Ibid.*, 5 October 1774.

28 *Ibid.*, 1 May 1775.

29 On the broader question of attitudes to parents and whether charity school trustees enforced rules against parents see Tomkins, 'Charity schools', p. 54.

30 Lemire, *Dress*, chapter 4; L. MacKay, 'Why they stole: women in the Old Bailey, 1779–1789', *Journal of Social History*, 32 (1999), pp. 623–39; P. Linebaugh, *The London Hanged: Crime and Civil Society in the Eighteenth Century* (London, Penguin, 1993), p. 254; D. Roche, *The Culture of Clothing: Dress and Fashion in the Ancien Regime* (Cambridge, Cambridge University Press, 1994), chapter 12.

31 Lemire, *Dress*, p. 7.

32 Welsh School Minutes, 22 February 172[1], 21 September 1720; this was a substantial sum, probably greater than the clothes were worth, intended as a deterrent.

33 *Ibid.*, 6 November 1749.

34 *Ibid.*, 22 February 1721; a similar arrangement was made at St Martin-in-the-Fields School in 1700: P. Cunnington and C. Lucas, *Charity Costumes of Children, Scholars, Almsfolk, Pensioners* (London, Adam & Charles Black, 1978), p. 147.

35 Lemire, *Dress*, chapter 5.
36 Welsh School Minutes, 27 February 175[1].
37 London Metropolitan Archives: St. Saviour's Girls' Charity School Southwark, Trustees and Subscribers Minute Book: A/NWC/1: 4 October 1709.
38 Welsh School Minutes, 7 September 1772.
39 MacKay, 'Why they stole'.
40 Welsh School Minutes, 17 August 1721.
41 Paulson, *Hogarth*, III, plate 3.
42 Welsh School Minutes, 4 December 1749.
43 *Ibid.*, 5 November 1770.
44 *Ibid.*, 16 January 172[3]; 1 July 1776.
45 *Ibid.*, 4 July, 1723.
46 *Ibid.*, 21 September 1720.
47 Unwin, 'Charity schools', p. 26.
48 St Saviour's Minute Book, 2 September 1707; 10 January 17[10]; 4 October 1709.
49 *Ibid.*, 9 November 1708.
50 *Ibid.*, 7 June 1709; 8 February 172[6]; 12 May 1730.
51 Church of England Record Centre: The Society of Patrons of the Anniversary of the Charity Schools, Minute Books of the Trustees for the Charity Schools in and about the City of London and Westminster, and weekly Bills of Mortality, NS/SP/1/1, 11 April 1712.
52 York University: Borthwick Institute of Historical Research, Minutes of the York Grey Coat School Ladies Committee, GCS1, 26 February 1791, 28 May 1791.
53 Tomkins, 'Charity schools', p. 64.
54 St Saviour's Minute Book, 2 September 1707.
55 *Ibid.*, 5 July 1720; 7 September 1725.
56 Welsh School Minutes, 5 February 1776.
57 *Ibid.*, 4 January 172[2].
58 *Ibid.*, 1 December 1777.
59 *Ibid.*, vol. 2: first page; the list is dated 26 December 1750.
60 *Ibid.*, 2 December 1776.
61 *Ibid.*, 5 June 1775; abuse and murder were sensitive issues. See B. Hill, *Servants: English Domestics in the Eighteenth Century* (Oxford, Clarendon, 1996), pp. 131–2; Tomkins, 'Charity', p. 66.
62 Welsh School Minutes, 5 August 1776, 2 September 1776, 7 October 1776.
63 H. Cunningham, *The Children of the Poor: Representations of Childhood Since the Seventeenth Century* (Oxford, Oxford University Press, 1992), p. 44.
64 Welsh School Minutes, 3 January 1757 (boy attending another school), 4 October 1773 (a boy's father has got him into the London Workhouse).
65 See for example, T. Hitchcock and J. Black (eds), *Chelsea Settlement*

    and Bastardy Examinations, 1733–1766 (London, London Record
    Society, 1999), pp. vii–viii.

66 Welsh School Minutes, 2 November 1772.

67 Rose, 'Evangelical', p. 54; the question is also addressed in Tomkins,
    'Charity'.

68 Welsh School Minutes, 8 January 172[9].

69 J. P. Malcolm, *Anecdotes of the Manners and Customs of London during
    the Eighteenth Century*, 2 vols (1810), I, pp. 58–64. For a contemporary
    account see *The London Chronicle*, 17–19 November 1763, p. 486.

70 Joanna Innes, '"The mixed economy of welfare" in early modern
    England: assessments of the options from Hale to Malthus (c. 1683–
    1803)', in M. Daunton (ed.), *Charity, Self-Interest and Welfare in the
    English Past* (London, UCL Press, 1996), pp. 139–80 (pp. 147–9);
    Eden, *State*, I, p. 465.

71 D. Andrew, 'On reading charity sermons: eighteenth-century Angli-
    can solicitation and exhortation', *Journal of Ecclesiastical History*, 43
    (1992), pp. 581–91.

72 *Public Advertiser*, 2 May 1775.

73 D. Andrew, '"To the charitable and humane": appeals for assistance
    in the eighteenth-century London press', in H. Cunningham and
    J. Innes (eds), *Charity, Philanthropy and Reform: From the 1690s to 1850*
    (Basingstoke, Macmillan, 1998), pp. 87–107.

74 Thomas Sherlock, *Sermon preached before … trustees of the Infirmary
    in James Street Westminster* (London, 1735).

75 *The Theological Works of Isaac Barrow, D. D.*, 6 vols (Oxford, Clarendon
    Press, 1818), II, Sermon 27: 'The nature, properties and acts and
    charity', pp. 35–60 (p. 50).

76 *The Works of William Paley D. D.*, new edn, 7 vols (London, 1825),
    IV, p. 153.

77 *The Works of Thomas Secker LLD*, new edn, 4 vols (Edinburgh, James
    Dickson, 1792), I, Sermon X, pp. 106–17 (p. 114).

78 Richard Richmond, *Sermons and Discourses on Several Subjects and
    Occasions* (London, 1764), Sermon 10: charity school sermon, Liver-
    pool, 1760, p. 139.

79 Secker, *Works*, III, Sermon CXXIX: 'On christian beneficence and
    liberality' before the Lord Mayor … and Governors of the several
    hospitals of the City of London (1738), pp. 444–59 (p. 447).

80 D. Owen, *English Philanthropy 1660–1960* (Cambridge, Mass., Har-
    vard University Press, 1964), chapter 2.

81 K. D. M. Snell, *Annals of the Labouring Poor: Social Change and Agrarian
    England, 1660–1900* (Cambridge, Cambridge University Press, 1985),
    p. 105; P. Sharpe, '"The bowels of compation": a labouring family
    and the law, c. 1790–1834', in Hitchcock *et al.*, *Chronicling Poverty*,
    pp. 87–108.

82 *Works of Isaac Barrow*, II, Sermon 31: 'The Duty and Reward of
    Bounty to the Poor', pp. 136–206 (pp. 156–7).

83 R. Skerret, *Sermon*, 'Almsgiving without Charity Unprofitable' before the Lord Mayor ... and governors of the several hospitals of the City of London (London, 1723).

84 *Works of Isaac Barrow*, II, p. 160.

85 James Carrington, *Sermon*, 'Benevolence the Genuine Character of Christianity' preached at the Anniversary Meeting of the governors and contributors to the Devon and Exeter Hospital (Exeter, 1758), p. 17.

86 Andrew, *Philanthropy and Police*.

87 P. G. Stanwood (ed.), *William Law, A Serious Call to a Devout and Holy Life* (London, SPCK, 1978), p. 120; John Walsh, *John Wesley 1703–1791: A Bicentennial Tribute* (London, Dr Williams's Trust, 1993), pp. 16–17.

88 C. Jones and G. Holmes (eds), *The London Diaries of William Nicholson Bishop of Carlisle 1702–1718* (Oxford, Clarendon, 1985), p. 714; R. L. Winstanley, *The Ansford Diary of James Woodforde* (Halesowen, Parson Woodforde Society, 1980), III, p. 37.

89 D. Andrew, 'Noblesse oblige. Female charity in an age of sentiment', in J. Brewer and S. Staves (eds), *Early Modern Conceptions of Property* (London, Routledge, 1995), pp. 275–301.

90 Francis Atterbury, *Sermon* before the Lord Mayor ... and governors of the several hospitals of the City of London (London, 1707), p. 4.

91 Sharpe, '"The bowels"', p. 102; Snell, *Annals*, p. 112.

92 *An Account of the Rise, Progress, and Present State of the Magdalen Hospital, for the Reception of Penitent Prostitutes* (4th edn, London, 1770), p. 410.

93 Matthew Hutton, *Sermon* preached before the President and Governors of the London Infirmary (London, 1746), p. 8; Hutton was subsequently Archbishop of York and Archbishop of Canterbury.

94 Joseph Roper, *Sermon* preached before the Lord Mayor, Aldermen and Governors of the Several Hospitals of the City of London (London, 1734); William Warburton, *Sermon* preached before the President etc. of the London-Hospital (London, 1767).

95 Welsh School Minutes, 6 June 1774.

96 Roper, *Sermon*, p. 10.

97 Hutton, *Sermon*, pp. 10–11.

98 Mary Astell, *The Christian Religion* (London, R. Wilkin, 1705), p. 203.

99 Thomas Francklin, *Sermons on the Relative Duties* (London, 1765), Sermon IV; Thomas Seaton, *The Conduct of Servants in Great Families* (London, 1720); William Nichols, *The Duty of Inferiours Towards their [Superiors]* (London, 1701).

100 *Methods Used for Erecting Charity Schools*, p. 10.

101 Welsh School Minutes: 1 November 1773; *Account of the Rise and Progress of the Lying-In Hospital for Married Women* (London, 1751), p. 13; A. Highmore, *Pietas Londinensis* (London, 1810), p. 205.

102 C. Jones, 'Some recent trends in the history of charity', in Daunton, *Charity*, pp. 51–63.

103 Tomkins, 'Charity'.
104 Secker, *Works*, III, Sermon CXXXV: 'Sermon Preached before the Governors of the London Hospital or Infirmary for the relief of sick and diseased persons, especially manufacturers and seamen in merchant service' (1754), pp. 558–75 (p. 559).
105 *Ibid.*, Sermon CXXIX, p. 451.
106 J. Guy, 'Archbishop Secker as a physician', in W. J. Sheils (ed.), *Studies in Church History: The Church and Healing* (Oxford, Blackwell, 1982), pp. 127–35.
107 Secker, *Works*, III, Sermon CXXXV, p. 566.
108 Andrew, *Philanthropy and Police*, chapters 5 & 6.
109 *Monthly Review*, 63 (November 1810), p. 277, on J. C. Curwen's *Hints on the Economy of Feeding Stock* (1808).
110 Hannah More, *The Cottage Cook, or, Mrs Jones's Cheap Dishes: Shewing the Way to do Much Good with Little Money* (London, Cheap Repository Tract, [1796]).

5
Crime, criminal networks and the survival strategies of the poor in early eighteenth-century London

Heather Shore

Introduction

> This morning one Rebecca Hart, a poor Woman belonging to the Parish of St. James's, was committed to Prison for stealing several Quantities of Coals, the Property of Mr. Nathan Robley. It was sworn against her that she had declared, 'It was no Sin in the Poor to rob the Rich; and that if it was, J— C— had died to procure the Pardon of all such Sinners.' The Prisoner all the Time she was before the Justice, appeared with uplifted Eyes, and behaved herself as if she had been engaged in her Devotions, appealing to Heaven for her Innocence, and invoking the most sacred Names as Witnesses of her not having committed a Fact, for which there appeared unquestionable Evidence.[1]

Rebecca Hart's challenge to the magistrates of Westminster and Middlesex provides an emblematic moment. In defending her transgression she appealed to her own spiritual moral economy; legitimisation provided by unanswerable heavenly authorities.[2] Yet Rebecca's appeal is not so common in the annals of the criminal.[3] The relationship between poverty and crime was rarely so straightforward. The eighteenth century has been exemplified as a period when the customary activities of the poor increasingly came under the orbit of the criminal justice system. Nevertheless, the model of social crime that has been constructed by historians of the shifting nature of criminal justice in this period does not sufficiently

address the study of urban crime.[4] Whilst historians have considered the criminalisation of the activities of the rural and
labouring poor in the eighteenth century, relatively few have
considered similar processes in urban environments. Moreover,
given the centrality of London in eighteenth-century discourse,
examination of the meanings and functions of crime in the capital
have been markedly thin on the ground.[5] Those who have done
have tended to concentrate (in the case of Peter Linebaugh) on
a specific set of dynamics shaped by emerging political conscious-
ness, and as a response to a patrician elite; or (in the case of John
Beattie) a more straightforward narrative of the social, economic
and demographic codas structuring crime in London and its
environs.[6] This chapter will consider the function and form of
crime and criminality in London parishes in the first half of the
eighteenth century. The discussion takes as its starting point the
idea that crime might be understood as part of the broader
makeshift economy of the poor.[7] Arguably the place of crime in
survival strategies has been inadequately assessed; the role of
criminal activity in the life-cycle merits closer examination than
it has thus far received. To what extent did criminal groupings
provide networks of support, information or protection? How far
can we argue that a criminal lifestyle offered a valid survival
strategy to those who were prepared to risk imprisonment, or
more seriously, transportation or death? The discussion that ensues
will be necessarily speculative, suggesting ways to read crime in
early eighteenth-century London.

Contemporary attitudes and models of criminality

The early eighteenth century was a period of heightened anxiety
about crime and order, and consequently one in which the combined forces of media attention, social policy and elite commentary
created a vision of the metropolis infested and overrun by organised criminality. Undoubtedly many of the most vivid
characterisations of eighteenth-century crime belong to this period.
'Real-life' criminals such as Jonathan Wild and the serial escapee
Jack Sheppard, as well as numerous highwaymen, whore-thieves,
and street-robbers were the subject of a rich vein of popular
literature: *Moll Flanders*, *Jonathan Wild* and *The Beggars Opera*
amongst them.[8]

Because of these characterisations and because of the publicity of crime in this period, the lives of early eighteenth-century criminals have been uncovered. At least superficially, we know far more about the 'real' criminals referenced through symbolic allusion in Hogarth,[9] Defoe and Fielding's work, than we do of those in the work of Charles Dickens for example.[10] These individuals were the more extreme examples of London criminality, made even more extreme by literary, and sometimes visual, characterisation.[11] Yet the vast array of material that was produced in this period provides insight into the criminal networks that existed. The term criminal networks refers less to the notions of organised crime that are implicit in elite commentary, but rather, as has been suggested elsewhere, to the networks and focuses of criminal exchange and communication that have traditionally been associated with urban life.[12] Yet arguably these networks had much more in common with the networks of neighbours, friends and relatives that supported local communities than they do with historical notions of the criminal underworld.[13] What might be seen straightforwardly as criminal behaviour by the authorities, might by the offender be viewed as solutions to poverty, dearth, crisis, under- and unemployment. Naturally such solutions often had a broader communal context. Even at the level of felony, a cursory glance at the records of the criminal justice system will indicate the petty and mundane nature of most crimes.[14] For example at the January Sessions of the Peace in 1727/28:

> Martha Rimus of St. Faith's, was indicted for stealing a Fan, value: 18s. the Goods of Robert Pickard; but the Fact not appearing to the Satisfaction of the Jury she was acquitted.
>
> John Thomas was indicted for stealing 3 Brass Candlesticks, on the 6th of this Instant, the Goods of Elizabeth Filks: but for want of sufficient Evidence he was acquitted.
>
> Mary Lewis, was indicted for stealing a Cap, value 3s. on the 13th of this Instant, the Goods of Richard Shervill, and found guilty to the Value of 10d.
>
> Robert Ramsey, was indicted for stealing a Pair of Shoes, value 3s. on the 30th of December last, the Goods of William Vox, and found guilty to the Value of 10d.
>
> Hannah Rowse, was indicted for picking the Pocket of William Smith, of a Silk Handkerchief, and 4 Shillings and 8 d in Money, but for want of sufficient Evidence she was acquitted.[15]

It is easy to imagine crimes (or non-crimes) such as these, as part of a broader life-cycle experience of the plebeian classes of the metropolis. Consequently, the workplace, domestic service, familial connections, sociability and street-life were all points in the lived experience that may have provided opportunities for theft.

One of the problems with studying the criminality of the poor historically is in the nature of the evidence. As Robert Jutte comments in the context of early modern Europe, 'Very few records tell us, however, how members of the marginalised groups themselves may have viewed their social world'.[16] For Olwen Hufton, in her study of eighteenth-century France, crime was an essential part of the makeshift economy:

> Theft, vagrancy extortion (*mendicité avec menaces*), prostitution, child abandonment, infanticide, the neglect of the aged, the exploitation of the crippled certainly represent the seamiest aspects of the problem of poverty, but they were an integral part of the struggle for self-preservation of the poorest sectors of the community.[17]

Whilst elite perception, and legal tools, drew divisions between the poor and the criminal, such divisions were not so sustainable in reality; a fact that did not escape the more astute commentators. In the eighteenth century many explanations were offered in the attempt to understand and solve the problems of poverty, indigence and crime. Defoe, like other of his contemporaries believed the causes to lie in luxury, sloth and pride.[18] In *Giving Alms no Charity and Employing the Poor a Grievance to the Nation* (1704) he criticised the workhouses and the various schemes undertaken to employ the poor usefully, arguing that this only encouraged the poor in their idleness; begging he saw as a direct consequence of what might be familiarly seen as eighteenth-century 'nannying'. Defoe identified begging as a national vice, thus the English were essentially lazy and would rather beg, thieve, or ultimately be supported in the workhouse than do an honest day's work. In contrast Bernard De Mandeville, in *The Grumbling Hive, or Knaves turn'd Honest* (1705) attacked 'virtuous society', suggesting that the acquisitive actions of thieves should be seen as enterprise, in much the same way as the actions of other outwardly more 'industrious' professions, such as lawyers and physicians:

> Whilst others follow'd Mysteries,
> To which few Folks bind Prentices;
> That want no Stock, but that of Brass,
> And may set up without a Cross;
> As Sharpers, Parasites, Pimps, Players,
> Pick-Pockets, Coiners, Quacks, Sooth-Sayers,

And all those, that, in Enmity
With down-right Working, cunningly
Convert to their own Use the Labour
Of their good-natur'd heedless Neighbour:
These were called Knaves; but, bar the Name,
The grave Industrious were the Same.[19]

Likewise Henry Fielding was well aware of the ironies that the criminal justice system brought to his court, commenting on the case of:

several Wretches who had been apprehended the Night before by Mr. Welch, were brought before Mr. Fielding and Mr. Errington; when one who was in a dreadful Condition, being all over covered with the Itch, was recommended to the Care of the Overseers; another who appeared guilty of no other Crime but Poverty, had Money given to her to enable her to follow her Trade in the Market.[20]

That same afternoon, 'Mr. Welch routed a Mob Gaming-house in Holborn, where he apprehended thirty idle Persons, all of them Apprentices, Journeymen and Gentlemen Servants, and all in the high Road to Ruin.'[21]

We are used to seeing the eighteenth-century criminal poor through the lens of commentators such as Fielding, Defoe and De Mandeville. The poor of course were part of the nation's political currency. Yet the poor man and the criminal were not easy bedfellows; the honest and industrious were set in opposition to the idle and disorderly. Contemporary notions of criminality were conditioned by manifold factors; to the traditional polarisation of deserving and undeserving could be added age and gender. In particular ideas about urbanity and crime were to sharply impact on policy from the late seventeenth century. For example, despite often anachronistic images of the highwayman haunting the commons up and down the countryside, the highwayman's Act passed in 1692 (and reaffirmed by Royal Proclamation in the ensuing years) very much reflected a fear of urban crime on urban highways.[22] The criminal, then, was often *seen* as a separate entity to the poor man. However, we must be careful of overstating such dichotomies, whilst serious crime and serious punishment may have identified and labelled the criminal, the more general shifts and overlaps of 'deviant' and 'normal' life in the metropolis were much more ambiguous. Paul Griffiths has recently suggested that we might see the relationship between criminal communities and other forms of support and sociability as 'overlapping circles'.

Thus in early modern London, he argues that 'A neat split dividing the worlds of criminals and citizens did not exist.'[23] In the *London Hanged*, Peter Linebaugh structured the narrative around his defining argument that in the context of eighteenth-century civil society, the crowd and the hanged were of much the same constituency: 'Research revealed the difficulty of distinguishing between a "criminal" population of London and the poor population as a whole. That is why we can say of the hanged that they belonged to the *poor*.'[24] Certainly, these were people who shared the same streets, occupations and alehouses. They weaved the same path between home or lodging-house, unemployment or underemployment, poor relief and charity. To echo Griffiths, their lives overlapped.

However, it is also clear that the London hanged got to that point because of difference; this was not just chance in the lottery that was being poor in eighteenth-century London. Rather a set of circumstances distinguished and led the criminal ultimately to the gallows. The account of the Ordinary of Newgate[25] of the 'Malefactors who were executed at Tyburn', gives us some indications to the formula that led to hanging.[26] Clearly recidivism was a key factor; hence the Ordinary built upon evidence of youthful misadventure and petty crime followed by a seemingly inexorable path to the robbery and burglary that were the key capital property crimes. Bad company, loose women and improvident 'associations' also marked out the criminal for execution. Thus 25 year old Peter Norman, who was executed in December 1730 for armed robbery, was an ex-apprentice, 'Since he was at his Freedom, he did not incline to work, but apply'd himself to Drinking, Gaming, Whoring, Thieving, Robbing and all Manner of Wickedness and bad Company, who hurry'd him headlong to Destruction.'[27]

Arguably those who mounted the scaffold were at the extreme end of a spectrum which included the disorderly poor, vagrants and beggars at the opposing end. They were not the same, but they *were* of the same constituency. Historians of eighteenth-century crime have been very aware of this spectrum and have subsequently concentrated their energies on a specific element of this criminality. Thus much of the work on the crimes of the labouring poor in the eighteenth century have been both researched and written through the lens of 'social crime'. Hence, the criminalisation of customary rights and perquisites have played a central role in histories of crime of the eighteenth century. This work has been based mainly on rural and coastal economies, where perhaps, the criminalisation of parts of the economies of makeshift are more visible.[28] However, various historians have sought to explore the meanings of petty crime both in the urban context, and in the workplace.[29] As we have seen above, much is known about elite perceptions and responses to crime in the eighteenth century; the role that it played in the lives of the urban poor has been less explored.

Clearly we know that urban poor communities had great recourse to the various charitable doles and benefits that were available.[30] Moreover, there is evidence that institutional forms of charity (and the term is used loosely) were also taken advantage of. For example Tim Hitchcock has suggested that beggars and the vagrant poor used the workhouse as a seasonal resource when the streets were less welcoming, and less profitable.[31] However, this was a fine balance: what seems clear is that for certain of the urban poor recourse to institutional provision meant risking labelling. Hence women who used the house of correction, or the city's Magdalenes in this way, risked becoming known as 'disorderly' or worse.[32] Moreover access to poor relief could not be assumed. Keith Wrightson has pointed out that parochial systems of relief were conditioned by an often punitive set of criteria:

> The system identified and isolated the poor as a group: stressing their otherness; markedly reinforcing the moral differentiation of the deserving and the undeserving; defining the boundaries of the community by the recognition of settlement and entitlement. The whole relief system was predicated on a recognition of eligibility which was discretionary, discriminatory and conditional. It could be remarkably generous; it could harshly exclude; it could be employed to discipline.[33]

This distinction between the institutions of poor relief and the wider world of the poor can also be seen in other parts of Europe. Thus Stuart Woolf, writing about the *Depots de Mendicité* in Napoleonic Tuscany, pointed out the limitations of the poor relief system, 'those poor unable to take advantage of any of the institutions set up for their assistance had to improvise ways of resisting hunger and cold. Some tried to solve their problems by theft and assault'.[34] Such responses to structural problems of poverty and dearth, however, belie a more proactive approach to criminality by the urban poor. Thus faced with a system of poor relief that, at least on the face of it, was heavily conditioned by notions of deserving and undeserving,[35] the poor sought more lucrative means of sustaining themselves. Workplace theft, begging and vagrancy, prostitution, petty theft, shoplifting, and receiving of stolen goods are all points on the continuum linking poverty and criminality. For the rest of this chapter three key 'deviant' activities (workplace theft, prostitution and receiving) will be considered in the context of the makeshift economy. Before this, in the next section, the impact of structural factors that affected access to poor relief will be explored.

The parish and the criminal

The main social and administrative unit in the eighteenth century was the parish, and whilst many parishes had a 'crime problem', certain London parishes were specifically identified as sites of criminality. These were not ghettos or enclaves in the sense that we might associate with the nineteenth-century metropolis, yet areas like St Giles, parts of Westminster, the Haymarket, Covent Garden, Drury Lane and Leicester Fields continued to exercise the attentions of local magistrates, parish officers and the vestry.[36] For most of its history, the parishes of London had controlled and ordered their poor with a combination of national legislation and local initiative. In the seventeenth century poor relief was organised by the parish vestry, who appointed an Overseer of the Poor to administer relief. Poor relief was an essentially face-to-face system, focused on the relationship between pauper and parish officer.[37] From the late seventeenth century this situation was gradually changing. Whilst parish relief on the one hand became more formal, moving away from the piecemeal system of doles and charitable hand-outs that supplemented the old poor law, it also moved away from outdoor relief.

In a period when institutional initiatives for the poor, criminal and general disorderly were being suggested by Quaker commentators, the administrators of parochial relief systems turned increasingly to solutions such as workhouses, charitable schools and even labour colonies.[38] For example in 1722 a scheme to provide for the poor of the parishes of St Martin's, St James and St Annes, Westminster, suggested setting the poor to work in a labour colony. This colony would not only make the poor self-supporting, but rather optimistically would provide the Corporation with profits of £20,000 a year.[39] This shift also corresponded with the emergence of the Society for the Reformation of Manners (SRM), who were at their height in London in the early decades of the century.[40] The Society's emphasis on cleaning the streets of the 'loose and disorderly' elided neatly with the shifting poor relief policy, many of the SRM initiated prosecutions resulting in committals to the metropolis Bridewells and Houses of Correction.[41] By the early eighteenth century, then, access to relief was not any more limited (if anything a broader stratum of people received relief at some point in their lives[42]), but the quality of relief had markedly changed. Thus the transformation of poor relief to a system that relied heavily on institutional forms of relief surely affected the ways in which the poor played the system.

Traditionally thinking about crime in London has been based on the idea that the city was essentially anonymous, with few ties of neighbourhood and kinship defining community relations.[43] Yet despite high levels of mobility, and the inevitable impact of continuous immigration, local knowledge and the importance of community networks should not be too readily dismissed. Despite the overwhelming size of London, daily life was closely based on the local parish.[44] Indeed criminals generally committed crimes in the parish in which they resided or in a neighbouring parish.[45] This suggests that, instead of being the rather anonymous and separate characters portrayed by elite sources, criminals were in fact very much part of the local neighbourhood. In fact they were the brothers and sisters, servants and apprentices, and well-known 'women of the town' that typified any metropolitan parish. For example, Mary Hollingshead was employed by Mary Hiltrop to iron the linen of her customers. When, in 1728, the pregnant Hollingshead stole four aprons belonging to John Nose, her employer begged for clemency to save her from transport-ation.[46] In the same year when Mary Coe, a poor washerwoman, was robbed of various goods from her house, she complained, 'in the Neighbourhood of her Misfortune, she learn'd, That a Women had been seen to come out of her House with two Bundles, and a Frying-Pan in her Hand; that she went with other Neighbours to Rag-Fair, and was no sooner got there, but they heard a Woman crying, *Who will buy a* Frying-Pan, *a Pair of* Tongs, *or a Poker*'.[47] Here we see the importance of work and neighbourly relations in the way the community responded to and dealt with crime.

Moreover, whilst parishes contained their fair share of vertical social relations the magistrates, the vestrymen, the local business-men and householders; the apprentices, the poor, and the criminal led lives that overlapped.[48] Thus in the spring of 1730 local tradesmen and respectable residents were becoming increasingly intolerant of the behaviour of the inhabitants of the less salubrious parts of the neighbourhood of Drury Lane. In July of that year, in response to petitions from the residents of St Martin-in-the-Fields and St Paul's, Covent Garden, which complained of the 'frequent outcrys in the night, fighting, robberies, and all sorts of debauchery committed by them all night long to the great inquie-tude of his majesties good subjects', a Committee of Justices was set up in order to enquire into the problem. The result of these petitions was a series of raids, organised by the joint efforts of the Westminster magistracy, local 'reforming' constables, and the input of the SRMs. By mid-July petitions from neighbouring parishes had extended the raids to St Margaret's, St Anne's, St John the Evangelist, St George's in Hanover Square and St James.[49] These raids, which resulted in fines and committals to the Bridewells, were based on extensive local knowledge. Thus in September 1730:

> Sir John Gonson, Justice Railton (the Chairman), Justice Blagny, and 6 or 7 more of his Majesty's Justices of the Peace of the Committee appointed at the last Westminster Sessions, for Suppressing the Night-Houses and other Disorderly Houses in and near Drury Lane, met at Covent Garden Vestry, and took several examinations concerning more of those sort of Houses, and have issued out warrants against several persons keeping the same, and bound over the Neighbours who complain'd of them, in recognisances to prefers Bills of Indictment against them.[50]

Moreover, local knowledge was not confined to neighbours but was also to be seen in the relationship between the offender and the magistrate. Thus magistrates like Gonson, De Veil and the Fieldings clearly had some familiarity with the subjects of their court. In August 1730, when Mary Harvey was committed to the Gatehouse after 'giving very saucy and abusive language to Sir John Gonson the Chairman', there is a real sense of the antagonism that had built up during the course of the disorderly house raids.[51] The lives of the magistrates and the condemned could and did overlap. John Gonson was 'insulted and threatened' in New Fetter Lane in November 1730.[52] Joseph Lucas, a robber active in the

1740s, apparently wrote wearily to his wife on the eve of his execution, 'Then we feared death as the greatest evil, now I embrace it as the greatest good, and am more afraid of having a reprieve to live again and be miserable, than I used to be of Justice De Veil and his Constables.'[53] Of course the Justices' role was multi-faceted. Whilst they had no real involvement in the daily distribution of poor relief, they were active in the Petty Sessions which heard settlement and bastardy examinations.[54] The crossover of their presence on both the petty and quarter session benches may well have closed down access to certain forms of relief for the criminal poor.[55]

Criminal networks and the makeshift economy

We have seen that the nature of and access to poor relief was changing in the early decades of the eighteenth century; this, along with other social and demographic factors, may have affected the access of certain of London's poor to relief. Moreover, this was a period in which there was a heightened concern about crime in the metropolis; the increased publicity of crime, and the willingness of neighbours and communities to confront 'criminals' in their midst meant that for some London poor, crime may not only have been an occasional resource, but a necessary adjunct to their makeshift economy. Such groupings and networks may have provided an alternative welfare strategy for certain sectors of the London poor. In the early eighteenth century, a central theme for commentators on crime was the prevalence of gangs. Thus elite commentary envisaged a city overrun by organised gangs of criminals thriving comfortably in an inverted world of robbery, gambling, whoring, vice and idleness. Pro-active magistrates like Thomas De Veil, and later Henry and John Fielding, were particularly articulate about their 'gang-busting' activities. In a biography published posthumously in 1748, the writer commented:

> But to return to Mr. De Veil, he saw very plainly, that to carry his point, and to become superior to others in his station, it was necessary for him to take more than ordinary pains; and in this, he was indefatigable, nor did he make any difficulty of exposing his person when it was necessary, in order to see his warrants executed, or to come at the bottom of remarkable villainies by several, and those sometimes long and tedious examinations. By these methods, by being

continuously in business, and by keeping very correct accounts of whatever passed before him, he came to make such discoveries, as alarmed one of the largest, and most desperate gangs, that ever infested this, or any other country.[56]

Certainly concerns about gangs and organised forms of crime were hardly new, but in the 1720s and 1730s concern about serious crime, and particularly street crime, was paramount.[57] This may have been partly influenced by the exposure of the activities of Jonathan Wild; it may also have had something to do with fears about demobilisation after the Treaty of Utrecht in 1713.[58] However, this is not a full explanation, and it is unclear why fears of crime were so heightened in this period. Nevertheless, newspapers, broadsheets, popular entertainments, and pamphlet literature were full of crime. This was period when the criminal biography was at its peak, when the ordinary of Newgate was flourishing, when Daniel Defoe was interviewing condemned criminals for the edification of an eager public.[59] In fact Defoe interviewed both Jonathan Wild and his apparent nemesis, Jack Shepherd.[60] The moral panic about crime in this period was very much Defoe's terrain, writing in 1731, 'The Mischief of Street-Robberies, which is the Subject of this Discourse, is grown up now to such a Height, especially in the City of London and Places adjacent, that it may very well be call'd Unsufferable.'[61] Clearly, however erroneous, the citizens of early eighteenth-century London had a strong sense of who their criminals were, what their nature was, how they were defined and recognised. They were not merely the poor but a group with their own codes of behaviour, closely connected, and ensconced in a criminal lifestyle. What is interesting about this commentary, and about the formulaic story of descent into 'bad associations' told by the Ordinary of Newgate and the authors of criminal biography, is the emphasis on community. Hence, the 'underworld' mirrored the 'upperworld' in its network of familial and friendship ties, support and help in times of dearth and crisis.[62] Many of the accounts of criminal lives romanticised the idea of community: In *Villany Exploded: or, the Mistery of Iniquity laid open*, an account of the activities of a so-called gang of street-robbers in Newgate written in 1728 at least in part by Daniel Defoe, included a 'Copy of Articles ... which were sign'd by a Gang of Street-Robbers and House-Breakers, who are now all, or most of them detected and executed'.[63] One of the articles stated, 'That whilst any Member of this Society lies in Newgate, or any other Gaol, he shall be allow'd one Shilling a Day, till he is clear, topp'd off, or transported'.[64] The bestowing of names based on the apparent leadership of the gang and, occasionally, territorial alignments, emphasised this notion of close-knit criminal communities. Thus Hawkin's Gang, Carrick's Gang, Dalton's Gang, the Gatehouse Gang and The Black Boy Alley Gang, were names familiar to the press and the courtroom in the early eighteenth century.[65] Yet how fixed were these so-called gangs? Judging by the level of informing by fellow 'gang' members the criminal networks of the metropolis were rather more fluid than the contemporary literature suggests.[66]

In the autumn sessions of the Old Bailey in 1726, an extensive series of indictments brought a group of female shoplifters to court. At the centre was the self-confessed thief, Mary Burton, alias Ravenscroft, alias Fenton, alias Holloway, alias Hatfield, formerly maid to Jonathan Wild, and evidence to the tune of £50 and a royal pardon. Between September and December of that year Mary gave evidence at eleven trials resulting in the executions of four of her accomplices, Katherine Fitzpatrick, Jane Holms, Sarah Turner and Mary Robinson.[67] At the trial of Sarah Turner, alias Lawson, whom along with Katherine Fitzpatrick later unsuccessfully tried to delay execution by pleading her belly, Burton described one of their outings:

> The 2 prisoners came to my room, and ask'd me to *go out*, which in our way of speaking signifies to go a shoplifting. I was not drest, and so they told me where they intended to go, and that they would wait for me, at a Brandy Shop in *St. Pauls Church-Yard*. They went, I drest myself and follow'd them, but before I came to the Brandy Shop, I saw them in the prosecutors shop, and went into them … *Fitzpatrick* took the silk out of the window, and put it under her hood, but there was a long edging to it, cut in little escallops, that had like to have betray'd us. She sold it for 3s. 6d. a yard, but *Sarah Turner* was angry with her, and said, she could have got 4s. for it.[68]

Burton had been approached previously by John Moone, the owner, with Richard Stone, of a shop at the Queen's Head and Anchor on Ludgate Hill, with the view to turning evidence. Clearly the activities of the women had been coming to the notice of local shopkeepers, as Moone remarked, 'These women, and others of their Profession, had been often at several shops in that neighbourhood, so that they were pretty well known.'[69] Moone advised Burton to give evidence, she refused but later voluntarily surrendered her evidence. Apparently Moone's was not the first or only attempt to divide the women. Justice Vaughan told the court how he had approached several of the women with the idea of giving evidence, but for one reason or another they were not reliable enough to be admitted, till 'Mary Burton came in a voluntary Evidence, and the Information that she then gave me, agrees in every particular with what she now swears in court'.[70] In giving evidence Burton describes the world of shoplifting that these women occupied, the receivers to whom they passed on their stolen goods, the lodging-houses they inhabited, the ale-houses in which they met.[71] This was a world of overwhelmingly petty crime, striking in its mundanity of stolen petticoats, pieces of satin, shop counters, wrappers and damask parcels.[72] For the shopkeeper victims, these women were local figures whom they knew well enough to approach. Nevertheless, implicit in the testimonies given at the Old Bailey was the language of profes-sionalism, a language later echoed by Burton, who describing the receiver Hannah Britton, stated, 'We went accordingly, and told her that we had spoke with a piece of Silk. She was well acquainted with our Profession, and knew that by saying, *we had spoke with it*, we meant, *we had stole it*.'[73] The definition of the professional criminal was inherently problematic, based as it was upon the fuzzy boundaries between the economy of crime and the economy of makeshift. Whilst such gangs or associations represent the rather more extreme resourcing of the makeshift economy, other crimes perhaps fit easier into such a model.

Crime, the life-cycle and the makeshift economy

Prostitution, begging and vagrancy, petty theft, receiving, shoplift-ing and employee theft were all activities to which the poor might resort in times of increased hardship, or as a way of supplementing a limited income. Indeed, in some cases of workplace theft, pilferage was seen as one of the customary perks of the job (though this view was not always shared by the employer).[74] Despite the contemporary stereotype of the career criminal, most offenders, even those who filled the pages of the Ordinary of Newgate's Account, had had some sort of employment or occupation, however menial. Indeed the apprenticeship story was central in the criminal mythology sustained in eighteenth-century crime narratives. Jack

Sheppard was apprenticed to a carpenter for six years until, only months before he was due to complete his indentures, he committed himself fully to a life of crime.[75] The thief and informer James Dalton was first apprenticed to his stepfather's trade of butcher (his own father having been executed); Thomas Neaves, 'the Noted Street-Robber', was also apprenticed to a butcher; the highwayman John Everett was apprenticed to a salesman, but left his master to enter the army; Edward Bellamy, formerly connected to Jonathan Wild, had been a tailor's apprentice.[76] Moreover, the moral story of the 'idle apprentice' was a key device in both criminal and conduct literature in this period. Yet whilst some apprentices may well have fed their desire for 'idleness and dissipation' by turning to a life of crime, it is worth questioning how far apprenticeship really figured in such men's lives. Using the Ordinaries Accounts, Peter Linebaugh found that 40 per cent of the 1,242 executed men and women for whom he had biographies, had been apprenticed to a trade.[77] However, as John Beattie points out, there are limitations to what information about apprenticeship can tell us, 'He might be an apprentice or might have completed an apprenticeship years before and not worked at that trade since; he might be a master or a journeyman; he might be prosperous or poor; employed or unemployed.'[78] Despite Linebaugh's calculations, specific information on apprentices is not always forthcoming in the Old Bailey Sessions Papers. In contrast, in early eighteenth-century London probably the most characteristic workplace theft to come to the attention of the courts was that committed by household and domestic servants. Thus in 1727, William Staples prosecuted his servant, Robert Beaton, who had stolen various goods from his master's house, including a watch, a ring and some money, 'It appeared that the Prisoner being the Prosecutor's Servant, had taken the Goods mentioned in the Indictment out of his Master's House, and carried them to his Mother's, who pawn'd them at the Rose in Rose-Alley, Golden-Lane ...'[79] Theft by servants was so common as to be frequently commented upon by contemporaries. Indeed, in 1713, when theft of goods to the value of 40s. or more, from a dwelling house was removed from clergy, this was aimed directly at servants: 'Divers wicked and ill-disposed servants, and other persons, are encouraged to commit robberies in houses by the privilege, as the law now is, of demanding the benefit of clergy.'[80] According to Linebaugh's calculations, sixty-two servants were hung between 1703 and 1772; twenty-one of these had robbed their masters.[81] Of course most of the crimes committed by domestic servants were not serious enough to end up on the gallows, but servants were a vulnerable group. As Bob Shoemaker points out, they were often hired on short-term contracts, with demand for their services fluctuating.[82] They were often suspected of opening houses to organised gangs of burglars; young women in particular could be vulnerable to the undercurrents of sexuality in a household.[83] Whilst servants might turn to pilfering from their households to supplement their income, unemployed female servants were one of the likely groups to turn to prostitution to stop the gaps.[84]

Stories of robberies and attempted robberies by prostitutes from the unsuspecting country innocent were the staple fare of early eighteenth-century literature; moreover this literature linked them closely to the cities' criminal networks. In his pamphlet on the Night-houses (essentially brothels and low-lodging houses), the author commented on the 'Seminaries of Thieves and Prostitutes, and also the Receptacles and Retreats of the Street-robbers, Murderers, Incendaries, and all the several Gangs of wicked People which are so much our Grievance and Terror ...'.[85] This imagining of the 'underworld' clearly spilled over into real life; indeed the disorderly house raids of summer 1730 were strongly conditioned by the apparent identification of gangs of prostitutes and thieves. Yet it is difficult to be sure about the shape and contours of prostitutes' involvement in crime, or for that matter, the involvement of poor women in prostitution. There does seem to be a strong connection between women's criminality and sexuality. In the Old Bailey Sessions, cases of women described by witnesses as whores stealing from their clients proliferate. The case of Hannah Wittermore, acquitted of privately stealing in September 1727 was typical. Hannah was picked up by Thomas Foaks (described as 'a ludicrous Tarpollian') on 18 of August, and 'carried to the Dog Tavern in Thames Street, where we drank four Pints of Wine, I pulled out my Watch, and she asked to look on it, I let her have it, and went to make Water, then asked for it again, she said she had put it in her —, but I did not feel there for it ...'.[86] Foaks eventually got his watch back from a pawnbroker, but nothing was proved against Wittermore. In such cases as these local knowledge was often displayed, thus when Sarah Martin and Sarah Mullenux were accused of stealing a watch from Peter Cox in 1727, they were described as 'a young Whore and an old Bawd';

the following year, when Mary Fowler was indicted of stealing a brass candlestick from the person of Robert Ward, it was noted that she:

> has for some Time kept a notorious Bawdy House in *White Horse Alley, Chick-Lane*, at which Place unthinking simple Sots have been frequently ensnared, gull'd &c, and several of the Strumpets have been brought out of the House to justice; but the *Mother* being in a fair Way for a long Voyage, it is hoped the Crew will be dispersed into other Quarters.[87]

Clearly reputation and local knowledge deeply impacted on women caught in the criminal justice system and indeed, in some cases, accused women used narratives of destitution to explain their fall. Thus Anthony Henderson describes the case of Anne Lumley, accused of theft in 1753, who told the court that she had been reduced to poverty when her husband had been killed on active service abroad.[88] Prostitution then may have been one of those deviant activities which poor women moved in and out of during their life-cycle. Indeed Defoe made pointed comments about the shifting world of prostitution and domestic service.[89] Moreover, there is a sense that once the parish officers associated claimants with prostitution, movement in and out of the trade became increasingly difficult, leaving the prostitute increasingly vulnerable to the temptations of crime.[90]

Peter King's work on female offenders and the life-cycle has shown that the late teens, and early twenties were the key years for vulnerability to indictment for property crime in the late eighteenth century.[91] However, in London and urban Middlesex, another significant period in the life-cycle can be identified. Thus amongst the accused at the Old Bailey, the age group from the early thirties to the mid-forties included a large proportion of women.[92] King has argued that involvement in receiving stolen goods is a major explanation for this peak. Thus half of those indicted for this offence were aged between 30 and 45.[93] Receiving, or fencing, was a particular area of concern for commentators on criminality in the eighteenth century. Many felt that the criminal law was poorly structured in the way it dealt with receivers. Receiving was not actually a felony in common law; the inherent problem was in the link between the receiver and the offender. Thus to convict a receiver, the thief had first to be convicted of felony. By 1718 receivers who were found guilty of being accessories to a felony could be transported for fourteen years. However, there were substantial difficulties in convicting receivers, providing a source of great annoyance and concern to Henry Fielding and Patrick Colquhoun.[94] Receivers were portrayed as a central feature of the world of organised crime, an agent linking the individual criminal to the broader networks of crime in the city.[95] John McMullen described the fence as a 'patron-sponsor' figure, 'overseeing and directing various forms of crime'.[96] Despite this mythologising of the receivers' role, the reality was rather less glamorous. Those accused of receiving almost invariably operated in a much more mundane guise. Thus they were pawnbrokers, old clothes shop keepers, publicans, lodging-house keepers.[97] In other words they occupied roles, ran trades or small businesses, at the heart of the community.[98] To some extent this explains why receivers were such a difficult group to criminalise: unlike other offenders they were not an easy group to label and demonise. Indeed they were central players in the interlinking of community and criminal networks in the metropolis, further reflected in the sets of relationships we see played out between thief and offender in the Old Bailey Sessions Papers.

Elizabeth Morris was indicted for receiving goods from the house-breaker William Norman in April 1733.[99] She was the mother of William Morris, who according to witnesses had been involved in the robbery from the house of Paul Rankin, in St James's Market. Elizabeth Morris kept a smith's shop at the 'Sign of the *Jack* and *Half Moon* in *Eagle-Court* by the New Church in the Strand'. According to one of the smiths she employed, William Hadly, 'Her chief Business is making Stove-Grates. I never knew that she brought any Goods but old Iron.'[100] A number of witnesses testified that Morris was the victim of physical abuse by her son William, and this had prompted some bad feeling in the neighbourhood. Francis Skelhorn, who sold Morris's Stove-Grates commented that:

> Some particular Neighbours may speak ill of her; on Account of her Son, who, indeed, had a vile Character. I have seen him beat her like a Stock-Fish, and break her Goods to Pieces before her Face.
>
> *C.* What particular Neighbours are those?
> *F. S.* Some that sent her Son to *Bridewel*.

Not only does this case show us the potential duality of the receivers' role, but it also shows how networks of neighbourliness could interact with the criminal justice process. Hence, the testimony of Francis Skelborn and William Hadly suggest that Morris was a victim of guilt by association, that neighbours intolerant of her son's behaviour have added to the process which has brought her to court.[101] The receiver then could be very much a part of the local community networks. Moreover, as in the Morris case, receivers often were bound to their suppliers by bonds of kinship: such as the Tanner family who were indicted for theft and receiving in January 1730.[102] Thus Martin Peter Tanner had stolen a gold ring, a watch case, some Bath metal buckles and some toys, from the toy shop of Henry Horton, for whom he worked as an errand boy, '. . . by his own Confession he had taken sundry Goods, at several times from his Master, and giving them to his Mother and Sister', Sarah and Diana Tanner. When the Tanners' house was searched various toys belonging to Horton were found. Martin and his mother were found guilty but his sister was acquitted.[103]

Whilst such cases as that of Morris and the Tanners were very typical of those found tried at the Old Bailey, in other cases the ties of criminal networks, rather than familial or neighbourly networks, were apparent. Andrew Dalton[104] in August 1730 described how he had sold ten gallons of liquor belonging to his master to Moll Harvey, whom we have met elsewhere.[105] Street-robbers Thomas Neaves and James Dalton, who both turned evidence in 1728, mentioned various women as well-known fences: Madame Toy, Susan Watts, Hannah Britton (who according to the *Lives of the Most Remarkable Criminals* was 'whipped from Holborn Bars to St. Giles's Pound').[106] But even in more stereotypical accounts of receivers (i.e. those operating in the context of gangs) kinship networks are still apparent. For example in the 1720s and 1730s, Moll Harvey worked closely with her sister Isabella Eaton, and various common-law husbands belonging to both of them.[107] Indeed when occupants of Harvey's house were thrown in the Roundhouse one Saturday night for 'fighting and quarrelling', Justice Gonson dismissed it as a 'Family Quarrel'.[108]

Conclusion

This chapter has explored the interweaving worlds of the poor and the criminal in early eighteenth-century London. By examining criminality through the lens of community, family and work it has attempted to show how crime might be read as a key element of the makeshift economy in this period. This is not to argue that the line between poverty and crime was indivisible, but rather the sharp dichotomies drawn by contemporaries were clearly not so tangible in reality. There is always a certain fluidity attached to behaviour identified as 'deviant', and in the eighteenth-century metropolis, developing systems of law enforcement, parochial authority and the organisation of poor relief had a significant impact on the way in which criminality was defined and responded to by local residents and neighbours. Clearly, in certain neighbourhoods, what the authorities defined as crime was tolerated to a greater or lesser extent. Prostitution, workplace pilfering and fencing all have their place in the canvas of the plebeian life-cycle. Moreover, kinship networks were not unusual within the groups identified by the authorities as gangs. Ultimately there can be no clear demarcation between the poor and the criminal in the eighteenth-century metropolis, subject as they were to a criminal justice system that whilst capable of negotiation and discretion also had clear ideas about how poor people should, or should not, behave.

Notes

1 *The Covent-Garden Journal*, No. 28, 7 April 1752, cited in H. Fielding, *The Covent Garden Journal and A Plan of the Universal Register Office* (Oxford, Clarendon Press, 1988), p. 422.

2 For a more formal definition and application of the 'moral economy' see E. P. Thompson, 'The moral economy of the English crowd in the eighteenth century', *Past and Present*, 50 (1971), pp. 76–136. For a recent reappraisal and broader application of the 'moral economy' see A. Charlesworth and A. Randall (eds), *Moral Economy and Popular Protest: Crowds, Conflict and Authority* (Basingstoke, Macmillan, 2000).

3 See R. Jutte, *Poverty and Deviance in Early Modern Europe* (Cambridge, Cambridge University Press, 1994), pp. 151–2.

4 For an overview on the historiographical handling of eighteenth-century crime, and particularly the impact of 'social crime', see J. Innes and J. Styles, 'The crime wave: recent writing on crime and criminal justice in eighteenth-century England', in A. Wilson (ed.), *Rethinking Social History: English Society 1570–1920 and its Interpretation* (Manchester, Manchester University Press, 1993), pp. 201–65.

5 J. Beattie, *Crime and the Courts in England, 1660–1800* (Oxford,

Clarendon Press, 1986); *idem*, 'The criminality of women in eighteenth-century England', *Journal of Social History*, 8 (1975), pp. 80–116; P. D'Sena, 'Perquisites and pilfering in the London Docks, 1700–1795' (unpublished MPhil, Open University, 1986); P. Linebaugh, *The London Hanged: Crime and Civil Society in the Eighteenth Century* (London, Allen Lane, 1991); *idem*, 'Tyburn: a study of crime and the labouring poor in London during the first half of the eighteenth century' (unpublished PhD, Warwick University, 1975); R. Shoe-maker, *Prosecution and Punishment: Petty Crime and the Law in London and Rural Middlesex, c. 1660–1725* (Cambridge, Cambridge University Press, 1991). Also see essays in L. Davison *et al.* (eds), *Stilling the Grumbling Hive: The Response to Social and Economic Problems in England, 1689–1750* (Stroud, Alan Sutton, 1992). Since the comple-tion of this chapter, John Beattie has published *Policing and Punishment in London, 1660–1750: Urban Crime and the Limits of Terror* (Oxford, Oxford University Press, 2001).

6 Linebaugh, *London Hanged*; Beattie, *Crime and the Courts*.

7 For a comparative discussion of the interplay between poverty and crime and the economy of makeshifts, see O. Hufton, *The Poor of Eighteenth Century France, 1750–1789* (Oxford, Clarendon Press, 1974), particularly part 3. See also P. Lane, 'Work on the margins: poor women and the informal economy of eighteenth and early nineteenth century Leicestershire', *Midland History*, 22 (1997), pp. 85–99.

8 See chapter 1, 'Literature/crime/society', in I. A. Bell, *Literature and Crime in Augustan England* (London, Routledge, 1991); P. Rogers, *Literature and Popular Culture in Eighteenth Century England* (Brighton, Harvester, 1985).

9 For Hogarth, particularly the Harlot's Progress, see R. Paulson, *Hogarth: Volume 1, The 'Modern Moral Subject' 1697–1732* (New Brun-swick, Rutgers University Press, 1991), especially pp. 241–52; J. Uglow, *Hogarth: A Life and a World* (London, Faber and Faber, 1997), pp. 193–7, 204–6, 209.

10 For example see G. Howson, *Thief-Taker General: The Rise and Fall of Jonathan Wild* (London, Hutchinson, 1970); R. Paley, 'Thief-takers in London in the age of the McDaniel gang, c. 1745–54', in D. Hay and F. Snyder (eds), *Policing and Prosecution in Britain, 1750–1850* (Oxford, Clarendon, 1989), pp. 301–41. For discussion of the 'reality' of Dickens's characters see J. J. Tobias, *Prince of Fences: The Life and Crimes of Ikey Solomons* (London, Vallentine Mitchell, 1974); see also P. Collins, *Dickens and Crime* (3rd edn, London, Macmillan, 1994).

11 For instance James Thornhill's (father-in-law of Hogarth) striking mezzotint of Jack Sheppard in his Newgate cell (Museum of London).

12 H. Shore, ' "Cross coves, buzzers and general sorts of prigs": juvenile crime and the criminal "underworld" in the early nineteenth cen-tury', *British Journal of Criminology*, 39 (1999), p. 11; P. Griffiths,

'Overlapping circles: imagining criminal communities in London, 1545–1645', in A. Shepard and P. Withington (eds), *Communities in Early Modern England* (Manchester, Manchester University Press, 2000), pp. 115–33, particularly 115–16, 120.

13 R. Samuel, *East End Underworld: Chapters in the Life of Arthur Harding* (London, Routledge and Kegan Paul, 1981). For a socio-anthropological view see M. Young and P. Willmott, *Family and Kinship in East London* (London, Penguin Books, 1962).

14 Bearing in mind that the best evidence we have comes from the higher courts, a broad range of much more trivial offences could be dealt with summarily. This could include offences as diverse as: 'vice (as defined by contemporaries), vagrancy and idleness, disobedient servants, certain types of petty theft and embezzlement, violations of the game laws, attending conventicles and other religious offences, and violations of a miscellany of economic and administrative regulations': Shoemaker, *Prosecution and Punishment*, pp. 35–6.

15 *The Proceedings at the Sessions of the Peace, and Oyer and Terminer for the City of London and on the King's Commission of Goal-Delivery of Newgate* ... (otherwise the *Old Bailey Sessions Papers*, hereafter *OBSP*), January 1727/28.

16 Jutte, *Poverty and Deviance*, p. 178.

17 Hufton, *The Poor*, p. 355.

18 See L. B. Faller, *Crime and Defoe: A New Kind of Writing* (Cambridge, Cambridge University Press, 1993).

19 B. De Mandeville, *The Grumbling Hive, or Knaves turn'd Honest* (1705), later incorporated into *The Fable of the Bees, or Private Vices, Public Benefits* (London, J. Roberts, 1714).

20 *The Covent-Garden Journal*, No. 49, 20 June 1752, p. 444.

21 *Ibid*.

22 4 Wm. and M, c. 8, s. 2 (1692); this statute was the first to establish a permanent reward, offering the sum of £40 for the apprehension and conviction of highway robbers, 'including those who robbed in the streets of the metropolis or other towns': Beattie, *Crime and the Courts*, p. 52.

23 Griffiths, 'Overlapping circles', p. 125.

24 Linebaugh, *The London Hanged*, p. xxi. This view of a threatening underclass is arguably much more apparent during the later nineteenth century, again in London, with the spectre of 'outcast London': see G. Stedman-Jones, *Outcast London: A Study in the Relationship Between Classes in Victorian Society* (Oxford, Clarendon Press, 1971); for an account of these shifting perceptions see the authors' introduction to J. Marriott and M. Matsumura, *The Metropolitan Poor: Semi-Factual Accounts, 1795–1910*, 5 vols (London, Pickering and Chatto, 1999), I, pp. xi-l.

25 For a description of the form of the Account see P. Linebaugh, 'The

Ordinary of Newgate and his account', in J. S. Cockburn (ed.), *Crime in England, 1550–1800* (London, Methuen, 1977), pp. 246–69.

26 John Beattie gives us some idea of the patterns of capital sentencing and execution for Surrey between 1722–48, which roughly corresponds to the period covered in this chapter. Thus in 1722–24, 41 people were executed (78.9 per cent of those sentenced to death); 1732–34, 8 (38.1 per cent); 1736–40, 36 (49.3 per cent); 1741–48, 26 (42.6 per cent). Later figures from three periods – 1749–75: 68 per cent; 1776–87: 73.1 per cent; 1788–1802: 53 per cent – show us that in each period the largest majority were hung for robbery or burglary. In fact, in all three periods there were never less than 76 per cent of the total executed for property crime: Beattie, *Crime and the Courts*, pp. 516, 536–7.

27 *The Ordinary of Newgate, His Account of the Behaviour, Confessions, and Dying Words of the Malefactors Who were Executed at Tyburn on Wednesday the 23rd of the Instant December, 1730* (London, John Applebee, 1730).

28 For example, A. Charlesworth, 'An agenda for historical studies of rural protest in Britain, 1750–1850', *Rural History*, 2 (1991), p. 42; P. King, 'Gleaners, farmers and the failure of legal sanctions in England, 1750–1850', *Past and Present*, 125 (1989); J. Rule, 'Social crime in the rural south in the eighteenth and early nineteenth centuries', *Southern History*, 1 (1979), pp. 1–16.

29 For example, Linebaugh, *London Hanged*; Beattie, *Crime and the Courts*; J. Styles, 'From an offence between men to and offence against property: industrial pilfering and the law in the eighteenth century', in M. Berg, P. Hudson and M. Sonenscher (eds), *Manufacture in Town and Country Before the Factory* (Cambridge, Cambridge University Press, 1983), pp. 173–210.

30 As Steven King has recently pointed out, London 'was the focus of a vast range of private acts and institutions which dealt directly or indirectly with relief and welfare. It had a complex array of alternative welfare sources, including the densest pawnbroking network in the country': S. King, *Poverty and Welfare in England, 1700–1850* (Manchester, Manchester University Press, 2000), p. 13.

31 For example, see T. Hitchcock, '"Unlawfully begotten on her body": illegitimacy and the parish poor in St. Luke's Chelsea', in T. Hitchcock, P. King and P. Sharpe (eds), *Chronicling Poverty: The Voices and Strategies of the English Poor, 1640–1840* (London, Macmillan, 1997), pp. 70–86; also T. Hitchcock, 'The English workhouse: a study in institutional poor relief in selected counties, 1696–1750' (unpublished DPhil, Oxford University, 1985).

32 A. Henderson, *Disorderly Women in Eighteenth Century London: Prostitution and Control in the Metropolis, 1730–1830* (Harlow, Longman, 1999), pp. 16–18.

33 K. Wrightson, 'The politics of the parish in early modern England',

in P. Griffiths, A. Fox and S. Hindle (eds), *The Experience of Authority in Early Modern England* (London, Macmillan, 1996), pp. 10–46, for this quote pp. 21–2. Whilst Tim Hitchcock has argued that developments in social policy from 1699 broke down the divisions between the pauper and the vagrant, this model is not so easily applied to crime. Hitchcock argues, 'In a sense, the creation of a sophisticated legal notion of settlement, with its certificates and system of removal, ensured that the sharp division between the vagrant and parish pauper, which had lain at the heart of the parallel development of legislation throughout the sixteenth century, no longer seemed clear': T. Hitchcock, 'The publicity of poverty in early eighteenth-century London', in J. F. Merritt (ed.), *Imagining Early Modern London: Perceptions and Portrayals of the City from Stow to Strype, 1598–1720* (Cambridge, Cambridge University Press, 2001), pp. 166–84, for this quote p. 182.

34 S. Woolf, *The Poor in Western Europe in the Eighteenth and Nineteenth Centuries* (London, Methuen, 1986), p. 109.

35 Obviously one response to this was to learn the language of the system. In early twentieth-century London, Arthur Harding's mother understood this: 'The whole thing was having your poverty well known to the people who had the giving of charity. They noticed that mother was a dead cripple, and that father was a loafer, and that she had children to bring up. And so she got on the list for any of the gifts which came from wealthy families, to distribute among the poor. They made out that she was "deserving". They were always asking whether we was good children or not, and whether we were clean, and whether we went to Sunday School.': Samuel, *East End Underworld*, p. 24.

36 For the development of such areas historically see J. McMullan, *The Canting Crew: London's Criminal Underworld, 1550–1750* (New Brunswick, Rutgers University Press, 1984); Griffiths, 'Overlapping circles'; Shore, 'Cross coves'.

37 T. Hitchcock, 'Paupers and preachers: the SPCK and the parochial workhouse movement', in Davison, *Stilling*, pp. 145–66, especially pp. 147–8.

38 *Ibid.*

39 *The Form of a Petition submitted to ... those Noblemen and Gentlemen who desire to subscribe what sums shall be necessary for relieving, reforming, and employing the Poor ...* (1722), cited in M. D. George, *London Life in the Eighteenth Century* (London, Penguin Books, 1966), p. 309.

40 See Shoemaker, *Prosecution and Punishment*; *idem*, 'Reforming the city: the Reformation of Manners campaign in London, 1690–1738', in Davison, *Stilling*, pp. 99–120.

41 Shoemaker, 'Reforming the city', pp. 99–120.

42 Hitchcock, 'Paupers and preachers', p. 147.

43 E. A. Wrigley, 'A simple model of London's importance in changing

English society and economy, 1650–1750', *Past and Present*, 37 (1967), pp. 44–70; Shoemaker, *Prosecution and Punishment*, pp. 10–11.

44 See J. Boulton, *Neighbourhood and Society: A London Suburb in the Seventeenth Century* (Cambridge, Cambridge University Press, 1987), particularly chapter 9, pp. 228–61. See also J. P. Ward, *Metropolitan Communities: Trade Guilds, Identity and Change in Early Modern London* (Stanford, Stanford University Press, 1997). How far these models can be adapted to the eighteenth century is of course a moot point. See Shoemaker, *Prosecution and Punishment*, p. 11.

45 Shoemaker, *Prosecution and Punishment*, pp. 273–4.

46 *OBSP*, June 1728.

47 *Ibid.*

48 Griffiths, 'Overlapping Circles', p. 125; Ward, *Metropolitan Communities*, pp. 46, 56, 71, 144.

49 London Metropolitan Archive, WJ/OC/2, folio 102.

50 *Daily Journal*, September 1730.

51 See *Daily Journal*, 18, 21 August, 2 November 1730; *London Journal*, 22 August 1730; *Daily Post*, 2 November 1730. For a case involving Mary Harvey and Justice De Veil, see *OBSP*, December 1732, no. 40, 41, pp. 15–18.

52 Gonson was threatened by two men 'on account of his committing to Bridewell ... one Luke Powel, alias Capt. Hop, a notorious Pickpocket. On this occasion Gonson was saved from further harm by the "Mob"': *Daily Journal*, 7 November 1730.

53 Cited in P. W. Coldham, *Emigrants in Chains: A Social History of Forced Emigrants to the Americas, 1607–1776* (Stroud, Alan Sutton, 1992), pp. 143–4. Of course, it is unlikely that these were Lucas's own words, and maybe not even his own sentiments; however, the extract does give some sense of De Veil's activity in this period. For further details about Lucas see Linebaugh, 'Tyburn', pp. 312–23, and appendix III, 'Examination of James Bye ...'.

54 T. Hitchcock and J. Black (eds), *Chelsea Settlement and Bastardy Examinations, 1733–66* (London, London Record Society, 1999), pp. xiii–xiv. De Veil, Henry and John Fielding and Saunders Welch were all active in Chelsea poor relief business.

55 It has been suggested that the poor themselves may have exploited the official relief channels: Lane, 'Work on the margins', p. 93.

56 *Memoirs of the Life and Times of Sir Thomas Deveil, Knight* ... (London, M. Cooper, 1748), pp. 34–5. For the Fieldings see P. Rawlings, *Drunks, Whores and Idle Apprentices: Criminal Biographies of the Eighteenth Century* (London, Routledge, 1992), pp. 24–6. See also Saunders Welch (High Constable of Holborn), *Proposal to Render Effective a Plan to Remove the Nuisance of Common Prostitutes from this Metropolis ... To Which is Annexed a Letter upon the Subject of Robberies, written in the year 1753* (London, 1758).

57 Beattie, *Policing and Punishment*, pp. 372–6.

58 A further period of heightened anxiety (and concern about gangs) followed the end of the War of Austrian Succession in 1748: Beattie, *Policing and Punishment*, p. 461; N. Rogers, 'Confronting the crime wave: the debate over social reform and regulation, 1749–53', in Davison, *Stilling*, pp. 77–98.

59 See M. Harris, 'Trials and criminal biographies: a case study in distribution', in R. Myers and M. Harris (eds), *Sale and Distribution of Books from 1700* (Oxford, Oxford Polytechnic Press, 1982), pp. 1–36; L. B. Faller, *Turned to Account: The Forms and Functions of Criminal Biography in Seventeenth- and Early Eighteenth-Century England* (Cambridge, Cambridge University Press, 1987); Rawlings, *Drunks, Whores and Idle Apprentices*.

60 D. Defoe, *A Narrative of all the Robberies, Escapes, &c. of John Sheppard ...* (London, John Applebee, 1724); *idem, A True and Genuine Account of the Life and Actions of the Late Jonathan Wild, etc ...* (London, John Applebee, 1725). See also Bell, *Literature and Crime*.

61 D. Defoe [attributed], *An Effectual Scheme for the Immediate Preventing of Street Robberies, and suppressing all other Disorders of the Night ...* (London, J. Wilford, 1731), p. 9.

62 For a discussion of the familial bonds to be found in 'gangs' see A. Farge, *Fragile Lives: Violence, Power and Solidarity in Eighteenth Century France* (Cambridge, Polity Press, 1993), pp. 152–7.

63 *Villany Exploded: or, the Mistery of Iniquity laid open; In a Faithful Relation of all the Street-Robberies, Committed by the Notorious Gang now in Newgate ...* (London, T. Read, 1728), p. 40.

64 *Ibid.*, pp. 42–4; also Linebaugh, 'Tyburn', pp. 319–20, n. 1, on the provisions of Mary Young's gang.

65 Similar alignments can be found in other periods: see Harding, *East End Underworld*.

66 The Black Boy Alley Gang, for example, were eventually broken when two of their members, William Harper (otherwise known as Old Daddy) and Anne Wells turned evidence. See the detailed City Minute Book, in the Corporation of London Record Office, SM 12. See also Paley, 'Thief-takers', especially pp. 304, 309, 318–19.

67 *OBSP*, September, October, December Sessions, 1726.

68 *OBSP*, September Sessions, 1726, trial of Sarah Turner alias Lawson, and Katherine Fitzpatrick.

69 *Ibid.*, trial of Jane Holms, alias Barret, alias Frazier.

70 *Ibid.*, trial of Katherine Fitzpatrick and Sarah Turner.

71 As Garthine Walker suggests in her work on gender and crime in early modern London, such networks could be gender related, 'The world of stolen clothes, linens and household goods was populated by women: women stealing, women receiving, women deposing, women searching, and women passing on information, as well as goods, to other women': G. Walker, 'Women, theft and the world of stolen goods', in J. Kermode and G. Walker (eds), *Women, Crime and*

the Courts in Early Modern England (London, UCL Press, 1994), pp. 81–105, for this quote see p. 97.

72 B. Lemire, 'The theft of clothes and popular consumerism in early modern England', *Journal of Social History*, 24 (1990), pp. 256–76.

73 *OBSP*, September Sessions, 1726, trial of Jane Holms, Mary Robinson and Hannah Britton alias Bradshaw. See also below, note 106.

74 Penelope Lane shows how the embezzlement of materials from the worsted industry in eighteenth-century Leicestershire was a significant part of the informal economy: Lane, 'Work on the margins', pp. 88–9. See also P. D' Sena, 'Perquisites and casual labour on the London wharfside in the eighteenth century', *London Journal*, 14 (1989), pp. 130–47; Styles, 'Embezzlement'. For a later period see B. Godfrey, 'Law, factory discipline and "theft": the impact of the factory on workplace appropriation in mid to late nineteenth-century Yorkshire', *British Journal of Criminology*, 39 (1999), pp. 56–71.

75 'G. E.', *Authentick Memoirs of the Life and Surprising Adventures of John Sheppard by Way of Familiar Letters from a Gentleman in Town* (2nd edn, London, 1724), cited in Linebaugh, *London Hanged*, pp. 14–15.

76 J. Dalton, *The Life and Actions of James Dalton (the noted Street-Robber) containing All the Robberies and other Villanies committed by him …* (London, R. Walker, 1730); T. Neaves, *The Life of Thomas Neaves, the Noted Street-Robber, executed at Tyburn, on Friday the Seventeenth of February, 1728–9, etc …* (London, R. Walker, 1729). For Edward Bellamy and John Everett, see G. T. Crook (ed.), *The Complete Newgate Calender, vol. III* (London, Navarre Society, 1926), pp. 47–52. See Linebaugh, *London Hanged*, pp. 184–92, 202, 205, for the link between the butcher trade and highway robbery.

77 Linebaugh, 'Tyburn', pp. 101–2. Linebaugh has discussed the problems of corroborating the Ordinary's Account in 'Ordinary of Newgate', pp. 262–4.

78 Beattie, *Crime and the Courts*, p. 249.

79 *OBSP*, September 1727, p. 3.

80 12 Anne, c. 7 (1713). Discussed in Beattie, *Crime and the Courts*, pp. 173–5.

81 Linebaugh, *London Hanged*, p. 249.

82 Shoemaker, *Prosecution and Punishment*, pp. 185–6.

83 See T. Meldrum, 'London domestic servants from depositional evidence 1660–1750: servant–employer sexuality in the patriarchal household', in Hitchcock, *Chronicling Poverty*, pp. 47–69. See also Beattie, 'Criminality of women', p. 92.

84 Shoemaker, *Prosecution and Punishment*, p. 186, although Henderson, *Disorderly Women*, pp. 14–16 demurs.

85 *An Effectual Scheme*, p. 36.

86 *OBSP*, September, 1727, p. 3.

87 *Ibid.*, p. 6; May 1728. There are no page or case numbers for this reference.

88 *Ibid.*, January 1753, p. 63. Cited in Henderson, *Disorderly Women*, p. 17.

89 A. Morton (pseud. for D. Defoe), *Every-Body's Business is No-Body's Business; or Private Abuses, Public Grievances: Exemplified in the Pride, Insolence, and Exorbitant Wages of our Women Servants, Footmen, etc.* (London, 1725), p. 7, cited in Henderson, *Disorderly Women*, p. 16.

90 As Robert Jutte points out prostitution could become a 'one-way ticket', *Poverty and Deviance*, p. 157; Hufton, *The Poor*, pp. 306–17. See Henderson, *Disorderly Women*, p. 17.

91 P. King, 'Female offenders, work and life-cycle change in late eighteenth-century London', *Continuity and Change*, 11 (1), 1996, pp. 61–90.

92 *Ibid.*, pp. 64–5, 82–3.

93 *Ibid.*, pp. 82–3. For women as receivers of stolen property see Walker, 'Women, theft and the world of stolen goods'. Penelope Lane also comments on the 1730s as a period of vulnerability for plebian women: Lane, 'Work on the margins', p. 86.

94 J. R. & M. A., with an introduction by Sir Basil Montagu, *Hanging Not Punishment Enough* (1701; reprint London, Longman & Co., 1812); H. Fielding, *An Enquiry into the Causes of the Late Increase of Robbers, with some Proposal for Remedying this Growing Evil, etc* (London, A. Millar, 1751), pp. 68–75; P. Colquhoun, *A Treatise on the Police of the Metropolis* (London, C. Dilly, 1796), pp. 187–209. See also Beattie, *Crime and the Courts*, pp. 189–90; L. Radzinowicz, *A History of the English Criminal Law: Vol. 3, The Reform of The Police* (London, Stevens & Sons, 1956), pp. 71–3, 253.

95 C. Hitchen, *The Regulator: or, a Discovery of the Thieves, Thief-takers, and Locks, Alias Receivers of Stolen Goods in and About the City of London ... by a Prisoner in Newgate* (London, W. Boreham, 1718).

96 McMullen, *The Canting Crew*, pp. 111–13, for these quotes see p. 111.

97 On the link between receiving and old clothes see Lemire, 'Theft of clothes', pp. 258–9, 269. On the link between receiving and pawnbroking see Tomkins in this volume.

98 McMullen, *The Canting Crew*, pp. 23–4.

99 *OBSP*, 4th Session, April 1733, no. 78, pp. 124–6.

100 *Ibid.*, p. 125.

101 *Ibid.* Morris was eventually acquitted, but William Norman was sentenced to death.

102 *OBSP*, January 1730, p. 24.

103 *Ibid.*, Martin Peter Tanner was sentenced to transportation.

104 I do not know if Andrew Dalton was any relation to James Dalton, the street robber who was executed in May of that year, or his brother Edward who was executed for murder in October 1732.

105 *OBSP*, August/September 1730, p. 7.

106 *OBSP*, May 1728, evidence of Thomas Neaves and James Dalton in several cases in the course of this session. Neaves, *The Life of Thomas*

Neaves, pp. 15, 21, 28–9; Dalton, *The Life and Actions* ..., pp. 10, 14–17; A. L. Hayward (ed.), *Lives of the Most Remarkable Criminals*, 3 vols (1735; reprint, London, Routledge, 1927), p. 534. Hannah Britton was tried at the Old Bailey for receiving in September 1726, see above note 73, and see also Rawlings, *Drunks, Whores and Idle Apprentices*, p. 104, note 6. Hannah Britton was transported to Virginia and is mentioned in volume I, of P. Coldham, *English Convicts in Colonial America*, 2 vols (New Orleans, Polyanthos, 1974–6), p. 34. Clearly by 1730 she had returned to her old haunts.

107 H. Shore, 'A noted virago: violence, sexuality and resistance, 1725–35', unpublished paper presented at the Long Eighteenth Century Seminar, in the Institute of Historical Research, January 2000. See also the case of Thomas Williams Junior and Thomas Williams Senior, who were indicted respectively for burglary and receiving, and were informed upon by fellow 'gang' member, James Nattris: *OBSP*, April 1730, pp. 16–17.

108 *Daily Post*, 3 November 1730; *Daily Journal*, 3 November 1730.

6

Pawnbroking and the survival strategies of the urban poor in 1770s York

Alannah Tomkins

Introduction

On 9 June 1778 a woman called Ann Moyser visited George Fettes's pawnbroker's shop in York to pledge a checked apron, for which she received a shilling.[1] On 14 October in the same year, the pawnbroker received a business call from the overseers of St Mary Castlegate parish in York. They claimed that the apron did not belong to Ann but to a parishioner of theirs called Sarah Wood. It is not clear whether the overseers considered the item to have been stolen, lent or pawned by Ann on Sarah's behalf, but they redeemed the apron for Sarah's use without producing the duplicate or ticket which had been issued to Ann in June. Despite this evidence and the sporadic entries in overseers' accounts about pledges redeemed with parish money, pawning by paupers was the exception rather than the rule; the pawnshop was the resort of a large number of people in York, predominantly the labouring poor in times of difficulty, but was rarely used by paupers. Nevertheless a close examination of the pawning practices of customers in general, and a comparison of customer names with the identities of city paupers, illuminates the range of ways pawning was employed and the interplay between pawnshop credit and parish relief in poor household economies. The aims of the chapter are ambitious, particularly given the difficulty of defining or characterising 'paupers'. The poor law might intervene at different points in the experience of households according to local custom, the economic conditions prevailing at different times, and the persuasive powers of individuals seeking relief. It would be impossible, for example, to ascribe economic status to people on the basis of the variety or quality of goods they pawned because one household might possess material wealth and receive relief while another might have scanty goods but have avoided technical 'pauperism'.

Such a consideration of the role of pawning in the eighteenth and early nineteenth centuries is long overdue; access to pawnshops and their uses have been largely overlooked by historians of welfare, despite acknowledgement of their crucial role in later periods.[2] Pawning has been listed among other strategies presumed to impinge on the English 'economy of makeshifts', but with no very clear sense of how it was used to make ends meet; the precise role of the pawnshop has perhaps been peculiarly difficult to determine given the paucity of detailed evidence (an issue discussed briefly in the introduction to this volume). Yet the manipulation of different forms of credit, and the conscious regulation of cash into and out of a household via strategic deployment of material possessions, would appear to be vital considerations in the solvency and viability of labouring families. The aim here is to reach beyond generalities into the specific, minute calculations which kept ordinary people afloat and generated prosperous business for the brokers themselves.

This chapter will look first at public perceptions of pawnbrokers and their likely clientele from contemporary printed sources. A brief overview of George Fettes's career as a pawnbroker in York, and some indication of the economic conditions prevailing in York in the second half of the eighteenth century, preface a detailed consideration of strategies used by customers to exploit pawnshop credit to the full. Finally a study of the income derived from both pawning and parishes by selected individuals gives some indication of the scale and function of the assistance offered by each.

Public perceptions of pawnbroking

Public opinion of pawnbrokers in the early and mid-eighteenth century was low; descriptions ranged from 'not very reputable'[3] to 'the chief agents of corruption ... the wretches by whom all wickedness is encouraged'[4] or 'Monsters in the Shape of Men'.[5] The bulk of published opinion was extremely critical. Meetings were allegedly held 'to invent new Schemes to grind the Face of the Poor'.[6] Doubts about the legality and propriety of living by moneylending, combined with anti-Semitism (given that the image of pawnbrokers was that they were typically Jewish), created a virulent, anti-pawnbroking press. Brokers were accused of using intermediaries such as the servants at bawdy houses, gambling dens and gin palaces to generate business and ruin families; the consequences were marked 'by the loss of life in many cases'.[7] Fielding characterised pawnbrokers themselves as 'Miscreants, which, like other Vermin, harbour only about the Poor, and grow fat by sucking their Blood'. He also echoed the persistent criticism that pawnbrokers frequently acted as the receivers of stolen goods, an anxiety which may have been sharpened by the difficulties associated with convicting receivers in the eighteenth century.[8] He referred to pawnbrokers's shops as 'fountains of theft', one of the numerous writers who alleged that thieves were encouraged or instructed and employed by pawnbrokers.[9] Furthermore, pawnbrokers were accused of corrupting the legal system to ensure they were not convicted, via private association.[10] Even writers posing as independent arbitrators, such as the author of the comments printed in the *Gentleman's Magazine* in 1745, were often partisan; the writer casually compares pawnbrokers with murderers.[11] Hogarth's 'Gin Lane' supplied a powerful derogatory image of pawnbrokers, and the picture remains a popular way to represent the terrors of eighteenth-century London life and poverty.

Pawnbrokers were popularly considered to be personally culpable for the uses to which their customers put them. If pawnbrokers were guilty of knowingly lending money on stolen goods then the accusation that they acted as receivers was just, but the practices of the poor in seeking credit were varied and opened up much greyer areas regarding the moral culpability attached to both borrowers and lenders. Writers questioned the integrity of a trader who would lend money to a servant or whore on valuables without enquiry, implying that their guilt lay in their unwillingness or inability to check the provenance of pawns.[12] Gin-drinking or gambling with money obtained on credit was held to be the fault of the moneylender. A milder but repeated accusation was that brokers accepted pawns from children without their parents' knowledge.[13] It was in the interest of opponent commentators to imply that the broker rather than the parent was 'at fault'. One writer highlighted some injustice with this type of criticism by pointing out that other trades were not held accountable for their customers' actions, citing the example of vintners who are free to sell wine even though people become drunk on it.[14] Another acknowledged that other traders' prosperity might depend on the supply of ready money to the labouring poor,[15] but this was a rare reflection in a period when the necessity for pawnbrokers was so often rejected.

Public (published) opinion of pawnbrokers and moneylending altered very little over the course of the eighteenth century. In 1797 Patrick Colquhoun railed against the practice of weekly pawning; typically a working family might pledge tools or other goods on Saturday to redeem their Sunday best, which would be pawned again on Monday morning. He concentrated his attention on the apparently unreasonable profits made by pawnbrokers from this practice (and the folly of 'insuring' in lottery tickets) without considering the alternatives open to the poor who continued to require some 'temporary accommodation'.[16] In the early nineteenth century, the author of *Pawnbrokers Detected and Dissected* bundled together 'Usurers, receivers of stolen goods, Jews, and men of the worst principles' as would-be deceivers of the poor.[17] There was no concession to the idea that the poor in question might legitimately consider pawning to be in their own best interests in the absence of alternative strategies.[18] The writer viewed the high rate of interest endured by people who frequently resorted to pawning as evidence that 'It is not the really industrious poor that make the most frequent use of these shops.'[19] The consequences of 'easy' credit were still considered to be drunkenness, crime and suicide. Also pawnbrokers continued to be criticised for the use made of them, especially by people who pawned several times a day (given the proportionately high rate of interest that was charged). The accusation that pawns were taken from children was modified to include the knowledge of parents and complicity of brokers so that the children grow 'lost to all becoming modesty'.[20]

There appears to have been a discrepancy between the type of pawnbroking which attracted intense opposition and the 'honest' trade. The quality of the service provided and the wealth of the clientele who used the shop, the 'tenor of the trade',[21] was determined by the goods which were considered to be acceptable collateral and the permanency or ad hoc nature of the business. There may have been pawnbrokers who organised theft and burglary but they were not necessarily the majority, or the same as the substantial pawnbrokers who wrote in defence of the practice of moneylending. One alleged convert to the necessity for pawn-brokers claimed in 1745 that people said to be pawnbrokers were really 'people of different professions'.[22] 'Pawnbroker' was a label which could be applied to any individual who lent money on material security, however slight, and the disreputable 'pawn-brokers' caught up in criminal proceedings were claimed to be first and foremost those who took pawns as a sideline (including gin sellers or keepers of disorderly houses).[23] Another less repu-table variation of the pawnshop was the 'dolly shop' which took low-value goods which pawnbrokers would not accept.[24] In addi-tion, James Lackington claimed that some establishments which advertised as pawnbrokers were in fact simple shops, where cus-tomers were over-charged when they thought that they must be getting a bargain in the form of an unredeemed pledge.[25] John Styles has found that criminal cases involving people who were described as pawnbrokers were few in comparison to those tra-despeople who accepted pawns informally, such as the owners of public houses.[26]

A pamphlet of 1744 rehearsed the arguments or 'apologies' of the 'honest' pawnbroker.[27] The writer latched on to the then relatively recent example of the failure of the Charitable Corpor-ation to assert that pawnbrokers were the most proper people to fill the role of supplying the poor with small sums. They were represented as substantial businessmen with stock of at least 2,000 items. Also, the pamphlet put the unusual view of the difficulties which pawnbrokers faced in honest trading. If pledges were left for a long time, they were dead stock bringing no return; when sold, they may not bring in the value of the money loaned especially if the clothes had gone out of fashion; in addition, if the goods were sold and the customer later returned to redeem their pos-sessions, the pawnbroker might face a law suit for their full value, 'aided and abetted by pettifogging attorneys'.[28] If only honest traders were relieved of such threats they could afford to charge lower interest, which (it was alleged) would constitute a genuine benefit to the poor. Furthermore it was argued that pawnbrokers needed to make enough to live and support a family. In fact, the writer of the *Apology* asserted that the interest charged was not an unreasonable reward for the service provided since if the poor person had to sell their goods instead of pawning them, they would not have been able to replace them without considerable loss, much greater than the interest charged by the pawnbroker. It was also claimed that pawnbrokers' return for their investment was modest in relation to the profit made by other traders for smaller outlay and over a shorter time. Many tradesmen had preserved their trade and credit via use of brokers. The pamphlet drew attention to the language routinely used when writing about pawnbrokers, that they 'incur infamy' as a result of the 'opprobrious language freely bestowed'.[29]

In response to accusations that pawnbrokers were in the habit of receiving stolen goods, and thereby gave encouragement to thieves, the *Apology* asked why more pawnbrokers were not convicted. It was alleged that pawnbrokers only became receivers by accident and even then they were often the one to expose the thief. The writer's resort to hyperbole is some indication of the impact made by past criticism, since he or she claimed that other traders might more easily steal a horse than a pawnbroker might look over a hedge; indeed, as the takers of valuable goods, pawnbrokers were themselves liable to be the victims of thefts.[30] Anxious to prove their probity, the London pawnbrokers announced their intention in 1753 to take the daily newspaper the *Public Advertiser* to try to identify any stolen goods presented as pledges and return them to their lawful owners.[31] A bill of 1752, which did not become law, had proposed that if a pawnbroker bought goods that had been advertised as stolen they would be guilty of a crime 'not yet named'.[32] John Fielding implied that pawnbrokers did not scan the papers so assiduously as he would have liked when he asserted in 1765 that 'if SUCH INFORMATIONS are properly attended to ... few Robberies will escape detection'.[33] An independent voice of support was raised by Campbell in his *London Tradesman*, where he contended that a pawnbroker's business did not inevitably encourage theft,[34] but commentators into the nineteenth century continued to allege that brokers did not do their duty and question their customers.[35]

Customers of pawnbrokers who felt cheated in some way by their transactions (and who could afford it) could technically choose to seek legal redress. If the pawnbroker refused to return goods, either because they had been sold or because the customer refused to pay the interest which had accrued, then the customer could bring a suit of trover to recover the value of the goods. Hence the complaint by one pawnbroker that people were likely to bring malicious suits to recover the value of the goods without returning the advanced loan.[36] There seems to have been some justice in the pawnbrokers' complaint in that they were punished for the wrongdoing of others. In 1752 a jury found against a pawnbroker, who had refused to return goods without the payment of money advanced. The fact that the goods had been pawned not by the owner of the goods but by his laundress suggests that the laundress was guilty of theft, but it was the pawnbroker who suffered since he lost both the money loan and the goods.[37]

This example helps to account for their need to associate, to meet the costs of defending such cases (and probably for mutual support in the face of public suspicion and hostility). The legal position of pawnbrokers and their customers was somewhat clarified by an Act of 1757.[38] This required pawnbrokers to keep a register, detailing the goods pledged, money lent, date and the name and address of the customer. If a person pledged goods on behalf of someone else, the owner's name was also noted. The customer could choose to pay for a ticket comprising a duplicate of the register details. The pawnbroker was obliged to take care of the goods and compensate customers for any loss of value resulting from neglect or wear and tear; however, it also gave pawnbrokers eventual rights over the goods, since items securing a loan of up to 10 pounds were forfeit after two years. There were also clauses to control illegal pawning, such as pledging stolen goods or piecework materials which were the property of an employer. Subsequent Acts sought to define the legitimate activities of pawnbrokers further, for example by stipulating in 1784 the interest which might be charged on loans of different sums over different durations.[39]

There was clearly room for a significant gulf between the public, printed opinion of pawnbrokers and the practical relationships which existed between pawnbrokers and their fellow tradesmen, and between pawnbrokers and customers. The opprobrium to which pawnbrokers were subjected in the press was not necessarily a feature of their everyday experience, particularly where the shop was long established and the business well regulated. Also, commentary focused on London pawnshops. In London, facilities for pawning were ubiquitous and some shops probably did offer a way to dispose of stolen goods. There was considerable scope for anonymity and evasion of the law; indeed in 1794, London was described in one novel as 'an inexhaustible reservoir of concealment'.[40] The situation was different in the provinces. Opportunities for anonymity were fewer, and established pawnshops were more sparsely distributed. By the end of the eighteenth century there were allegedly 431 pawnbrokers in the provinces throughout the country who bought licences,[41] principally located in substantial towns (pawnbroking being 'an urban phenomenon').[42]

The provincial picture of pawnbroking, which was relatively unconsidered by contemporaries and has been inadequately studied by investigations into the broad spectrum of welfare facilities, forms the main focus of this chapter. Melanie Tebbutt has demonstrated that in the 1870s, pawnshops were most prevalent in industrial, manufacturing areas, particularly in Lancashire and the Black Country.[43] This pattern was already evident by the end of the eighteenth century when pawnbrokers outside London were already clustered in the north-west and the midlands.[44] Therefore, the evidence supplied by the pledgebook of George Fettes, working in the almost anti-industrial atmosphere of 1770s York, cannot be used confidently as a proxy for patterns of pawning in general. Nevertheless, there was probably little uniformity in the practices of different populations in different regions; even in the late nineteenth century 'industrial pawnbroking was itself hardly uniform'.[45] An investigation of the surviving pledgebook will at least shed some light on the situation in York.

George Fettes, pawnbroker, and the city of York

The evidence indicates that George Fettes, the York pawnbroker of the 1770s, was one of the 'honest' pawnbrokers whose protests of innocence were occasionally heard above the general din of disapproval. He had an established shop in Lady Peckett's Yard off Pavement in the town centre (see figure 6.1).[46] The surviving pledgebook of 1777 and 1778 is itself the earliest evidence of his business, which was the only pawnbroking firm in York to be listed in the 1781 directory. Fettes was listed with a second pawnbroker, Thomas Palmer of Swinegate, in the *Universal British Directory* of 1798. Fettes carried on trading until he sold the business at some time between 1823 and 1827.

George Fettes had been born into a family of substance; his father was an Edinburgh merchant and his cousin Sir William Fettes later founded the Edinburgh school of the same name. He

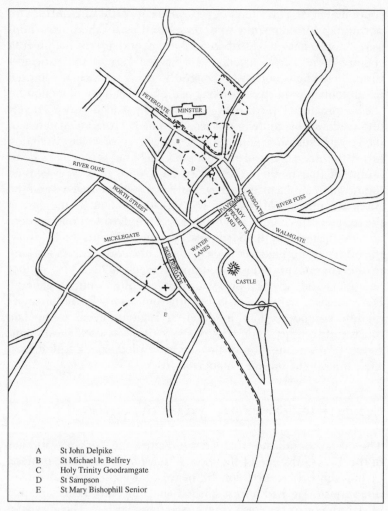

A   St John Delpike
B   St Michael le Belfrey
C   Holy Trinity Goodramgate
D   St Sampson
E   St Mary Bishophill Senior

Figure 6.1 Map of York

was a young man in his early twenties during the years when the pledgebook survives; in later years he came to be well regarded by his fellow traders and citizens in York. He was elected a commoner to the city council by 1798, served as Sheriff for the city in 1802 and thereafter was one of the 24 city aldermen. His financial and trading experience was presumably influential in his being appointed one of the first directors of the York savings

bank, established in 1816. He and his wife Elizabeth were both
Wesleyan Methodists and were valued members of the congregation. George was a 'President of the prayer leaders' and fellow
Methodist John Pawson remembered his 'great kindness' at the
time of his (Pawson's) marriage in 1785.[47] Fettes was a friend of
John Wesley who stayed with him on his visits to York. The
pawnbroking trade clearly did not stand in the way of this relationship, although it may have been the subject of some friendly
raillery between the two men. In Wesley's only recorded letter to
Fettes he wrote 'Prove these two points – first that pawnbroking
is necessary, secondly that it is lawful (in England) – and you will
satisfy your affectionate brother John Wesley.'[48]

York might be eligible for the 'leisure town' status accorded
to Shrewsbury. In the early eighteenth century Defoe referred to
York as a place of 'good company and cheap living; a man
converses here with all the world as effectually as at London' but
enjoying 'no trade indeed, except such as depends upon the
confluence of the gentry'.[49] In 1745 he was echoed by another
commentator: 'the chief support of the city, at present, is the
resort to and residence of several country gentlemen with their
families in it'. It has been described as the social and intellectual
capital of the north between the seventeenth and the nineteenth
centuries.[50] Nevertheless, by the 1770s not all of its visitors thought
it a particularly vibrant social centre. One of Horace Walpole's
correspondents described it in 1771 as 'this dullest of all provincial
towns'.[51]

In the 1770s the city of York's population was gradually increasing, since the inhabitants numbered approximately 12,000
in 1760 but had reached 16,145 in 1801;[52] however, York did not
experience any of the economic upheaval associated elsewhere
with industrial development, technological change or reorganisa-
tion of employment. This was considered by contemporaries to
be a result of 'the restrictive policy of the corporation' which
tended to discourage outside manufacturers from settling in York.
The corporation attempted to enforce the freedom regulations
strictly throughout the eighteenth century; it was still being urged
to 'open the gates to all tradesmen and manufacturers inclinable
to settle among us' in 1790.[53] York's chief economic importance
remained its role in the regional economy, as a centre of wheat
and dairy distribution. This remained true well into the nineteenth
century, despite relatively rapid population growth after 1800.[54]

Coincidentally, York had been a notable centre for moneylending in the sixteenth century, but this function had seemingly declined in importance well before the 1770s.[55]

The absence of any significant manufacture in the city was cited by one contemporary as a significant cause of the distress of the poor; the experience of poverty caused by people's 'life-cycle' was exacerbated by restricted employment opportunities. Nevertheless the picture of York presented by the evidence of formal relief was unremarkable. The number of paupers in York was around 500 in the 1720s, amounting to around 5 per cent, a typical proportion of urban populations.[56] The poor were managed by individual parishes, of which there were 28 in 1777, but overseers of the poor were supervised by the corporation which compiled statistics relating to poor rates and expenses in a central 'Poor Book'. Proposals to found a workhouse were considered in 1729 and 1737–39, but schemes to cover the whole city failed. In 1768 several parishes chose to unite for the purpose of running a joint workhouse which was established in Marygate, but individual parishes continued to administer their own funds and to pay outdoor relief.[57]

In addition to rated relief, inhabitants of York parishes could claim assistance from a relatively long list of privately-funded charities which provided almshouses, cash for apprenticing and other benefits. It was claimed in 1833 that the wealth of charities in some parishes made them particularly desirable as places of settlement; parents prevented children from taking apprenticeships if it meant they would lose a settlement in a parish with munificent charities, and outsiders would strive to acquire settlements in such places.[58]

Finally, as Armstrong has observed, York was to become the focus of Rowntree's influential report on poverty at the end of the nineteenth century, making it an intriguing subject for the study of poverty in earlier periods.[59]

Pawnshop customers

George Fettes held a key position in this framework of urban development and the experience of poverty. He kept a pledgebook recording customers and their pledges in accordance with the law of 1757. He or his shop assistants recorded the date, the name and address of customers, the goods pledged and the sum advanced. If the items were redeemed the date of redemption was commonly entered but the source is faulty in that notes of redemptions become more rare towards the end of the volume. On the last day when the book was used to enter pledges, 26 December 1778, no redemption dates were written down, presumably because it was too much trouble to look up the initial entry in an old book once a new book was in use in the shop. One redemption after December 1778 was noted, because the customer waited six years to collect his goods: George Parrott, after pledging his silver watch during York race week on 22 August 1777, only came back for it on 29 May 1784.[60]

A simple statistical breakdown and analysis of this very rich source sheds new light on the place of pawnbroking in the lives and strategies of the urban poor. Fettes received a total of 10,879 pledges in the eighteen months from July 1777 to December 1778. The pace of business fluctuated according to the weekly, monthly and annual requirements of customers but also according to Fettes's willingness to loan money; the book only records loans made rather than loans requested. The number of pledges accepted (Figure 6.2) fell from an average of 33 a day in February 1778 to a low of 17 in July 1778. The possible causes of this downturn in trade include the appearance of a trading rival or an improvement in the financial fortunes of York's labouring poor.[61] The economic complexion of the two years 1777 and 1778 was very different and it is likely that increasing hardship had some part to play in making Fettes more reluctant or less able to accept pledges. In 1777 England enjoyed something of a boom; the Yorkshire woollen cloth industry enjoyed considerable prosperity, with the output of broadcloth increasing.[62] Admittedly the harvests were good in both years ('prodigious' in 1778[63]), but the crucial difference between the years was caused by the entry of the French into the American War of Independence. Britain had been at war with the American colonists since 1775, but French involvement raised the stakes and intensified the British effort. Consequently, there was a hike in taxation rates and financial crisis threatened. Ashton's analysis of contemporary statistics and comment identifies 1777 as a peak of prosperity, with signs of decline in late 1777, and sudden crisis in the first months of 1778.[64] The construction industry suffered a serious depression 1778–84, a common feature of wartime in the eighteenth century, and the

Yorkshire cloth industry experienced a sudden depression. It was said that 'trade of every kind seems to be at a perfect stand owing to an uncommon great and general scarcity of money' and there were 623 bankruptcies in 1778 as opposed to 471 in 1777. The rate of custom at Fettes's shop suggests that he initially responded to this sudden demand for money by meeting customers' requirements but was limiting his advancement of credit later in the year. Either he was suffering himself from the shortage of money and unable to take advantage of his customers' desire for cash, or he became more cautious about making loans, fearing that if redemptions were sluggish he would be left with a large, unprofitable, perishable 'dead stock'.

The weekly pattern of pawning is clearly visible from the database. Customers were most keen to pledge their property on Saturday or Monday, with these days seeing 23 per cent and 21 per cent of business respectively. The remaining pledges each week were shared between the other four working days. This broad pattern conceals a wide variety of usage by different types of customer. Some people only entered the shop once during the eighteen months covered while others might visit several times a day. One strategy employed by customers was to pledge several items at the same time but in separate lots and redeemable on separate tickets. This meant that goods could be redeemed one at a time although it did mean buying a ticket for each pledge. On 2 October 1777 Henry Richardson made eight pledges of individual items of clothing for between three and six shillings each; he redeemed them over the next ten months, between 1 November 1777 and 22 August 1778.

In addition to the pledges made by customers the book contains the dates when goods were redeemed. Analysis of a small sample of redemptions (for two weeks in September 1777[65]) showed that the average time lapse between pledge and redemption was 56 days, but this bland average conceals three basic types of behaviour in pledging and redemption by customers. Half of all pledges were short term, with a quarter destined to be redeemed within one week and another quarter collected within a month. The majority of the remaining items stayed in the shop for longer periods of 29 days or more. On 3 September 1777 Frances Smith pawned a brown calamanca gown for 4s. and returned for it nearly a year later on 31 August 1778. Some goods were never redeemed; 14 per cent of pledges left with Fettes went unclaimed. It was

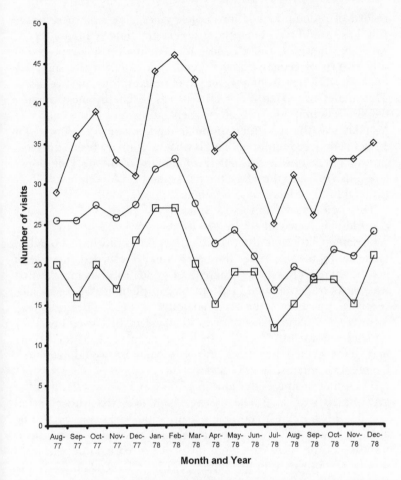

-⊖- Overall/monthly avg -⊟- Fri avg -◇- Sat avg

Figure 6.2 Pledges accepted by George Fettes

asserted in the *Gentleman's Magazine* in 1745 that many items were considered unlikely to be redeemed if left with the pawnbroker for more than 15 months. Therefore, items pledged in September 1777 and not redeemed by December 1778 could be assumed to have been abandoned by their owners.

It is difficult to trace the weekly redemption pattern of goods since this requires a calculation of what weekday the date of redemption fell in the case of each individual pledge. Also, the record of redemptions is incomplete since goods pawned before July 1777 could have been redeemed at any time without a record surviving; however, there is no particular reason to suppose that the pattern of redemption for goods not listed in the surviving book was different from any sample of redemptions that are listed. This analysis revealed that Saturday was by far the most popular day for redemptions, with 30 per cent of pledges being collected. Monday was the next most popular day, but only accounted for 14 per cent of redemptions. This is what might have been expected. Presumably, Saturday was pay day for many of the working population in York and therefore the day when people were most likely to be able to redeem pawned goods.

The amounts of money advanced for pledges were usually considerably below their 'value' to their owners, but may have represented little less than the pawnbroker could have hoped to make by their sale. Fettes only occasionally recorded the sale of goods; there were two lone entries of goods sold during the first two weeks of September 1777 out of 236 pledges. Where he also recorded the amount he received for the sale, it does not seem to indicate a particularly high profit margin. In November 1777 he sold a gown for 10s. 6d. which had been pledged for 9s.; he may have gained less from this sale than he would from the payment of interest by the owner.

The smallest sum Fettes lent in 1777 and 1778 was 2d. and the greatest 10 guineas.[66] The average loan over the whole period was 3s. 9d. but the majority of loans totalled 2s. or less.[67] The average amounts loaned rose significantly in August each year at the time of the races (the main focus of the York social season);[68] in the seventeen months August 1777 to December 1778 the average amount loaned on each occasion was between 3s. and 4s. during twelve of the months but rose to 5s. 5d. and 4s. 10d. in August 1777 and 1778 respectively. Visitors to the town were among Fettes's wealthier clients, able to pledge more valuable goods. William and Thomas Bradley of Newton on Derwent both pledged their watches in August 1777 and Thomas also pledged his greatcoat, coat and waistcoat. Thomas literally lost the coat from his back and the Bradleys both had to wait until a return trip to York in November to redeem their property.[69]

Most of the goods which Fettes accepted as pledges could be characterised as items of adult clothing, but he also routinely lent money on soft furnishings, household metalware such as irons and cutlery and more valuable pieces such as watches and jewellery.[70] This is the pattern repeated in evidence of nineteenth-century pawnbroking and this aspect of pawnbrokers's business has been used to illustrate the vibrancy of the second-hand clothing trade in the eighteenth century.[71]

The predominance of women's clothing, particularly aprons and gowns, reflects the gender balance of Fettes's clients. Women represented the majority of his customers, and made more repeated visits than men (suggesting a central role for women in northern household economies). During the sample two weeks in September, the most frequent male customers each visited the shop three times. By comparison, twelve women visited the shop on four or more occasions and Sarah Beeforth made pledges at 15 different times (more than one pledge per day when the shop was open). A database of customers' names[72] was edited and condensed to derive a guesstimate of the number of individual customers who visited Fettes's shop between 18 August 1777 and 26 December 1778 (see appendix, pp. 192–3). This guesstimate gives 2,200 people of whom 1,349 or 61 per cent were definitely women. This is a somewhat lower figure for female customers than might have been expected given that women were more likely than men to be counted twice in making the guesstimate. Women who married and therefore changed their name during the eighteenth months of the pledgebook would inadvertently have been counted twice. The total figure of 2,200 suggests that, in a town of 12–14,000 people, 15–17 per cent of the population resorted to this pawnbroker and had pledges accepted.[73]

The pledging of clothing and household goods by women to raise credit supplies circumstantial evidence for an overlap between the pawning poor and those guilty of theft. The same sorts of goods were the most popular targets for both male and female thieves but were disproportionately stolen by women who were also more active in pawnshop transactions than men. It is likely that this overlap (which may or may not have arisen from a causal connection) exacerbated public suspicion of pawnshops. Confusingly, in late eighteenth-century London the connection between pawnshops and theft was drawn explicitly when women pleaded *not* guilty to theft, on the grounds that they had pawned goods on behalf of others or with permission rather than as a strategy for converting stolen property into cash; 'these were instances of women's borrowing networks gone wrong'.[74]

The York evidence can only show that *overt* borrowing, or pawning on behalf of others, was not very common. The law of 1757 required Fettes to keep a record when goods were pawned by one person on behalf of another, and there are only 52 instances of this practice between August 1777 and December 1778 accounting for only 0.5 per cent of all pledges. Also, there is no discernible pattern to these pledges for others. People may have been acting on behalf of friends, relatives, employers or tourists staying locally. Twice in 1778, pledges from John Hare were brought by Nurse Hare, presumably a relation, whereas items belonging to Mrs Wood of North Street were brought by Mrs Aspinall of Petergate (addresses at some distance from each other). Catherine Woodhall of Thursday Market sent her apprentice to the shop with four silver teaspoons on 29 August 1777 but never came by to redeem them. Robert Hepworth, who was staying at Judges Lodgings, persuaded (or paid?) Widow Aldridge, an almswoman who was otherwise a stranger to the pawnbroker's, to take a coat, waistcoat and silk gown to be pledged. Presumed cases of borrowing are occasionally discernible, where the same item (such as a watch identified by a manufacturer's number) was pledged more than once by two or more different people, but it would be impossible to trace anonymous items (such as most clothes) moving between pawnshop customers.

Customers were mainly drawn from the city of York itself, with tourists being the exception rather than the rule. Assuming the list of 2,200 people to provide a fair reflection of the individuals involved, the largest contingent came from Walmgate and North Street, locations on the south side of the city a little way distant from the centre. Between 2 and 5 per cent of customers were drawn from each of Fossgate, Goodramgate, Petergate and Micklegate, large thoroughfares leading into the city centre, and from the Waterlanes and Skeldergate, poor areas on the banks of the Ouse. Other addresses accounted for fewer than 2 per cent of all customers. This picture is broadly in line with a study of addresses taken from pledges rather than separate customers.[75] It suggests that customers were drawn to the shop regardless of its distance from their homes. People may have been drawn in by its proximity to their place of work or to places where ready money might be spent such as gambling dens or alehouses (one of the greatest fears of the anti-usury pamphleteers), but it is more likely that the need for cash drove people to walk any necessary distance.

Paupers and the pawnshop

The paucity of sources like Fettes's pledgebook has led to a neglect of pawnbroking as an alternative strategy for the eighteenth-century poor; the subject has received more attention for the nineteenth century. During the latter, Treble found that pawnshop credit was obtained for four different types of need; access to short-term (often weekly) credit, seasonal pawning to cover longer periods of difficulty, pawning to pay for costs associated with sickness such as doctors' bills or loss of earnings, and steady pawning in periods of unemployment. Yet it is important to distinguish between all people who had desperate need of credit and the individuals best placed to obtain it from pawnbrokers, since there were different gradations of poverty. Pawnbrokers were most accommodating for clients with regular wages and were wary of unemployment.[76] Beverley Lemire has rightly observed that pawning in the eighteenth century 'was not restricted to the indigent, to the destitute, or to the recipients of charity'.[77] In fact the services of the reputable, established pawnshop were virtually denied to the destitute because, as in the nineteenth century, 'there were certain sections of the working classes who were treated as unacceptable risks'.[78] There was a reduced chance that they would be able to redeem their goods and pay the interest, leaving the broker with their (typically) low-value goods. The destitute were compelled to turn to dolly shops, or moneylenders requiring little or no security, where the rate of interest was even higher.[79]

Commentators in the eighteenth and early nineteenth centuries who deplored the practice of pawning tended to demonstrate a masterly lack of understanding of the cash-flow problems of the labouring poor. Until the end of the eighteenth century,[80] writers were largely unaware of the intimate minutiae of poor household budgets but relied instead upon suppositions formed from a position of relative financial security. It is notable that writers were invariably men enjoying relative financial security whereas pawnshop customers were typically poor women. Such views were (justifiably?) said to demonstrate 'Ignorance of the Sudden and Unexpected Disappointments and Embarrassments, which not only People of the lower Rank, but even those of a higher Station are liable to'.[81] Occasionally a more balanced independent view was available. The assertion 'the industrious poor could as well do without butchers, bakers and brewers, as they could subsist without some such conveniency of borrowing money' was reported second-hand and not wholeheartedly endorsed by the writer,[82] but Campbell stoutly declared 'they are so necessary to the poor ... I cannot comprehend almost how they can live without the Pawnbroker'.[83] Those who wrote actively in defence of pawnbroking described the clientele of pawnbrokers as 'chiefly among the industrious poor, and working part of mankind, who have little or no credit at all, and who, for want of some such assistance, must come upon the parishes they belong to, or be starved'. Pawnbrokers were characterised as providing much-needed assistance in the period between the onset of a crisis and a resort to the parish, and preventing people from falling on rates and this view received inadvertent confirmation in other texts.[84] Such writers correctly perceived pawning as typically an alternative expediency to parish relief, not an auxiliary service.

The process by which individuals or households fell into utter destitution (a state partly defined by a scarcity or absence of any goods to sell or pawn) could be lengthy and the pawnshop could be crucial to this process. In addition to providing access to credit, pawning without redemption was an obvious way for people's material stock to decline. Yet (as I mentioned in the introduction to this chapter) parishes could intervene at different points in the process for different people. Any group of people on parish relief might encompass a wide range of material wealth, from those rich in goods to those who had reached destitution.[85] This means that very few assumptions can be made about people identified as paupers without additional information about the point they have reached in the process of destitution. The only thing that can be said about them is that they are sufficiently needy to have attracted the attention of the poor law authorities, for which the threshold could be relatively or surprisingly high in terms of material wealth.

The number of Fettes's customers who were also in receipt of parish relief is few. In order to find paupers among the pawnshop customers, I compiled the names of the poor receiving some kind of parish relief during the years 1777 and 1778 in the parishes where overseers accounts survive for these years. The five parishes with good accounts are St Michael le Belfrey (the parish with the largest population in York in 1801), St Sampson, St Mary Bishophill senior, St John Delpike and Holy Trinity Goodramgate. These parishes contained 20 per cent of the town's population in

1801, so if pauper customers were drawn from parishes in proportion to the total population, any overlap between known paupers would represent 20 per cent of the total number of pauper customers. Unfortunately, it is unlikely that paupers were drawn from parishes in proportion to the total population because some areas of the city were poorer than others and more likely to be home to customers; the number of pauper customers found is likely to underestimate the total because some of the most popular addresses for customers fall in parishes with no surviving overseers' accounts.

A total of 201 paupers were found receiving parish relief in 1777 and or 1778, of whom 16 were deemed to be customers from a correspondence of names and addresses. A further 38 paupers may possibly have been customers but there was some inconsistency between the pauper's name and address and that of the customer. This gives a total of 54 people who might have been both paupers and customers. Taking only probable individuals, and assuming they represent 20 per cent of all probable pauper customers, then only 4 per cent of Fettes's customers belonged to the parish poor. If the 'possibles' are included then the total rises to 12 per cent. Even if this underestimates the total extent of overlap between paupers and pawnshop customers by half, then over three-quarters of Fettes's customers were not paupers at approximately the same time they made use of his shop. However, it is likely that many more customers would technically become paupers over the course of their life-cycle, given the gradual, incremental nature of the process of decline into destitution.

In finding pauper customers, some were easier to identify than others. For example, the overseers of St Michael le Belfrey paid relief to Joseph Armitage's wife, so it was legitimate to look for both Joseph and Mrs Armitage of Petergate in the pawnbook; in contrast, there were a number of customers called Turpin who may have been related to one another, but it was only legitimate to collect references to Jane Turpin from the overseers' accounts since she was the only pauper named.

There are a couple of references in the overseers' accounts to goods redeemed by the parish during 1777 and 1778. In 1778 the overseers of St Michael le Belfrey paid to redeem from pawn clothes belonging to Mary Wilson's child, and paid twice to redeem the clothes of Elizabeth Gleddill's child. These clothes may have been placed with Fettes before the start of the surviving pledge-book, because there is no record of them being pawned. Alternatively, this is a fragment of evidence that paupers (or some individuals among paupers) had access to credit from some other source, possibly some less reputable moneylender than Fettes, who required less in the way of security and more in the way of interest.

Parish officers had an interest in monitoring the disposal of goods by paupers because parishes occasionally decided to appropriate material possessions when paupers entered the workhouse or died. Their authority to do so was wholly assumed (it was not authorised by law) and was not always exercised.[86] Entries in parish accounts to a person's goods being carried to the workhouse, and becoming subsumed into parish property in subsequent inventories of workhouse property, or the acknowledgement that a portion of parish income derived from the sale of paupers' goods, is the only (sporadic) evidence for the practice.[87] It was presumably easier for parishes to assume ownership where a pauper died without dependents or local kin to assert a claim to whatever scanty goods remained. In Leeds, paupers were periodically forced to surrender their goods when entering the workhouse, a strategy on the part of the parish which increased the severity of the 'workhouse test' and reduced the number of relief claimants.[88] In Mansfield the workhouse rules required every inmate to bring their goods and chattels with them, although this may not have been consistently enforced.[89] There was a similar condition attached to workhouse entry in Lincoln, but there paupers could take their goods away with them again if and when they left. Claiming pauper goods for the parish may have been only an occasional strategy to defray some of the costs of keeping a person over the preceding years, but it suggests an element of self-interest in parish scrutiny of pauper possessions and their disposal by pawning or other means.

An associated problem for parishes (and also for charities and other agencies which supplied free clothing or access to household goods) was the illegal pawning of parish goods by paupers for their private gain. In some places, the parish 'mark' was fixed to clothes, household wares and even furniture to prevent or inhibit their theft and subsequent disposal. Such a strategy presumably made it easier for parish officials to identify goods and for reputable pawnbrokers to avoid the charge of receiving stolen goods; it was not a guarantee, however, that theft would not occur.

Individual people used the pawnshop in different ways but the variety of their usage was not decidedly conditioned by whether they were a pauper at the same time. All types of customers employed a number of different strategies in maximising their use of the pawnshop. The only identifiable difference between pauper customers and all customers was that paupers on average redeemed their goods much more quickly; on average customers repaid their loan after 56 days whereas paupers took an average of only 25 days. It is difficult to know what to make of this given that each average conceals such a wide range of behaviour. It may possibly suggest that the poorer people became, the more short-term their strategies or the more central the pawnshop became to their survival.

The main obstacle to determining patterns of use by different types of customer lies in the difficulty of categorising individual customers as representatives of the independent labouring poor or as parish paupers; I could not be certain that a customer who was not a pauper in one of the five parishes studied was not a pauper in one of the other 23 parishes listed in the 1777 overseers' returns to parliament. Individuals are also indistinguishable as members of a particular trade or as domestic servants since there are very few occupational labels recorded against customers' names. Also, there was virtually no overlap between the tradesmen listed in the York directory of 1781 and the pawnshop's customers.[90] It was said in 1745 that it would be injurious for the reputation of a trader even to enter a pawnbroker's shop; tradesmen who were tempted to pawn were advised instead to admit their virtual insolvency.[91] If there was a stigma for tradesmen in approaching a pawnbroker they might have tried to use intermediaries, but such a practice is not disclosed by a study of the few items reported to have been brought on someone else's behalf.

One of the only identifiable groups of customers is the almsmen and women who lived in one of the many almshouses or 'hospitals' in York; at least 19 were operational in the 1770s.[92] Almspeople are recorded amongst Fettes's customers by virtue of their address being given as the almshouse; however, only 13 men and women are listed in this context, seven of whom only used the pawnbroker once or twice and none of whom visited more than 13 times. A number of the almshouses paid a stipend to inhabitants in addition to providing accommodation, so these charity recipients could rely on a regular 'wage' or income. The infrequency of their custom suggests either that this rendered them less liable to the sudden

need for credit, or that the regularity of their income did nothing
to persuade Fettes to accept their pledges. The few charity customers there were seemed to use the pawnshop for very long-term
credit, since their average time before redemption was 67 days,
much longer than paupers and even longer than the average for
all customers of 56 days.

It is not possible to compare the use made of Fettes's shop with
Treble's categories of the reasons why credit was sought. For
instance, it is likely that a number of the customers in York did
need a short-term loan as a result of illness, but it is not now
possible to determine which individuals became involved in this
way. It is possible to look at some of the patterns of custom, which
are critical to understanding the experience of poverty which did
not fall within the scope of formal parish agencies. There were
people who only used the shop once or twice during the period
covered by the pledgebook. Pendock Vane or Vame, apprentice
to the barber-surgeon John Firth of Coney Street, pawned a silver
watch on 18 July 1777 and redeemed it on 4 November of the
same year but did not place any further pledges before the end
of the volume.[93] Others came in periodically over the eighteen
months, perhaps on a monthly basis but not necessarily to a
predictable pattern. Ann Plaister's address was 'Mr Telford's
Nurseryhouse'; she was presumably an employee of John and
George Telford, seedsmen with premises in Tanner Row.[94] She
made eight pledges in September 1777, a further three in October
and she reappeared periodically over the following months. She
can be found pawning twice in the final week for which the book
applies in December 1778. Some customers used the shop intensively over one or two months and then slackened off, or did not
reappear in the book. An example of this sort of usage, which
might best be characterised as episodic, is provided by the Beeforths who lived in the Shambles. Sarah Beeforth visited the shop
15 times during the first two weeks in September 1777, pledging
various items of clothing and shoes. One pledge was redeemed
the day after it was pawned, while another remained in the shop
until the following March. She visited the shop between three and
six times each week for the following seven weeks. During the
fifth week Elizabeth Beeforth also of the Shambles and possibly
a member of Sarah's family and/or household appeared as a
customer. In the seventh week Richard Beeforth of the Shambles
made pledges; there is circumstantial evidence that Sarah and

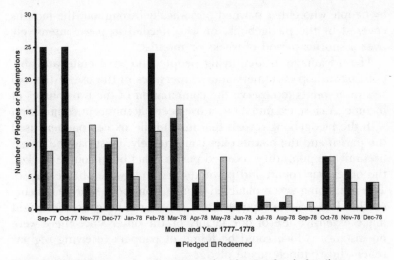

Figure 6.3 Pledges and redemptions by the Beeforth family

Richard were connected in some way because they both pledged items used in patten-making. On 8 October Sarah pawned a patten-maker's knife which remained unredeemed in December 1778 while Richard pawned four pairs of patten irons on 1 November and redeemed them on 8 November. After the end of the seventh week (Saturday 1 November), the Beeforths were obviously better off, redeeming more goods than they pledged in November (Figure 6.3). They remained occasional customers until their next period of particular difficulty in February 1778. From March to May they were net redeemers, and then made only a handful of visits to the shop until October; up to December 1778 the shop experienced a small concentration of custom from them, which was trailing off by the end of the year.

The sheer number of customers, the doubts about whether an individual listed on one occasion was the same person recorded on another day (with a slightly different spelling for their name, or a different address), and the fact that it is difficult to determine whether people lived with or were related to one another, makes it impossible to know whether there were more complex patterns of credit-seeking at work in York's poorer households. Nevertheless, the broad picture of pawnshop use illustrates these three patterns at work. There were many people who visited the shop only once or twice, but the majority of pledges are accounted for by people who either pawned periodically throughout the months covered by the pledgebook, or who needed to pawn intensively over a shorter period of weeks or months.

The advantage in identifying people who were quite probably both pawnshop customers and paupers lies in the use of the two sets of accounts to observe the combination of the two sources of income. A close examination of overseers' accounts in conjunction with the pledgebook reveals that nine of the sixteen paupers used the parish and the pawnbroker consecutively; most pawned goods up until the point they received parish relief but a couple worked the other way round and pawned once they were off the parish. The remaining seven obtained money from both sources concurrently. The evidence points to a situation where people might make extensive use of one facility or the other since there were no instances which could be found of paupers receiving regular relief who routinely made pledges.

Mary Budd and Mary Prince are both examples of customers who used the pawnshop energetically, if in very different ways. Mary Budd used the shop before she took relief. She worked systematically, pledging a large, fairly fixed bundle of goods on a monthly basis. She pledged her four gowns, her two black satin cloaks and a long list of other goods on the same ticket, left them with Fettes for about a month, and redeemed them only to pledge them again later the same day or the next day. She did this ten times between September 1777 and July 1778 (and made smaller pledges on four other days). She received between £4 and £5 pounds for her bundle; £5 in September 1777 which dropped down to a low of £3 and 15s. in July 1778. Fettes was being shrewd in dropping the amount he would advance on her bundle; he also began to insist that the bundle would be forfeit if she did not redeem it within one month. Whatever resources she was able to utilise monthly to redeem her clothes, they ran out after July 1778. The bundle was pledged for the last time on 31 July 1778 and shortly before Christmas she became a pensioner in the parish of St Sampson receiving 2s. per week. Mary Prince was a much more frequent visitor to Fettes's shop, pawning between one and thirteen times a month, making 112 visits between 19 August 1777 and 5 December 1778. She pawned adults' and childrens' clothes, flat irons and a Bible on one occasion for small sums ranging between 4d. and 3s. 6d. A handful of items remained unredeemed by December 1778 and some items were left for long periods of three months or more but the majority of her pledges were redeemed within ten days. She fell into difficulty towards the middle of November 1778, went to St Sampson's parish for help and was given a shilling a week for four weeks.

The Armitages were relatively unusual because they received their relief first, before they needed to pawn, but Joseph Armitage and his wife were only on the fringes of pauperism since they received just a single handout of 3s. in 1777 and no relief in 1778. They pledged clothes and bedlinen with Fettes on seven occasions between January and September 1778 and redeemed the earlier pledges between March and September 1778, but by December 1778 their last three pledges, including a gold ring, remained unredeemed. An alternative picture is presented by Robert Turner. He was a pensioner in St Mary Bishophill senior parish receiving 4s. per week from November 1777 onwards; he only visited the pawnshop once, on 9 April 1778, to pledge a green silk waistcoat for 4s. 2d. He collected it on 2 July and apparently did not return again.

Conclusion

The case of George Fettes provides the opportunity to test the operation of provincial pawning in the context of a hostile, critical press which tarred all pawnbrokers with a metropolitan brush. He was a respected businessman with a vibrant trade which stretched from the tourist visitors who came for the races to the poorest inhabitants of York's streets and alleys. Furthermore, the pledge-book supplies vital information about the experience of poverty in York. The routine finding that approximately 5 per cent of the population stood in need of parish relief is given context by the fact that 15–17 per cent of the town's inhabitants made use of this one pawnbroker in the relatively short period July 1777 to December 1778. Different styles of usage can be identified among Fettes's clientele. Customers might use the shop once, possibly pawning a single valuable item, to help them cope with a particular crisis. Others used the shop persistently but not necessarily frequently to deal with periodic, recurrent problems or shortfalls. Brief periods of intense pawning followed by a lull in activity or disappearance from the pledgebook can be labelled episodic, emanating from a period of crisis which either permitted short-term recovery or signalled an important stage in absolute material decline into destitution (and thereafter an absence of goods to pawn). The role of the pawnshop in the process of either independent survival or decline into dependency can be charted, particularly in the case of individuals who went on to receive parish relief. The strategies employed by the poor who dealt with Fettes's pawnshop were limited by whether he was willing to accept their pawn, by the amount he advanced, and by their ability to redeem their goods. Nonetheless, individual people exploited the essential flexibility of pawning to cover routine expenses, regain their financial equilibrium following a crisis, or stave off deeper destitution for so long as their material wealth would allow.

Appendix

The names attached to over 10,000 pledges were conflated to give a guesstimate of the number of individual people who made use of the pawnshop during the period 18 August 1777 to 26 December 1778. The pledgebook begins in July 1777, but the entries for a number of days are torn or very faint so it was decided to start a comprehensive list from the date when the vast majority of pledges were readily legible.

There were two basic problems attached to this exercise, first relating to changes in customers' circumstances and, second, relating to variation in notation by the pawnbroker or his assistants. Regarding changes of circumstance, it was likely that a number of Fettes's female customers got married during the 17 months under study and changed their surnames, meaning the same individual would be pledging but under two different names; however, it was not thought justifiable to search the marriage registers of York's 28 parishes to identify which women this applied to, and find what their names became. Therefore, the list is likely to overestimate the number of separate female customers. Also, both men and women were able to change address during the same 17 months, but every variation of address in the pledgebook might indicate a different person. Therefore Dorothy Batty, for example, has been counted four times because a woman or women with this name and surname were listed at four different addresses. This is an extreme example but demonstrates how the number of both men and women are probably overestimated.

The second problem concerns the wide variation of spellings enjoyed by different names and the range of possible 'addresses' which might refer to the same location in the city of York. Ruth Creaser lived in Walmgate, but was Ruth Cassia of the same address in fact the same woman? It is likely she was, but there was no way to formulate a rule for the conflation of such names. A relational database which compares the extent of correspondence between letters of a name would not have helped much in this instance because there is very little similarity between Creaser and Cassia. Also, the same person might be recorded under different addresses which, on consultation of a map, appear to apply to the same approximate area of the city. William Addy was recorded at Holgate Lane and also living outside Micklegate Bar. The exact location of Holgate Lane is not now known but Holgate was outside Micklegate Bar so it seemed legitimate to conflate the two. Other cases were not so clear-cut.

These difficulties reduce the accuracy of the resulting list to such an extent that the number of 2,200 people reached by these means is little more than an informed guess. Without parish reconstructions for the 28 York city parishes the total picture can never be obtained. Nevertheless, given the number of names in the list which could not conceivably be conflated, the number 2,200 provides a figure to work with to determine approximate proportions of male and female customers, the geographical spread of customers and other calculations.

Notes

1 York City Archives, pawnbroker's pledgebook, 1777–78.
2 For example, D. Vincent, *Poor Citizens* (London, Longman, 1991), pp. 92–3.
3 R. Campbell, *The London Tradesman* (London, T. Gardner, 1747), p. 296.
4 *Gentleman's Magazine*, xv (1745), p. 410.
5 J. Stow, *Survey of the Cities of London and Westminster ... Corrected, Improved,, in the Year 1720 by John Strype* (6th edn, London, 1754), I, 474 quoted in B. Lemire, 'Consumerism in preindustrial and early industrial England: the trade in secondhand clothes', *Journal of British Studies*, 27 (1988), p. 14.
6 *A Plain Answer to a late pamphlet intitled The Business of Pawnbroking Stated and Defended* (London, W. Bickerton, 1745), p. 4.
7 *Ibid.*, p. 8.
8 J. M. Beattie, *Crime and the Courts in England 1660–1800* (Princeton, Princeton University Press, 1986), pp. 189–90.
9 H. Fielding, *Amelia* (London, Croscup and Sterling Co., 1751), quoted in H. Fielding, *An Enquiry into the Late Increase of Robbers* (London, 1751), edited by M. Zirker (Oxford, Clarendon, 1988), pp. 125–30.
10 *A Plain Answer*, pp. 3–4.
11 *Gentleman's Magazine*, xv (1745), p. 461.

12 *A Plain Answer*, pp. 6–7.

13 *Ibid.*, pp. 11, 27; however, it is not impossible that the adult poor actively used children as their intermediaries and messengers.

14 *An Apology for the Business of Pawnbroking* (London, 1744), p. 57.

15 *Gentleman's Magazine*, xv (1745), p. 699.

16 Report of Colquhoun's publication of *An Account of the Meat and Soup Charity established in the Metropolis*, contained in *The Times*, 20 March 1797 and *Gentleman's Magazine*, lxvii (1797), pp. 856–7.

17 *Pawnbrokers Detected and Dissected: or the poor man's adviser* (London, 1809), p. 4.

18 Only J. Bentham, *Defence of Usury* (London, T. Payne & Son, 1787) went so far.

19 *Pawnbrokers Detected*, p. 8.

20 *Ibid.*, p. 44; it is likely that observations of this sort qualify as the misinterpretation of parent/child relations which Pollock has identified when the middle and upper classes tried to comment on the lives of the poor: see L. A. Pollock, *Forgotten Children: Parent-Child Relations from 1500 to 1900* (Cambridge, Cambridge University Press, 1983), p. 61.

21 M. Tebbutt, *Making Ends Meet: Pawnbroking and Working-Class Credit* (Leicester, Leicester University Press, 1984), p. 3.

22 *Gentleman's Magazine*, xv (1745), p. 700.

23 *Ibid.*

24 Tebbutt, *Making Ends Meet*, p. 13.

25 J. Lackington, *Memoirs of the forty-five first years of the life of James Lackington* (London, 1795), pp. 226–7.

26 J. Styles, 'Clothing the North: the supply of non-elite clothing in the eighteenth-century north of England', *Textile History*, 25 (1994).

27 *An Apology*; some of the views expressed in this pamphlet had been aired earlier, see *Daily Post Boy*, 26 April 1731.

28 *An Apology*, p. 16. There was also some legitimacy in the claim that clothes could depreciate if they went out of fashion. Towards the end of the eighteenth century breeches made of leather were entirely replaced by cloth alternatives such as corduroy, meaning that there was no domestic market for secondhand leather trousers; see Lemire, 'Consumerism', p. 17.

29 *An Apology*, pp. 16, 26.

30 *Gentleman's Magazine*, liv (1784), p. 711 reports a case of 1784 where a pawnbroker's apprentice stole jewellery in his master's keeping.

31 J. Black, *The English Press in the Eighteenth Century* (London, Croom Helm, 1987), p. 60.

32 *Gentleman's Magazine*, xxii (1752), p. 41.

33 *The Public Advertiser*, 1 January 1765, quoted in B. Lemire, 'The theft of clothes and popular consumerism in early modern England', *Journal of Social History*, 24 (1990), p. 259.

34 Campbell, *London Tradesman*, pp. 296–7.

35 *The Poor Man's Friend, or the Frauds of the Pawnbrokers Exposed* (London, H. Chance, c. 1835), pp. 6–7.

36 *An Apology*, pp. 15–16.

37 *Gentleman's Magazine*, xxii (1752), p. 284.

38 30 Geo 2 c. 24.

39 24 Geo 3 c. 42.

40 W. Godwin, *The Adventures of Caleb Williams* (Oxford, Oxford University Press, 1982), p. 254.

41 B. Lemire, 'Peddling fashion: salesmen, pawnbrokers, taylors, thieves and the second-hand clothes trade in England c. 1700–1800', *Textile History*, 22, 1 (1991), p. 82.

42 K. Hudson, *Pawnbroking: An Aspect of English Social Hhistory* (London, Bodley Head, 1982), p. 31.

43 Tebbutt, *Making Ends Meet*, pp. 3–4.

44 Lemire, 'Consumerism', p. 12.

45 Tebbutt, *Making Ends Meet*, p. 6.

46 I am indebted for much of the information contained in this paragraph and the next to the work completed by Alison Backhouse: A. Backhouse, 'The wormeaten waistcoat – the pledge book and owners of a pawnbroker's business', *York Historian*, 14 (1997).

47 J. Telford (ed.), *The Letters of the Rev. John Wesley* (London, Epworth, 1960), VII, p. 77.

48 *Ibid.*, letter of 3 August 1781.

49 D. Defoe, *A Tour Through England and Wales* (London, J. M. Dent & Sons, 1959), II, pp. 230, 234.

50 D. M. Palliser, *Tudor York* (Oxford, Oxford University Press, 1979), p. 1. Drake in 1745, quoted in P. M. Tillott (ed.), *Victoria County History for Yorkshire, City of York* (London, Dawson for London University Press, 1961), p. 215.

51 A. McInnes, 'The emergence of a leisure town: Shrewsbury 1660–1760', *Past and Present*, 120 (1988); W. S. Lewis (ed.), *Horace Walpole's Correspondence* (New Haven, Yale University Press, 1955), XXVIII, p. 23, letter from William Mason at York dated 21 September 1771.

52 Tillott, *V. C. H. City of York*, p. 212; P.P. *Abstract of the answers and returns made pursuant to ... 'An act for taking an account of the population of Great Britain'* (1802).

53 Tillott, *V. C. H. City of York*, pp. 215–16; *York Chronicle*, 27 August 1790, quoted in A. Armstrong, *Stability and Change in an English County Town: A Social Study of York 1801–1851* (Cambridge, Cambridge University Press, 1974), p. 20.

54 Armstrong, *Stability*, pp. 27–36.

55 Palliser, *Tudor York*, p. 280.

56 Drake, quoted in Tillott, *V. C. H. City of York*, p. 215; P. Slack, *Poverty and Policy in Tudor and Stuart England* (London, Longman, 1988), p. 72.

57 S. Lambert (ed.), *House of Commons Sessional Papers of the Eighteenth Century* (Wilmington, Delaware, 1975), p. 31 for 'Abstracts of the returns made by the overseers of the poor 1777'; Tillott, *V. C. H. City of York*, pp. 226–9.

58 *York Herald*, 30 November 1833.

59 Armstrong, *Stability*, p. 37.

60 The contents of the pledgebook are ideally suited to conversion to a computer database and this enormous task has been undertaken by Alison Backhouse. The database allows for easy statistical analysis of the numbers of pledges taken, the days of the week most favoured by customers, the types of goods pledged and the values of pawns: see Backhouse, 'Wormeaten waistcoat'. At the time of writing the database is not complete, so findings are based partly on Mrs Backhouse's analysis of pledges July to December 1777 and partly on my own less ambitious databases of the pledgebook contents.

61 Backhouse, 'Wormeaten waistcoat', p. 40.

62 T. S. Ashton, *Economic Fluctuations in England 1700–1800* (Oxford, Clarendon, 1959), p. 130.

63 *Ibid.*, p. 23.

64 *Ibid.*, pp. 40, 100, 105, 130, 161–2, 172–3.

65 These two weeks were chosen for two reasons. First, the quality of the accounts is less good at the start of the volume (some pages are torn), but it seemed appropriate to select a period towards the start of the book where the record of redemptions was likely to be fullest. Second, race week occurred in August and pledges made at that time were not necessarily typical because visitors to the town had distant addresses and pledged goods of higher value than usual. Therefore the first two weeks in September 1777 were chosen for close analysis.

66 Backhouse, 'Wormeaten waistcoat', p. 40.

67 Based on the sample of two weeks in September.

68 Tillott, *V. C. H. City of York*, p. 245.

69 York City Archives, pawnbroker's pledgebook, 19–21 August 1777.

70 For a statistical breakdown of items pledged and an illustrative list of the more unusual pledges taken by Fettes see Backhouse, 'Wormeaten waistcoat', pp. 35–7.

71 B. Lemire, *Dress, Culture and Commerce* (Basingstoke, Macmillan, 1997), pp. 105–12.

72 My own, rather than that compiled by Mrs Backhouse.

73 This calculation allows customers who were visitors to the town to account for approximately 150 people.

74 Borrowing, like pawning, stands witness to the precariousness of life, where commodities other than cash became effective currency: L. MacKay, 'Why they stole: women in the Old Bailey, 1779–1789', *Journal of Social History*, 32 (1999), pp. 625, 628, 630–4.

75 Backhouse, 'Wormeaten waistcoat', p. 35.
76 J. H. Treble, *Urban Poverty in Britain 1830–1914* (London, Batsford, 1979) p. 132.
77 Lemire, 'Consumerism', p. 23.
78 Treble, *Urban Poverty*, pp. 131–3.
79 *Ibid.*, p. 133; for an account of a complex, early twentieth-century strategy involving a street moneylender, a credit draper and an established pawnshop, see J. Burnett, *Idle Hands: The Experience of Unemployment, 1790–1990* (London, Routledge, 1994), pp. 188–9.
80 Principally, D. Davies, *The Case of Labourers in Husbandry* (London, Robinson, 1795) and F. M. Eden, *The State of the Poor* (London, Routledge, 1928), first published 1797; consideration of pawning is largely absent from both of these works. Labourers in husbandry might have had restricted access to urban pawnshops but Eden's trawl of budgets only uncovered one pawnshop customer, a Bristol labourer.
81 *An Apology*, p. 39.
82 *Gentleman's Magazine*, xv (1745), p. 697.
83 Campbell, *London Tradesman*, p. 296.
84 *Gentleman's Magazine*, xv (1745), pp. 578, 698; Eden, *State of the Poor*, p. 191.
85 P. King, 'Pauper inventories and the material lives of the poor in the eighteenth and early nineteenth centuries', in T. Hitchcock, P. King and P. Sharpe, *Chronicling Poverty: The Voices and Strategies of the English Poor 1640–1840* (Basingstoke, Macmillan, 1997).
86 For instance, there is no mention of this practice in M. Nolan, *Treatise on the laws for the relief and settlement of the poor* (London, 1805).
87 For example, see Shropshire Records and Research Centre, P250/L/2/1, Shrewsbury Holycross overseers' accounts, workhouse inventory 1750; Borthwick Institute, St Michael le Belfrey workhouse masters' accounts 1744–56, removal of Ann Weatherill's goods to the workhouse, 12 November 1745; Oxford Record Office, Mss dd par Oxford St Peter le Bailey b. 18, redistribution of Elizabeth Cooling's goods 1765; requisitioning of goods was practised more extensively in seventeenth-century London: see J. Boulton, 'Going on the parish: the parish pension and its meaning in the London suburbs, 1640–1724', in Hitchcock *et al.*, *Chronicling Poverty*, pp. 35–6.
88 P. Anderson, 'The Leeds Workhouse under the Old Poor Law, 1726–1834', *Thoresby Miscellany*, 17 (Thoresby Society, 1980), pp. 91, 98.
89 J. D. Chambers, *Nottinghamshire in the Eighteenth Century* (London, Cass, 1966), p. 240.
90 *Bailey's Northern Directory* (Warrington, William Ashton, 1781).
91 *Gentleman's Magazine*, xv (1745), pp. 460–1.
92 Tillott, *V. C. H. City of York*, pp. 422–6.

93 York City Archives, pawnbroker's pledgebook, 18 July 1777; Back-house, 'Wormeaten waistcoat', p. 37; B.L. Eg 2572.
94 *Northern Directory*, p. 317.

7
Kinship, poor relief and the welfare process in early modern England

Sam Barrett

Overview – the 'problem' of kinship

Historiographical writing on the depth and functionality of kinship in early modern England is limited. It is also contradictory. On the *extent and depth of kinship networks*, for instance, early commentators such as Peter Laslett were clear that English households tended to be relatively small and simple and that, because of demographic constraint (migration, 'background' mortality, epidemic mortality and relatively late marriage ages), such families were located within relatively shallow kinship networks.[1] Microsimulation exercises appeared to confirm this view, suggesting that 'achievable' levels of kinship in most localities remained low throughout the early modern period.[2] Other early commentators, focusing on particular social, religious or regional groups, were not so sure. Lawrence Stone suggested that, notwithstanding negative demography, nominal kinship networks amongst the aristocracy and gentry could be both deep and extensive,[3] while Gilbert noted that nonconformist groups such as Quakers were tied into very deep kinship connections which could be used in business, an idea that has become a commonplace of the Industrial Revolution literature.[4]

More recent analysis of the extent and depth of kinship networks has not proved any less contradictory. Painstaking empirical work by Cooper and Donald has revealed that in suburban Exeter the extent of local kinship networks (and of kinship co-residence) is substantially understated using conventional census analysis because of the tendency for many of those standing in contractual relationships to local families to in fact be kin by blood or marriage.[5] Reay has also sought to question the idea of shallow kinship networks. Focusing on rural villages in nineteenth-century Kent he argues that while extended families were comparatively rare, well over one half of all families by 1851 were related to at least one other, that perhaps a further 10 per cent who had no kin in their village nonetheless had kin in immediately adjacent villages (which meant only small distances to travel given the small size of southern parishes) and that even if complex families containing kin were relatively rare, kin nonetheless lived in proximate residence to each other, creating de facto extended families.[6] Other commentators have found less to take issue with in the views of Laslett. Keith Wrightson, for instance, has calculated that in the Essex village of Terling, only 33 per cent of all families had kinship connections by blood or marriage with others in the same community.[7] In mid-nineteenth-century south-east Surrey, Evelyn Lord found that for ten rural communities kinship density was at best on a par with, and usually much lower than, the kinship densities identified by Wrightson for Terling well over 100 years earlier.[8]

The purpose of my chapter is not to address this literature on the extent and depth of kinship directly, though a quantitative measure of kinship density is important for establishing the limits of potential kinship involvement in the economy of makeshifts. Rather, I think that historiographical division over the extent and depth of kinship networks feeds directly into division over the *functionality of kin* in the welfare arena and particularly over the question of *whether (and if so at what level) kin provided welfare in substitution for, or support of, the poor law and charity*.[9] On the one hand, commentators such as Cressey, Fissell, King and Thane suggest that kin *must* have been an important part of the economy of makeshifts, a way for poor people to avoid poor relief or a means to supplement poor relief which, as King shows, was always and everywhere inadequate to hold body and soul together.[10] Cressey, for instance, concludes that for families 'most of the time their dealings were limited to those closest to them but the potential existed to bring even distant and latent kin into a close and effective [welfare] relationship'.[11] Fissell for Bristol and King for Yorkshire provide some support for this idea. They show that those obtaining medical or other relief were disproportionately those who lacked dense kinship networks in their locality.[12] In these cases, the poor law might act as a partial substitute for kinship networks, though neither author seems to provide support for the contentions of Peter Laslett that weak kinship networks necessarily generated more generous or more encompassing poor law systems.[13]

Other contributors to the debate have argued that many local poor law authorities tried to create a care partnership between (often stretched) kinship networks and community resources. Both Thane and Botelho suggest that the elderly in the eighteenth and nineteenth centuries were likely to be subject to these sorts of implicit agreements as their working capacity was curtailed, and in the absence of formal retirement agreements of the sort that we see in some continental countries.[14] The poor law, for instance, could pay rent for elderly people living with relatives, effectively sharing the full cost of providing for such old people and giving poor families valuable cash flow. Lynne Hollen Lees suggests that such partnerships, aimed at ensuring the survival of the family unit and the coherence of the kinship and neighbourhood networks of poor people, might have been the norm and could, at least until the nineteenth century, guarantee a basic level of community support to poor people within their kinship networks for long periods of time. Using vestry minute evidence from nineteenth-century Lancashire, one of the most parsimonious of all English counties in relief levels and eligibility, King supports this idea.[15]

There are, however, alternative and competing lines of historiography. Sandra Cavallo, for instance, echoes Michael Anderson in suggesting that family members often conflicted over the issue of welfare and that where families did provide welfare the respective obligations of donor and recipient were strictly limited by negotiation. In fact, she suggests, institutions played a large part in the coping strategies of poor people, and might effectively act as surrogate kin. Her data is for Italian communities, but the lessons are probably portable.[16] Meanwhile, David Thomson, dealing with the experience of paupers in the initial decade of the new poor law in Bedfordshire, argues that despite well-known legal provisions that some of the kin of paupers were obliged to care for them where they had the means to do so, in practice welfare was a community rather than a familial responsibility. Either because they were not able, or because they chose not to, families did not form either a large or consistent part of the welfare process.[17] Crowther likewise sees a decisive shift in the balance of provision during the nineteenth century (though with counties such as Kent continuing to enforce the 'liable relative clause' which was little changed by the 1834 Poor Law Amendment Act) as the economic position of families moved decisively against offering material support at times of life-cycle stress.[18] McIntosh traces a decisive negative shift in family support for paupers at a much earlier date. She suggests that 'A contrast between formal and informal or between public and private care would likewise have puzzled Elizabethans' and shows that in late sixteenth-century Hadleigh over one-third of all people in receipt of welfare also had fairly extensive and economically secure local kinship networks. By the late seventeenth century, however, her own evidence and that of Wales and Newman Brown suggests that for certain groups of the poor the community was becoming the main plank of welfare and kinship was being relegated to the backwaters of the economy of makeshifts.[19] These differences over the timing of any transition in the role of kin are important, and would be magnified considerably if we had more numerous local studies available. However, the stark contrast between the two ends of the historiographical spectrum on the role of kinship in the economy of makeshifts is clear to see.

Of course, there are many good reasons for these different levels of contradiction. Kinship density could change rapidly in any locality (due to mortality crises, for instance) as well as experiencing longer-term trends. It is thus difficult, even with the best of sources, to trace the exact dynamics of kinship in a given community over time, and even more difficult to put community experiences together in order to pin down regional typologies of either kinship depth or functionality.[20] A further problem, however, is that reconstructing the density of kinship and its functionality is problematic given the level and quality of English record keeping and survival. English sources are considerably less rewarding than those on the continent,[21] and for any individual community we have to undertake complex multiple source record linkage in order even to begin uncovering kinship networks and reading their meaning. The potential pitfalls in this sort of record linkage are numerous – kinship connections tend to get lost as we link between sources of different types; considerable numbers of in-laws, stepchildren, half-children or adopted children complicate decisions on who is really (and functionally) related to whom; and repeated movements between communities could create an extensive localised kinship network which the historian simply does not detect when looking at individual communities [22] – but the rewards are considerable.

This chapter will use family reconstitutions linked to a range of supplementary data for six communities in the West Riding during the eighteenth and nineteenth centuries, in order to reconstruct the depth of local and regional kinship networks and then to elaborate the place of kinship in the economy of makeshifts. Utilising over 18,000 discrete family histories I will suggest that kinship densities in the West Riding woollen district were very high, that we can detect a broad inverse relationship between kinship density and community level poor law spending, as Fissell and King have suggested, and that there was a broad positive relationship between kinship density and receipt of charity. However, the existence of such a relationship does not mean that those with dense kinship links never received poor relief. I will demonstrate that the poor law often provided resources to those with kin in response to sudden crisis such as illness, giving the kinship group time to marshal the material and human resources which kept their relatives off longer-term relief. Finally, I will use narrative evidence to try and pin down the character of the support that kinship networks were able to offer in the late eighteenth century.

Places and sources

The West Riding of Yorkshire is certainly the most fully reconstituted of all eighteenth- and nineteenth-century counties. By the mid-1990s no fewer than 23 townships in the county had been subject to family reconstitution, and this chapter uses some of these reconstitutions and contributes to the stock with new studies. It covers six townships in four large parishes. Tong and Cleckheaton (1801 populations 1,637 and 1,336 respectively) were part of the very large parish of Birstall and were reconstituted by Hartley Thwaite. They have been subject to extensive demographic analysis as part of the 26-reconstitution sample used by Wrigley and Schofield in 1997.[23] Horsforth in Guiseley parish (1801 population 2,099), Otley (1801 population 2,014) and Armley and

Bramley (1801 populations 2,695 and 2,562 respectively[24]) were townships in the western part of the sprawling parish of Leeds and were reconstituted by the author as part of a study of kinship in the woollen and worsted districts of the West Riding.[25]

This collection of townships makes an ideal framework for the study of the role of kinship in welfare provision for several reasons. First, the townships were all in relative proximity to each other, allowing us to talk (albeit not definitively) about localised rather than simply community-based kinship networks. The townships were also staging points for migrants on the way to, and returning from, Leeds itself, easing some of the uncertainties of record linkage created by heavy short distance migration in early modern communities.[26] A second reason for the suitability of this collection of townships is that while they are all nominally located in the woollen district of the West Riding, they had very different occupational structures, allowing a contrast of the scale, depth and functionality of kinship networks across a number of different socio-economic typologies which may have wider echoes with communities elsewhere. There is not the space here to conduct a detailed anatomisation of any one community, and in any case both the general and the specific occupational and economic history of the West Riding and its individual townships has been drawn by others.[27] Briefly, though, Horsforth and Otley were centres of woollen cloth production organised under the artisan system whereby essentially small-scale producers combined, at family level, textile production with farming and other income generation strategies. Armley combined agricultural production with textile production organised through the putting-out system, which drew around one-third of male workers in the town into a proletarian relationship with Leeds merchants by the 1780s at the latest. However, as Mr James Ellis testified before the 1806 enquiry into the state of the woollen industry, the township also had its fair share of resident master manufacturers who, as well as spinning and weaving on their own account, also put out work to other families in Armley and its surrounding hamlets.[28] Bramley was a centre for the preparation of wool and the finishing of woollen cloth, with scribbling, carding and fulling mills surrounded by independent yeomen clothiers often maintaining substantial farms and organising putting-out networks in other townships. Tong and Cleckheaton were more balanced villages, combining some mining and quarrying with textile production, agriculture and, especially in the case of Tong, service industries such as baking and milk production for surrounding industrial townships.[29]

However, the most compelling reason for looking at these townships is the volume and clarity of the archival collections relating to them. While none of the townships have continuous parish register sources, the Bishops' Transcripts are excellent and more than compensate for the gaps. Moreover, while these townships, like the rest of the West Riding, have considerable numbers of nonconformist places of worship, survival of the nonconformist registers is really very good.[30] More than this, though, the reconstitution evidence can be linked to poor law accounts, charity records, diaries and a variety of other material, such as the credit book of the Bramley scribbling miller Joseph Rogerson, that can throw light on the complex patchwork of the economy of makeshifts in this part of the West Riding.[31]

Kinship and the economy of makeshifts in Yorkshire

To locate the relationship between the economy of makeshifts and kinship in these communities, we must initially turn to the width and depth of local kinship networks. As one might expect of this subject, historians agree on neither the best way to measure kinship connections nor on the nature of the relationship that must exist for a person to be regarded as part of a kinship group.[32] However, Table 7.1 uses family reconstitution evidence to quantify the depth of kinship networks in the six communities for the whole period 1700–1820, employing a cut-off point at the level of first cousins to determine what does and does not constitute kinship. Clearly, whatever the socio-economic composition of the individual townships, the extent of kinship networks was considerable. The levels of interrelationship found here are twice or three times those found in Essex or Surrey, though they are also consistent with kinship densities detected by King and by Coster for other Yorkshire communities.[33]

There was a broad tendency for those communities with the greatest reliance on rural industry to have the densest kinship networks from an early date. This makes sense. As local witnesses before the 1806 enquiry into the state of the woollen industry testified, putting-out jobs were plentiful and there was still an expectation that young men in this area of the West Riding could

Table 7.1 Kinship density (%) in six West Riding towns, 1700–1820

Place	Related to 0	Related to 1	Related to 2	Related to 3+
Otley	18	22	35	25
Horsforth	19	25	26	30
Tong	24	30	26	20
Cleckheaton	27	28	29	16
Armley	23	26	20	31
Bramley	29	32	20	19

climb to achieve economic independence. James Ellis noted, 'I was not kept constantly to weaving and spinning; my master fitted me rather for a master than a journeyman.' More importantly, the woollen industry provided plenty of jobs for other members of the family, even as hand spinning came to be replaced by mechanised spinning. Ellis also noted in response to questions about the treatment of raw wool 'that we employ inferior people, women and children, to do, any person may do that'.[34] The economic imperative to move longer distances that we might see in the midlands or the rural south was thus missing and consequently kinship densities were higher. This did not mean, though, that families in these villages had few kinship links in surrounding villages. Many of those with no apparent connection in one township appear to have had connections in another not too far away, while most of those with multiple kinship links in one community also had dense links with another.

Of course, these observations provide a static picture. Table 7.2 suggests that there were important fluctuations in kinship densities over the course of the period 1700–1820. The strongest growth in the density of kinship links was in Bramley, which also had the most diversified economy of all six townships. Kinship densities remained strong in Horsforth, but they weakened notwithstanding rural industrialisation. In Armley, densities improved over the same period, but then fell back in the first two decades of the nineteenth century. These movements are intriguing. They confirm a very broad positive relationship between kinship densities and rural industrialisation while at the same time suggesting that a more diversified local economic structure could underpin spectacular growth in the extent and depth of kinship networks. They also suggest that kinship networks could be subject to not inconsiderable erosion or dilution according to local demo-economic circumstances. To take just one example, the decline in kinship density that we see in Horsforth between the late eighteenth and early nineteenth centuries is almost entirely accounted for by a two-year surge in adult and child mortality (reflecting the onset of smallpox, followed by typhus, measles, whooping cough and a fatal fire at the local fulling mill) in the late 1790s. This high mortality diluted the kinship connections of those who were related to two or more families in the locality, but it also removed the kinship connection for 29 families that had previously had a kinship link to only one further family in the locality. Within limits, then, kinship networks were physically volatile and it will be important to bear this in mind when we come to look at the welfare role of such networks. The key point though is that, by the early nineteenth century, kinship in these communities had reached virtual saturation point, testimony to a very different society from the sort that we see in Keith Wrightson's Essex or Evelyn Lord's Surrey.

Table 7.2 Kinship density over time in six West Riding towns, 1700–1820

Place	*1700–49*	*1750–99*	*1800–20*
Otley	84	82	87
Horsforth	87	82	74
Tong	58	74	78
Cleckheaton	65	72	77
Armley	72	81	74
Bramley	42	67	76

How did these figures manifest themselves on the ground? Every community had its core groups such as the Spacie family of Horsforth, who were related in some way or other to the majority of families in the township, and all communities also had a judicious helping of those who were just linked to one other family grouping or indeed none at all. But was there anything that particularly distinguished the kin-rich from the kin-poor? An initial observation is that the weakest kinship links were not always or indeed usually a reflection of the experience of recent in-migrants. Given substantial and growing levels of intra-township marriage and strenuous efforts on the part of migrant families to make marriage connections with more established groups in the host community, migrants often did rather well in achieving connectedness. Commentators such as Betts have observed similar features in other parts of the country.[35] Nor did certain occupations have a greater tendency to generate strong kinship networks than others. Proletarianised weavers often had kinship densities on a par with substantial artisan clothiers, and they in turn often exceeded the kinship densities of local farmers.

There are, however, two factors that do mark out families with the highest kinship densities from the rest in all six communities. First, the most interconnected kinship groups were disproportionately likely by the later eighteenth century to have a substantial nonconformist character. Methodist, Moravian, Independent and Baptist circuits criss-crossed the West Riding industrial district, clearly facilitating chain migration and inter-marriage within the religious grouping, pushing up kinship densities. Second, and without exception, in all six communities families with weak or non-existent kinship networks were also families that had what we might style 'high-pressure' demography, with high marital fertility, high infant death rates and relatively low marriage ages. We will return to these characteristics later. In the meantime, the general message is clear – that kinship networks could be both extensive and of considerable depth in the West Riding.

They might also be nominally functional. Table 7.3 traces bequests made in all of the surviving wills for the six townships that could be traced at the Borthwick Institute and in local archives (where copies of wills are often preserved in family collections) between 1700 and 1820. In contrast to the picture drawn by Coster, we can see that testators in the West Riding woollen district showed no tendency to concentrate bequests on immediate co-resident family. Indeed, while Table 7.3 does not make it clear, if anything the range of kinship recognised in wills actually increased after 1750. This may be a reflection of a lower tendency for children and other kin to leave communities as industrialisation kicked in (and hence they were more visible at the time of will-making) or it might reflect a conscious engagement with a range of kin. In the case of Bramley the evidence from the early nineteenth-century diary of Joseph Rogerson, linked to the reconstitution of the township, suggests the latter. Rogerson mentioned almost all of his available local kin (though he rarely specified an exact blood or marriage relationship) in the diary.[36]

Table 7.3 Bequests in West Riding wills, 1700–1820

Place	Nuclear family	Siblings	In-laws	G'children, nephews, neices	Cousins	Others
Otley	36	21	10	16	8	19
Horsforth	37	14	8	15	9	17
Tong	64	8	2	8	4	14
Cleckheaton	59	8	2	9	4	18
Armley	52	12	4	11	7	14
Bramley	57	7	4	8	3	21

Source: Family reconstitutions and 452 wills drawn from the collection of the Borthwick Institute and West Riding family collections.
Note: All figures are percentages of bequests. Only those with definite (stated or from family reconstitution) kinship links are used in the table. Some 364 of the 4,200 bequests are thus omitted.

What role was there, then, for this extensive, deep and nominally functional kinship network in providing or supplementing welfare in this part of the West Riding? An initial way into this question is provided by Table 7.4 which relates kinship density and poor law spending in the six townships over the period 1750–1820.[37] The table provides two index numbers for each community to ease comparison. The first takes the average density of kinship over all six communities for the whole period 1750–1820 as 100 and relates individual community kinship figures to this baseline to see if they are above or below average for the West Riding woollen district. The second takes average *per capita* poor law spending (to allow for different population sizes) in all six communities for the period 1750–1820 as 100 and relates per capita spending in the individual communities to this baseline to show whether they are above or below average.[38] We can see clearly that there was a broad relationship between above average kinship density and below average poor law expenditure.[39] Of course, there are many ways to read this table. A limited rate base may have constrained the supply of welfare through the poor law and thus forced families to fill the gap. Alternatively, poor law officials may have consciously restricted welfare supplies to force families to step into the breach. Or the poor law may have found itself as a fallback to kinship action, coping with extreme problems or reacting to short-term changes of circumstance which overwhelmed the coping abilities of kinship networks.

Some guidance on how we might read the situation is provided

Table 7.4 Kinship density and poor relief spending in six West Riding communities, 1750–1820

Place	Index of kinship density	Index of spending relief
Otley	110	79
Horsforth	101	96
Tong	99	108
Cleckheaton	97	116
Armley	100	99
Bramley	93	126

Note: Mean kinship density = 77 per cent, indexed at 100. Mean per capita poor relief spending was 30s., indexed at 100.

by Table 7.5, which, for the period 1750–1820, contrasts the index of kinship used above with an index of monthly pension payments (the average monthly pension payment over all six communities representing 100) and an index of the percentage of the population in receipt of relief (the proportions of the population on relief in the six communities in 1801, 1811 and 1821 representing 100). Below average poor law spending in communities with higher kinship densities clearly represents both fewer people on relief at any given time and lower mean relief payments for those who did obtain relief. Again, the meaning of this table is not unambiguous, but I think that what we see here could be kinship support limiting the role of the poor law in some communities and its absence extending the role of the poor law in others, as Laslett and others have suggested. Vestry records for Horsforth[40] provide some credence for this speculation. Between 1780 and 1802, the vestry received 474 applications for relief from those who had no kin or were linked to just one other family and they accepted over 90 per cent of these applications. By contrast they received 121 applications from those that we might style 'kin-rich' and they turned down 66 of them. Only cases which concerned individual and family illness seem to have been worthy of support. Some of this willingness to turn down applicants with kin represents religious tension between an anglican vestry and a group of 'kin-rich' people who were disproportionately nonconformist, but there *was* clearly an expectation that kin would provide welfare support in this community.

Table 7.5 Kinship density, monthly pensions and percentage of the population in receipt of poor relief, 1750–1820

Place	Index of kinship density	Index of pensions	Index of % on relief
Otley	110	81	83
Horsforth	101	93	95
Tong	99	104	100
Cleckheaton	97	110	108
Armley	100	99	98
Bramley	93	121	129

Note: Mean kinship density = 77 per cent, indexed at 100. Mean pension payment = 5s., indexed at 100. Mean percentage on relief = 5.6, indexed at 100.

Certainly, an extensive welfare role for kin makes sense when set against other evidence from this part of the West Riding. It is clear, for instance, that even in the nineteenth century, as lunatic asylums and workhouses proliferated, relatively few of the lunatic poor from the West Riding actually ended up in them. Poor law records suggest that a combination of community and family action came to the rescue of some of the lunatic poor, but, for others, family care must have been the first and only alternative.[41] An extensive welfare role for kin also makes sense when set against the wider communality and reciprocation that we can see in this area of the West Riding. Thus Mr Hainsworth reported to the 1806 committee of enquiry into the state of the woollen industry that

> Some master clothiers, when the trade has been bad, would work for other masters, and they have given on another work ... the clothiers belonging to our own place of course we employed first in order to keep down the rates ... You mean that some of the masters have worked for hire? Yes, when trade has been bad they have taken goods to make for other masters, in order to keep their families by their labour.[42]

This said, it would be wrong to imply from this aggregate analysis simply that dense kinship links reduced poor relief bills and gave the poor law a fallback role. To draw more definitive conclusions, we need to know the nature of the kinship relationships of the individuals who received relief and to understand in rather more depth the wider economy of makeshifts in which they were engaged. Nominal linkage between reconstitution data and poor law and charity accounts can provide the bedrock for this sort of deeper investigation.

What, then, was the kinship status of those who received relief? At individual level things are not as clear-cut as the aggregate analysis would imply. As we would expect on the basis of the discussion so far, many recipients of poor relief lacked kin. However, others were tied into very extensive kinship networks, as we might perhaps also expect from the work of Hollen Lees, Thane and King which stresses that the poor law sought to generate a resource partnership with kin to cope with individual level destitution. While we could draw detailed examples from all of the communities, the situation in Bramley perhaps best illustrates this latter point. Table 7.6 attempts to categorise poor relief recipients for the period 1780–1820 according to the depth of their kinship links, and we can see that three of the most well-connected people in the township appear on the relief lists. This confirms that risks of poverty were widely distributed throughout early modern communities. It might also be read as suggesting that kinship networks were unable to cope with certain sorts of need – the community-wide crises which plunged some or all of the family members into penury and which were particularly characteristic of the period 1780–1820, or perhaps even sudden crises linked to illness.

Table 7.6 Poor relief recipients and their kinship links: Bramley, 1780–1820

Kinship depth	Absolute number	% of claims
Related to 7+	3	1.0
Related to 5–7	8	2.6
Related to 3–5	21	7.0
Related to 1–3	38	12.6
Related to 1	92	30.6
Related to 0	84	46.2

Note: Total number of claims (902) includes 54 for which no definitive kinship relationship could be established in the reconstitution.

Figure 7.1 gives more clarity to these ideas. It categorises poor relief recipients according to *both* the depth of their kinship network *and* the length of time spent on relief and highlights the fact that while well-connected people did get relief (and in Bramley

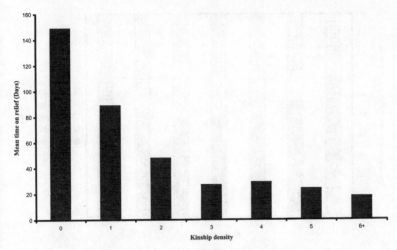

Figure 7.1 Length of time on relief and kinship depth

and the other townships well-connected people also record the top ten biggest individual or family payments of poor relief) the least well-connected people in the township stayed on relief longest. This is consistent with the situation identified by King in the nearby parish of Calverley, and with the case studies used by Fissell around Bristol.[43] It seems, then, that being well connected could prompt overseers and vestries to allocate substantial short-term payments to meet sudden need, but made it less likely that individuals would need (or the poor law would support) a longer-term relationship with the welfare system. Those with less kin or no kin found themselves in a longer-term relationship with the communal welfare system, both because of their lack of kinship and because of their high pressure demography. The poor law in Bramley was not resource starved, but might be said to adopt a conscious policy of working with kin to optimise kinship support of the needy. This is precisely what Thane and other commentators have suggested.

Meanwhile, still concentrating on Bramley, we can also see a difference in the type of relief given to those with strong kinship links compared to those with weak ones. Figure 7.2 demonstrates a clear tendency in Bramley (followed more or less clearly in all of the other townships analysed here) for late eighteenth-century sickness relief or 'investment' payments to be the focus for those

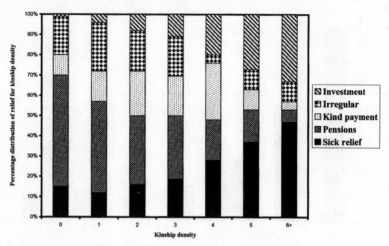

Figure 7.2 Payment type and kinship links in Bramley

with rich kinship networks, while pensions and irregular cash payments were the primary focus for those without. There are several potential readings of this evidence, but it seems clear to me that the immediate onset of sickness (often manifested at family rather than individual level) disproportionately under-pinned the application of the 'kin-rich' for poor relief and that poor law authorities were willing to provide such relief (as they did in Horsforth) until kinship and religious care networks could mobilise people and resources to cope with the situation.

Yet we should beware of lumping people together into the simple categories 'kin-rich' and 'kin-poor', as Table 7.7 begins to suggest. Using a system of index numbers, this table measures the degree to which families with certain kinship characteristics were over- or under-represented amongst those on poor relief. It takes the kinship systems in force in all six communities in 1811 (chosen because we have supplementary listings to the census data for four communities in this year[44]) and allocates families to one of several typologies.[45] The classification exercise is re-peated for families on poor relief in 1811 and by indexing the numbers in each typology amongst poor families against the 'expected' numbers in each typology based upon mean presence in the wider community, we can see whether certain types of kinship situation were over-represented (and hence have numbers above 100), under-represented (and hence have numbers below

100) or exactly represented (and hence have 100 as an entry) amongst those who received poor relief. What we see is the expected over-representation of those without kin in the poor law accounts. However, there was also a very strong tendency for individuals and families without living male relatives on the father's side to appear in the relief system, whatever the exact nature of the residual kinship network. Paradoxically, though, the most important male relatives in predictive terms were not fathers, but uncles or brothers. Those without these kinship links were disproportionately likely (compared to their wider presence in the six townships) to appear on poor relief, and to stay there for some time. Of course, Table 7.7 does not prove unequivocally that uncles and brothers were disproportionately likely to offer material support to pauperised relatives, but diary evidence of functional kinship links between poor relatives and these two groups in other regions is substantial.[46]

Table 7.7 The over- and under-representation of kinship typologies amongst those on relief in six West Riding communities, 1811

Typology	*Presence index*
Without any local kin	174
With kin of all kinds	55
Without father	103
With/without father and without immediate male kin on father's side	139
Without mother	90
Without kin on mother's side	100
With female kin only	84
With distant kin only	110

We return to this question of kinship functionality amongst those who received poor relief shortly, but a chapter attempting to locate the importance of kinship in the economy of makeshifts must also be concerned with those who did not get poor relief as well as those who did. This group comprises two sub-groups: those who applied for poor relief but were refused (whether or not they subsequently managed to get the local poor law officials to agree with them) and those who never applied for poor relief. The groups were by no means distinct when we consider life-cycles as a whole, but for the moment this categorisation is a convenient fiction. In common with almost all studies, data on the first category (such as vestry records or pauper letters) are not common, while data on the second category of person are positively scarce.

Let us concentrate first on those who were turned down for relief and the state of their kinship relations. While partial vestry records survive only for Horsforth, Tong and Otley[47] and for the period 1783–1811, a brief analysis of the decisions taken by these vestries is instructive. By the later eighteenth century around 15–20 per cent of those who applied to the poor law were denied relief in the three townships, with a strong tendency to employ moral criteria in making decisions on relief applicants. There is not the space here to deal with the sentiments employed by the vestries, but because we have reconstitution evidence available what we can do is to say something about the kinship relationships of those denied relief. The complex tabular results of this linkage exercise can be found elsewhere;[48] two particular observations might be made, however. First, and perhaps not surprisingly given the conclusions drawn above, those with good kinship connections on the male side were disproportionately likely to be turned down for relief. Second, individuals and families whose kinship connections were dense through marriage rather than blood were also disproportionately likely to be turned down. There are many potential interpretations of this experience, but one might be that poor law authorities were less likely to enter into resource partnerships with diluted than with tight kinship networks. In particular, it might be the case that poor law authorities liked to deal with an unchallenged authority figure, a character frequently missing from kinship networks extended through marriage. More work in this sort of vein needs to be done before we can draw any more definitive conclusions.

Meanwhile, discerning the kinship relations of those who were poor but did not apply for poor relief is a thorny problem. Tom Arkell suggests that for any community it is possible to assemble a range of measures of need in addition to the normal poor law accounts.[49] One of his measures is those who pay no rates but who also do not (at the same point in time) receive poor relief. Unfortunately, contiguous rate and poor relief data exist for only three of the six townships (Horsforth, Tong and Bramley[50]) and for the period 1760–83. A brief consideration of this data reveals that almost 20 per cent of all people in the three townships paid no rates but received no poor relief, testimony to the existence of a considerable poor underclass.[51] Table 7.8 makes more use of the data, and we might draw two key lessons from it. First, that those on the margins of poverty were moderately connected to wider kinship networks. Second, that it was not at all unusual for a substantial ratepayer to have relatives in the poor underclass in the same township and at the same point in time. In one sense there is nothing particularly surprising about the latter observation in particular. If non-ratepayers were just solvent enough to escape the clutches of the poor relief system then relatives, even richer relatives, may have been unwilling to make transfer payments (other than perhaps to forgive debts already contracted) or may not have been called upon. Yet we could turn this idea on its head and suggest that transfers of resources or people between richer and poorer households within a defined kinship group was what kept non-ratepayers from the clutches of the welfare system in the first place. Such was the case for Nathaniel Hargreaves, who petitioned the Horsforth vestry for relief in 1789, noting that his uncle had paid his rent for the last two years 'but his long illness now means that he has much need of his purse at present'.[52]

Table 7.8 Kinship characteristics of non-ratepayers and non-relief recipients in six West Riding townships, 1760–83

Kinship depth	Absolute number	% of non-ratepayers
Related to 7+	32	5.9
Related to 5–7	54	9.9
Related to 3–5	104	19.4
Related to 1–3	192	35.4
Related to 1	86	15.8
Related to 0	74	13.6

Another way into the question of the kinship relationships of those who did not get poor relief, and also a way into the question of the value of kinship links in material terms, is to look at the overlap between those who received poor relief and those who received formal charity, and to contrast the kinship depth of those who received poor relief, those who received charity and those who received both. In this exercise, we are lucky that all of the six townships under the microscope here are blessed with good survival of charity material.[53] Table 7.9 attempts this sort of linkage exercise for the six townships in aggregate.[54] We might draw three important conclusions from this table.

Table 7.9 Kinship connections of charity and poor law recipients in six West Riding communities, 1780–1810

Receiving	Related to 0	Related to 1–3	Related to 3–5	Related to 5+
Poor relief only	1223	532	375	131
Charity only	156	242	394	189
Poor relief and charity	78	43	31	19

First, that the overlap between those who received relief and those who received charity at the same point in time was in most townships and at most times limited. Even in late eighteenth-century Tong, the township with by far the most overlap, only 45 per cent of those who received poor relief also received charity at the same point in time. Second, the trustees of local charities were disproportionately likely to recognise the poverty and need of people with good kinship connections, and to do so over long periods. This is perhaps not surprising given the terms under which many benefactions were made, and the wider need to show respectability in order to receive charity, something which could be done by pointing to dense kinship connections. In other words, we must be interested in kinship not just for the material and emotional benefits that it might offer, but because kinship provided a gateway to other welfare avenues, something that has been insufficiently stressed in the historiography thus far. Finally, it is clear that the attitude of charity trustees towards those with and without kin was fluid. While I do not have the space to show it here, there is more than a hint from the record linkage exercise that as the nineteenth century progressed the role of charity began to change as the balance between the relative levels of charity and poor law expenditure moved decisively towards the latter. Certainly by the 1830s, increasing numbers of those with little or no local kinship came to rely on charity. This may reflect a change in migratory patterns, the changing dynamics of local policy or a change in the nature of poor relief and need in the run up to the new poor law, but only more research will enable us to say which. What is clear is that kinship interacted in complex ways with the changing constellation of the economy of makeshifts over time.

Looked at collectively, these tables and figures generate ambiguous and complex results. The common thread, though, is the idea that not having kin (or not having particular sorts of kin) is an important predictor of long-term relationship with the poor law. While the high pressure demography of the 'kin-poor' may have contributed to this relationship, it was not the main driver. By contrast, having rich kinship relationships could not always keep individuals and families out of the relief system in the short term, but kin could be a very important component (presumably along with religious self-help) in the long-term welfare patchwork.

The problem with these conclusions is that they *infer* a strong role for kinship in the economy of makeshifts rather than showing it (or quantifying it) directly. Of course, in the absence of the contractual, legal and other data available to continental family historians even an indirect commentary of this sort is valuable and novel. This chapter has added weight to the contentions of Pat Thane, Lynne Hollen Lees[55] and others that kinship *must* have been an important part of the welfare safety net for early modern families. It has also reinforced ideas from Fissell and King that the poor law was disproportionately a welfare system for the 'kin-poor'. But can we say more? What was the level and form of help offered by families to their needy kin? What activated kinship support, and what served to end it? Was kinship support particularly likely at certain times of life-cycle need and less at others? And who organised the transfer of material, human or emotional resources between households within a kinship network? Oral historians have begun to ask questions such as these for the twentieth century, but the early modern period offers us fewer avenues for exploration. Let us deal briefly with two.

First, the help offered to kin by Jonathan Snowden, an Armley clothier. As well as employing outworkers in several Leeds out-townships, Snowden held land in Armley, Guiseley and Calverley. In other words, he was a wealthy man and thus perhaps not as representative as one might like. This said, Snowden's surviving pocket account books[56] (1770 to 1796, with a break between 1780 and 1783) reveal that he was very well endowed with needy relatives. Between 1775 (when he started recording all of his expenditure rather than just business expenses) and 1796, Snowden appears to have made 122 gifts or loans to relatives in Armley or elsewhere. On average he disbursed twenty-six pounds per year to relatives and while it is not always easy to discern the residence of those relatives, most can be traced back to Armley. By relating disbursements to the life-cycles revealed in family reconstitution, we can see that Snowden made three types of payments – small 'one-off' payments before or just after the marriages of his nephews, nieces and grandchildren; periodic small payments to relatives who were overburdened with children; and more regular payments to relatives who can be identified as recipients of charity or poor relief. In other words, Snowden was disbursing resources in exactly the way that the aggregate analysis of the relationship between kinship, poor relief and charity would suggest. Interestingly, he also finances the transfer of human resources, paying for the apprenticeship of one of his nephews and buying clothes for a niece to become a servant in the household of her aunt. Snowden was clearly aware of the life-cycle stages that could throw otherwise independent people into poverty, and he appears to have acted *before* the onset of the constellation of influences that would trigger the slide into destitution. We thus have at least some answers to my rhetorical questions.

A second avenue of investigation confirms much of what we can learn from Snowden. Pauper letters written back to the vestries of Horsforth and Otley from townships throughout the West Riding are replete with the language of kinship support or lack of it.[57] Thomas Day, for instance, wrote to the Horsforth Vestry in 1787 from Batley. He requested payment of his rent and a small regular pension, citing an inability to get work after a finger injury. However, he added that 'My family and mee has no kin in this place and wee cannot get one penny of credit'. The two were probably linked in practice as well as linguistically, highlighting the indirect importance of kinship in the economy of makeshifts. Robert Spacey, overseer of Bramley, wrote to the Horsforth vestry in 1790 on the subject of William Hornby who 'is in a wretched state, havinge no worke and beeing almoste blynde he has been cared for by his sister Charlotte Eastwood these years since and his board paid by Jas Hornby, but now his condicion cannot be borne no longer'. The withdrawal or overwhelming of kinship welfare support thus carried serious consequences. Other paupers looked forward to richer kinship networks and the support that they might offer. Edward Parker wrote back to Horsforth from Pudsey in 1793 asking for relief and telling the vestry that his son, John, would soon be setting up business in Pudsey and would pay back the money granted by the vestry as well as offering long-term support. In short, there was in practice, in expectation and in rhetoric, a considerable role for kinship support in the economy of makeshifts and in addition to the poor law.

Conclusion

To the very specific question of the value of kinship in the wider economy of makeshifts, we can perhaps draw three fairly concrete answers. First, it seems likely that kin provided direct material support, particularly in the medium and long term, allowing people to keep away from the poor relief system or to supplement income from the community. Second, it seems likely that having or not having dense kinship networks determined access to other elements of the economy of makeshifts such as, in this particular analysis, charity. Finally, while it is clear that different individuals and families would have relied on kinship support with different intensities at different stages of the life-cycle or in response to different causes of poverty, those with access to particular constellations of kin, notably male blood relatives, may have been particularly likely to turn to kin as a first rather than a last resort. We should beware of assuming, however, that an economy of makeshifts, even if it included poor relief and material support from kin, generated a consistently sufficient income for poor people. As Rose points out for nineteenth-century Nottinghamshire, 'the elderly pieced together a very meagre subsistence'[58] and others in this volume have made similar points.

Notes

1 On household size and structure see P. Laslett, 'Size and structure of the household in England over three centuries', *Population Studies*, 23 (1969) and *idem*, 'Mean household size in England since the sixteenth century', in P. Laslett and R. Wall (eds), *Household and Family in Past Times* (Cambridge, Cambridge University Press, 1972). On the issue of demographic constraint, see P. Laslett, 'Family, kinship and collectivity as systems of support in pre-industrial Europe: a consideration of the nuclear hardship hypothesis', *Continuity and Change*, 3 (1988). For regional differences, see R. Wall, 'Regional and temporal variations in English household structure from 1650', in J. Hobcraft and P. Rees (eds), *Regional Demographic Development* (London, Croom Helm, 1978).

2 See J. E. Smith and J. Oeppen, 'Estimating numbers of kin in historical England using demographic microsimulation', in D. S. Reher and R. S. Schofield (eds), *Old and New Methods in Historical Demography* (Oxford, Clarendon, 1993). From a different angle, see M. Anderson, 'The emergence of the modern life-cycle in Britain', *Social History*, 10 (1985). See also P. Laslett, *A Fresh Map of Life* (Cambridge, Cambridge University Press, 1989), who suggests that at least one-third of women reaching age 65 would have had no surviving children. For a sceptical view of the value of microsimulation, see S. Ruggles, 'Family demography and family history: problems and prospects', *Historical Methods Newsletter*, 23 (1990).

3 L. Stone, *Family, Sex and Marriage in England, 1500–1800* (London, Weidenfeld and Nicholson, 1977).

4 A. Gilbert, *Religion and Society in Industrial England: Church, Chapel and Social Change, 1740–1914* (London, Methuen, 1976). Also K. Honeyman, *Origins of Enterprise* (Manchester, Manchester University Press, 1982) and R. Grassby, *Kinship and Capitalism: Marriage, Family and Business in the English-Speaking World, 1580–1740* (Cambridge, Cambridge University Press, 2001).

5 D. Cooper and M. Donald, 'Households and hidden kin in early nineteenth century England: four case studies in suburban Exeter', *Continuity and Change*, 10 (1995). For other literature on the problems of terminology in kinship analysis, see N. Tadmor, 'The concept of the household-family in eighteenth century England', *Past and Present*, 151 (1996) and M. Chaytor, 'Household and kinship: Ryton in the late 16th and early 17th centuries', *History Workshop Journal*, 13 (1982); also O. Harris, 'Households and their boundaries', *History Workshop Journal*, 13 (1982).

6 B. Reay, 'Kinship and the neighbourhood in nineteenth century rural England: the myth of the autonomous nuclear family', *Journal of Family History*, 21 (1996) and *idem*, *Microhistories: Demography, Society and Culture in Rural England, 1800–1930* (Cambridge, Cambridge University Press, 1996).

7 K. Wrightson, 'Kinship in an English village: Terling, Essex, 1500–1700', in R. M. Smith (ed.), *Land, Kinship and Life-Cycle* (Cambridge, Cambridge University Press, 1985).

8 E. Lord, 'Communities of common interest: the social landscape of south-east Surrey 1750–1850', in C. Phythian-Adams (ed.), *Societies, Cultures and Kinship, 1580–1850* (London, Leicester University Press, 1993). See also R. Wall, 'Elderly persons and members of their households in England and wales from pre-industrial times to the present', in D. Kertzer and P. Laslett (eds), *Aging in the Past: Demography, Society and Old Age* (Los Angeles, University of California Press, 1995); T. Sokoll, *Household and Family Among the Poor: The Case of Two Essex Communities in the Late Eighteenth and Early Nineteenth Centuries* (Bochum, Verlaag fur Regionalgeschichte, 1993); *idem*, 'The

household position of elderly widows in poverty: evidence from two English communities in the late eighteenth and early nineteenth centuries', in J. Henderson and R. Wall (eds), *Poor Women and Children in the European Past* (London, Routledge, 1994), pp. 207–24, and *idem*, 'Old age in poverty: the record of Essex pauper letters 1780–1834', in T. Hitchcock, P. King and P. Sharpe (eds), *Chronicling Poverty: The Voices and Strategies of the English Poor* (Basingstoke, Macmillan, 1997).

9 In part of course historiographical division on this issue reflects the fact that the welfare role of kinship has been tied up with wider theoretical and practical discussion of the general strength of early modern families. For a discussion of the positive and negative ends of the spectrum of opinion on this issue, see S. King and J. Timmins, *Making Sense of the Industrial Revolution* (Manchester, Manchester University Press, 2001).

10 S. A. King, *Poverty and Welfare in England, 1700–1850: A Regional Perspective* (Manchester, Manchester University Press, 2000).

11 See C. Pooley and S. D'Cruz, 'Migration and urbanization in north west England c. 1760–1830', *Social History*, 19 (1994); C. Pooley and J. Turnbull, *Migration and Mobility in Britain Since the 18th Century* (London, UCL Press, 1998); D. Cressey, 'Kinship and kin interaction in early modern England', *Past and Present*, 113 (1986).

12 M. Fissell, 'The sick and drooping poor in eighteenth century Bristol and its region', *Social History of Medicine*, 2 (1989) and S. A. King, 'Reconstructing lives: the poor, the Poor Law and welfare in Calverley, 1650–1820', *Social History*, 22 (1997).

13 Laslett, *A Fresh Map of Life*. See also M. Gorsky, 'The growth and distribution of English friendly societies in the early nineteenth century', *Economic History Review*, LI (1998).

14 L. Botelho, 'Aged and impotent: parish relief of the aged poor in early modern Suffolk', in M. Daunton (ed.), *Charity, Self-Interest and Welfare in the English Past* (London, UCL Press, 1996) and P. Thane, 'Old people and their families in the English past', in *ibid*, pp. 113–38. Also *idem*, *Old Age in the English Past* (Oxford, Oxford University Press, 2000). On retirement arrangements elsewhere, see T. Held, 'Rural retirement arrangements in seventeenth to nineteenth century Austria: a cross community analysis', *Journal of Family History*, 7 (1982).

15 L. Hollen Lees, 'The survival of the unit: welfare policies and family maintenance in nineteenth century London', in P. Mandler (ed.), *The Uses of Charity: The Poor on Relief in the Nineteenth Century Metropolis* (Cambridge, Cambridge University Press, 1990) and *idem*, *The Solidarities of Strangers: The English Poor Laws and the People, 1700–1948* (Cambridge, Cambridge University Press, 1998). Also S. A. King, 'The English proto-industrial family: old and new perspectives', *History of the Family*, 6 (2003).

16 S. Cavallo, 'Family obligations and inequalities in access to care in northern Italy, seventeenth to eighteenth centuries', in P. Horden and R. Smith (eds), *The Locus of Care: Families, Communities, Institutions and the Provision of Welfare Since Antiquity* (London, Routledge, 1998).

17 For different representations of these views, see D. Thomson, 'The decline of social security: falling state support for the elderly since early Victorian times', *Ageing and Society*, 4 (1984), *idem*, 'Welfare and the historians', in L. Bonfield, R. M. Smith and K. Wrightson (eds), *The World we Have Gained* (Oxford, Clarendon, 1986), *idem*, 'The elderly in an urban-industrial society: England 1750 to the present', in J. M. Eekelaar and D. Pearl (eds), *An Ageing World: Dilemmas and Challenges for Law and Social Policy* (Oxford, Clarendon, 1989) and *idem*, 'The welfare of the elderly in the past: a family or community responsibility', in Pelling and Smith, *Life, Death and the Elderly*.

18 M. A. Crowther, 'Family responsibility and state responsibility in Britain before the welfare state', *Historical Journal*, 25 (1982).

19 M. J. McIntosh, 'Networks of care in Elizabethan English towns: the example of Hadleigh, Suffolk', in Horden and Smith, *Locus*. See also T. Wales, 'Poverty, poor relief and life-cycle: some evidence from seventeenth century Norfolk', in Smith, *Land*, and W. Newman-Brown, 'The receipt of poor relief and family situation: Aldenham, Herts, 1630–90', in *ibid*.

20 M. Anderson, 'Some problems in the use of census-type material for the study of family and kinship patterns', in J. Sundin and E. Soderlund (eds), *Time, Space and Man: Essays on Microdemography* (Umea, Umea University Press, 1977) argues that we should not even try to construct such typologies, but should instead focus on variations in kinship patterns within communities.

21 See the contributions to S. Woolf (ed.), *Domestic Strategies: Work and Family in France and Italy, 1600–1800* (Cambridge, Cambridge University Press, 1991) and A. Janssens, *Family and Social Change: The Household as a Process in an Industrialising Community* (Cambridge, Cambridge University Press, 1993).

22 A. G. Darroch, 'Migrants in the nineteenth century: fugitives or families in motion', *Journal of Family History*, 6 (1981).

23 The Birstall reconstitutions are available from the Cambridge Group for the History of Population and Social Structure or in the library of the Yorkshire Archaeological Society in Leeds: see E. A. Wrigley, R. S. Davies, J. E. Oeppen and R. S. Schofield, *English Population History From Family Reconstitution 1580–1837* (Cambridge, Cambridge University Press, 1997).

24 These figures are drawn from Edward Parsons, *History of Leeds and adjoining towns* (Leeds, 1848) and, because they cover only the town and not adjoining hamlets, differ from figures given by other historians.

25 S. Barrett, 'Die protoindustrielle Entwicklung und Verwandschaft in Acht Gemeinden Yorkshires (1650 bis 1837)' (unpublished PhD, University of Marburg, 1998).

26 See S. Ruggles, 'Migration, marriage and mortality: correcting sources of bias in English family reconstitution', *Population Studies*, 46 (1992).

27 See P. Hudson, *The Genesis of Industrial Capital: A Study of the West Riding Wool Textile Industry* (Cambridge, Cambridge University Press, 1986); M. Yasumoto, *Industrialisation, Urbanisation and Demographic Change in England* (Nagoya, Nagoya University Press, 1994); D. Gregory, *Regional Transformation and Industrial Revolution: A Geography of the Yorkshire Woollen Industry* (London, Macmillan, 1982).

28 *Report From the Committee of the Woollen Manufacture of England With Minutes of Evidence and Appendix, 1806 (268) III* (Shannon, 1968).

29 It is also important to note that each of these villages was relatively isolated – no new roads to Leeds were built before 1820 and the existing roads were notoriously narrow and winding – and that while they were junior parts of larger parishes they nonetheless remained self-governing with their own clergy, overseers and churchwardens.

30 A comprehensive list of contemporary chapels is provided by E. Parsons, *The Civil, Ecclesiastical, Literary, Commercial and Miscellaneous History of Leeds, Bradford, Wakefield, Dewsbury, Otley and the District Within Ten Miles of Leeds* (Leeds, F. Hobson, 1834). Bramley and Cleckheaton were particular hotbeds of Methodism and Congregationalism respectively. Full details of the parish register and Bishops Transcript locations, the treatment of gaps and other problems with the registers, and the linkage process employed in family reconstitution can be found in Barrett, 'Die protoindustrielle', appendix 1.

31 See E. Hargrave and W. B. Crump, *The Diary of Joseph Rogerson, Scribbling Miller of Bramley, 1808–1814* (Leeds, Thoresby Society, 1936). Comprehensive demographic and kinship analysis can be found in Barrett, 'Die protoindustrielle'.

32 There is not the space here to report in detail the competing methods. Broadly however, the choices are between a cohort model of the sort employed in P. R. Uhlenberg, 'A study of cohort life-cycles: cohorts of native born Massachusetts women, 1830–1920', *Population Studies*, 23 (1969), double-counting models of the sort employed in Wrightson, 'Kinship in an English village', the iterative model reported by A. Bideau and G. Brunet, 'The construction of individual life histories: application to the study of geographical mobility in the Valserine Valley (French Jura) in the nineteenth and twentieth centuries', in Rehr and Schofield, *Old and New*, or simply measures of absolute and relative kinship density. For the purposes of this chapter I use the iterative model of Bideau and Brunet. I am taking no account here of the as yet inadequately specified but potentially very important kinship models advanced by Tadmor.

33 King, 'Reconstructing'; W. Coster, *Kinship and Inheritance in Early Modern England: Three Yorkshire Parishes* (York, Borthwick Institute, 1993).

34 *Report From the Committee*, p. 16.

35 P. F. J. Betts, 'Marriage alliances, household composition and the role of kinship in nineteenth-century farming', *Local Population Studies*, 66 (2001).

36 Hargrave and Crump, *The Diary*.

37 Only after 1750 does poor law data for all six townships become sufficiently reliable to undertake the comparisons which follow.

38 These figures are calculated from: West Yorkshire Archive Service (hereafter WYAS) Leeds, 'Horsforth Churchwarden Accounts 1700–58'; 'Horsforth Parish Accounts, 1730–1820'; 'Overseer Accounts of Armley, 1750–1818'; 'Parish Accounts of Birstall 1740–1830'; ' Otley Churchwardens Account' and Yorkshire Archaeological Society (hereafter YAS) 'Overseer accounts of Bramley'.

39 Communities with lowest levels of relief expenditure were also those with the most intra-community marriages. It could thus be argued that, like friendly societies, the institution of considerable local inter-marriage was a reflection of weak regional poor law systems and was itself a coping system.

40 YAS, 'Vestry minutes for Horsforth township'.

41 For early work on admissions to asylums, see J. K. Walton, 'Lunacy in the Industrial Revolution: a study of asylum admissions in Lancashire, 1845–50', *Journal of Social History*, 13 (1979). For more recent work, see R. Adair, J. Melling and B. Forsythe, 'Migration, family structure and pauper lunacy in Victorian England: admissions to the Devon county pauper lunatic asylum 1845–1900', *Continuity and Change*, 12 (1997). D. Wright, 'Familial care of idiot children in Victorian England', in Horden and Smith, *Locus*, adopts a more sceptical view of the role of the family in the nineteenth century. A. Suzuki, 'The household and the care of lunatics in eighteenth century London', in Horden and Smith, *Locus*, echoes these concerns suggesting that lunatic children were often forced out of the household and into dependence upon the community at life-cycle pressure points such as old age of parents or the birth of new children in younger families.

42 *Report From the Committee*, p. 8.

43 King, 'Reconstructing'; Fissell, 'The sick'.

44 Detailed in Barrett, 'Die protoindustrielle', 376–89.

45 Of course, families which showed multiple characteristics had to be allocated according the best guess yardsticks, but the vast majority of families slotted more or less easily into my categories.

46 See for instance the help afforded to his brother and his nephews and nieces by the Lancaster merchant William Stout: J. D. Marshall, *The Autobiography of William Stout of Lancaster, 1665–1752* (Manchester,

Manchester University Press, 1969). The Coventry ribbon weaver Joseph Gutteridge also notes a cash injection by his brother 'from his own limited store' to the Gutteridge household at a time of economic crisis: see V. Chancellor (ed.), *Master and Artisan in Victorian England: The Diary of William Andrews and the Autobiography of Joseph Gutteridge* (London, Mckay, 1969).

47 WYAS Leeds: 'Horsforth township minutes, 1779–1821'; 'Minutes of the 24 men of Tong, 1783–1811'; 'Otley vestry minutes 1750–1832'.

48 Barratt, 'Die protoindustrielle', pp. 274–99.

49 T. Arkell, 'The incidence of poverty in England in the later seventeenth century', *Social History*, 12 (1987).

50 WYAS Leeds: 'Horsforth parish book'; 'Tong rate assessments 1672–1837'; YAS 'Bramley rate lists, 1666–1857'.

51 Of course, most of these people would subsequently go on to claim relief, or had done so in the past, but this is not the point at issue here.

52 YAS D/1/23/3, 'Pauper letters'.

53 WYAS Leeds: 'Popplewell Charity Accounts'; 'Hainsworth Charity'; 'Returns of the Hainsworth Charity', 'Horsforth Township Book'; 'Sir Walter Calverley Charity Accounts'; 'Cleckheaton Township Records'; 'Shuttleworth Charity'; 'Hargeaves Charity Accounts'.

54 We should beware of concentrating too much on exact figures as opposed to order of magnitude. Cross-source and cross-period record linkage of this sort is notoriously difficult, and up to one-fifth of the links on which the figures are based might be termed 'best guess'. Since linkage errors are likely to be randomly distributed, concentrating on orders of magnitude should blunt the force of this problem.

55 Thane, 'Old age'; Hollen Lees, *Solidarities*.

56 I am grateful to Ruth Snowden for the use of this book from her family collection and for bringing it to my attention when I talked in Leeds.

57 YAS D/1/23/3, 'Pauper letters'.

58 Rose, 'Widowhood', p. 287.

8
Making the most of opportunity: the economy of makeshifts in the early modern north[1]

Steven King

Overview

The introduction to this volume suggested that the old poor law has been subject to a positive historiographical makeover by some welfare historians. To commentators such as David Thomson and Martin Daunton, the old poor law was a flexible, increasingly humane (by design or simple loss of control) and frequently generous *system* which came to represent the *central plank* of the welfare strategies of many people by the opening decades of the nineteenth century.[2] There is persuasive empirical support for this point of view, with various authors mining bland poor law account books to show that over the course of the long eighteenth century the poor law came to relieve more people (sometimes at more generous levels), to recognise *relative poverty*, to pay for a greater range of goods and services and to relieve people for longer, than had been the case before.[3] In pioneering work linking family reconstitution evidence and poor law accounts, Richard Smith has clearly shown the development of more expensive pension strategies, the changing composition of relief lists and a widening of the services provided by the poor law from the late eighteenth century.[4] Peter King has used pauper inventories from Essex to show that poor law authorities there were willing to recognise relative as well as absolute destitution, and to intervene to preserve the household possessions of those who faced sudden need.[5] And Steve Hindle has analysed the vestry minutes, charity accounts and poor law book of Frampton in Lincolnshire to show that, at least for its *settled* poor, the community could demonstrate considerable paternalism to those in need.[6]

Of course, there were stark variations in local practice. This was to be expected given that the 1601 codification act which implemented the old poor law had established for all parishes a duty to relieve the deserving poor but had allowed local administrators to decide both who was deserving and who not, and on the form and generosity of relief. Rate-saving was thus always a temptation, and in most places we see periodic attempts to cut back the scale and cost of the relief list, something which becomes more generalised after 1820. Ultimately, however, the *system* appears to have coped moderately well with the three types of poverty which dominated the 'national' picture – endemic, trade-related and life-cycle.[7] Indeed, for many access to poor relief had become a 'right' by the later eighteenth century, and overseers had to tread a sensitive path between the competing demands of economy and customary treatment of different groups of poor people. Little surprise, against this backdrop, that we can find evidence up and down the country of poor law administrators setting out in advance a 'tally' of relief payments which would apply to different classes of paupers over the forthcoming year.[8]

The 'problem' that the poor law was obliged to confront was severe even in the late seventeenth century. Keith Wrightson's perceptive analysis of economic life starts from Gregory King's observation that 62 per cent of families (containing 51 per cent of the population) were decreasing the wealth of the kingdom in 1695 and suggests that such levels of poverty must be understood against the backdrop of slim profit margins in agriculture for most farmers, seasonal working patterns which depressed annualised income, frequent payment of wages in forms other than cash, and demographic uncertainty.[9] Such influences on the economic lives of some 70 per cent of the population were to remain in force after 1750 and were augmented by trade-cycle fluctuations, structural unemployment, the vagaries of an increasingly urbanised labour market and increasing levels of sickness amongst the population even as life-expectancy improved. By the early nineteenth century inherited poverty was common and whole life-cycle poverty was the lot of an increasing proportion of the population even in better times.[10]

But how much of the poverty problem did the old poor law really confront and alleviate? For communities in the mainly rural south and east, the positive makeover of the old poor law seems apposite. While the Bedfordshire parishes analysed by David Thomson may have been unrepresentative in their generosity, providing up to 80 per cent of local wages rates to some welfare recipients, even critics such as Hunt do not question Thomson's central theme, that the poor law and yearly welfare had become synonymous for poor people in many southern and eastern communities.[11] Faced with the breakdown of the family economy, southern de-industrialisation, the loss of alternative earning opportunities from common land and fields, pressed by population increase in some places and population stagnation elsewhere, and forced to confront big changes in the economic position of women and children, the poor law in the rural south and east in particular may have had little option but to intervene in a major way to guarantee welfare and social stability. Even here, though, we have recently been urged to take a more holistic view of the welfare process.[12]

This call is even more relevant for other areas of the country. When the numbers of poor and the amount spent on them by the poor law started to be systematically recorded from the early nineteenth century there were very wide regional differences. It was Lancashire and surrounding counties that had the lowest levels of per capita poor relief spending. The picture is not uniform – Richard Smith shows, for instance, that the Lancashire township of Woodplumpton was incredibly generous to its poor[13] – but on balance the argument that Lancashire, the West Riding and Cumberland and Westmorland relieved fewer people and at lower levels of relief than, say, Surrey or Essex, is compelling. So how might we explain these sorts of regional difference, and indeed sub-regional variation in the role and scope of the poor law? Variation may reflect differences in the scope or character of the underlying poverty problem between different counties and communities. Or it may reflect the fact that some places had much tougher poor law criteria for relief than others. Certainly Midwinter, talking of early nineteenth-century Lancashire, believed that the poor were actually better off under the new poor law than the old because of the 'chilly appraisal of misfortune' which had underlain administration of the old poor law in this county.[14] Or regional and sub-regional differences in the scale and scope of poor law expenditure might reflect the fact that some places were substantially under-resourced compared to the money available for poor law administrators elsewhere. The cost of basic foodstuffs, clothing and rent may also have been somewhat lower in some regions than in others, necessitating a less central role for poor relief in the everyday needs of poor people. Yet an alternative explanation might be the strength and variety of alternative welfare networks in some counties, and some communities in those counties, than in others.

Deciding between these different explanations involves conducting more regional studies, and then comparing them. This chapter aims to make a contribution to this process. For the rural and rural industrial north-west in the period 1750–1834, and using both aggregative analysis and a detailed community study, it will address four themes. First, what alternative welfare strategies were available to families and communities in a low poor law expenditure regime? Second, how did exploration of those strategies change over time? Third, how did these strategies interact with the poor law, taking the holistic view that John Broad appeals for? Finally what sort of living could welfare strategies yield in totem? Answering these questions should allow us to begin writing regional histories of the economy of makeshifts, much as we have written regional histories of the poor law, and allow us to begin the complex task of reconstructing welfare as it might have looked to contemporaries rather than welfare as it looks to the historian. Initially, though, we must be precise about the role of the poor law in welfare in the north-west.

The character of the poor law in the north-west

That aggregate poor relief bills rose across the north-west in common with other areas of the country is not to be doubted. But in many communities this reflected more an increase in the number getting relief than a sustained increase in generosity.[15] Figure 8.1 aggregates individual monthly *pension* payments during the period 1806–9 for seven randomly chosen north-western townships.[16] The bulk of pension payments were very low indeed, and crude estimation of wage rates suggests that regular relief amounted to no more than between one-seventh and one-fifth of the adult wage in the areas concerned. Of course, there was a willingness on the part of some poor law administrators to provide 'extra' payments in cash or kind for things like fuel, clothing or for sickness, hence adding to overall income from the communal

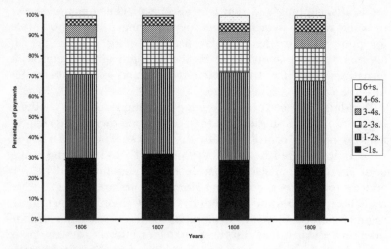

Figure 8.1 Monthly pension payments in seven north-west townships

pot, but even the most generous system in this sample did not do much to supplement pensions *consistently* in this way. Other communities were more generous, but even in generous places such as Woodplumpton in Lancashire or Troutbeck in Westmorland we can detect periodic and sometimes more sustained drives to cut the extent of relief lists and the payments of those who could not be thrown off altogether. Steve Hindle found that in Frampton the vestry policed communal and poor law resources in order to identify and get rid of 'foreigners' but even in relatively generous north-western communities, vestries and overseers stringently policed those entitled to poor relief rather than just those who were not. This sort of experience is by no means unique to the north-west, but its prevalence suggests no central role in welfare for the poor law, as Margaret Hanly has suggested elsewhere in this volume. Clearly, many of those in receipt of regular relief in the north-west must have been obtaining substantial welfare supplements from elsewhere, even if we accept that poor law payments were meant mainly for individuals rather than families.

We should also remember that not only were relief levels relatively low, but many people were turned down for relief and do not therefore figure in surviving poor law accounts. We can begin to explore this issue, though not as systematically as might be

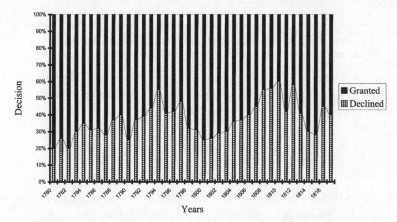

Figure 8.2 Vestry decision-making in three north-western townships

Number of decision in totem: 614

desirable, by looking at vestry records. These survive for around 8 per cent of north-western communities, and Figure 8.2 records the aggregate outcome of the decision-making process in three such places between 1790 and 1812.[17] It suggests that in some years upwards of one half of all people who applied for relief were turned down. Some were denied because they were not considered poor enough, others because they had kin on whom to draw, others because they had some moral failing in the eyes of the vestry. A few examples are illuminating. Thus, in Colne in June 1793, the vestry decided not to relieve James Foulds, but that, 'Jas Foulds is to be allowed 2s. a week by his son for another month, he being at present very sick.'[18] This vestry might also monitor the way in which previous relief was used by the applicant as one of the criteria for granting further help. In March 1794, for instance,

> The wife of Wilson Hargreaves of Watershead applied for relief but was refused because she had ... sold clothing and other things given to her by ye contribution to ye late fund for the benefit of the individual poor.[19]

Similar themes can be detected in other sets of vestry records. Thus in the Lancashire township of Garstang (already mentioned by Margaret Hanly in this volume) in 1815, Molly Crossley, made application for something towards buying coals. At the meeting of the 1st of August she said she could go on with 6 shillings allowed her towards her rent. The committee think that she should not so soon trouble the town again after the former promise.[20]

In November of the same year, the vestry balanced the circumstances of John Pedder and found them satisfactory, despite the fact that his income was well below the norm in the town. They noted,

Jno Pedder attended and wanted some relief. He admits being in constant employ ... earning 6s a week plus meat. He has only a wife and 3 children. Resolved that he is to have no further relief.[21]

Even being abandoned by one's spouse was no necessary cause for relief to be granted, as Alice Wakefield found out,

Alice Wakefield, the wife of John Wakefield who has run away with another woman, attended wanting relief. Her goods have been seized hold for rent. She has had a series of ill health which has brought her to her present distress – she has only 1 daughter 16 years of age a weaver at home to support her at present. Resolved nothing to be done. To have a ticket for Brindle if dissatisfied.[22]

Other applications were turned down in a more cursory manner. William Kendall was denied relief because he, 'keeps 2 or 3 dogs and which are a great annoyance to the children going to school'.[23] Of course, it is difficult to establish just how poor these people were, but even if we accept that half of applicants who were turned down were simply trying their luck, this would still leave a substantial core of poverty not addressed by the poor law, and one perhaps complemented by a core of those who were poor but too proud to apply for relief in the first place.

Moreover, we might also remember that even where people were granted relief, it did not always come in the form in which they asked for it. Widow Varley went to the Colne vestry asking for her rent to be paid. The vestry resolved that, 'Widow Varley's rent to be paid and the same is to be stopped out of her allowance.'[24] Widow Etherington came to the Halliwell vestry in 1797 looking for a pension of two shillings per week and came away instead with a bag of potatoes.[25] Nor was decision-making 'consistent' when viewed from the modern perspective. In Garstang some recent widows coming to the vestry were granted (small) pensions without comment; others who came with equal need and family circumstances were denied altogether, presumably because of some moral failings or other parameters of judgement (appearance, dress, or the way a pauper approached the vestry) which necessarily remain closed to us. The texture of the vestry records as a whole – showing often repeated applications on the part of people judged unworthy of relief – does much to suggest even to a casual reader that there really was a poverty problem being brushed under the carpet in these townships.

Of course, there are powerful reasons for thinking that any community keeping good vestry records might be atypical. Such communities certainly demonstrated the interest in tight administration which the Webbs thought to be absent and we might thus expect them to be vigorous in their application of relief only to those with severe and demonstrable need. Typical or not, it is important to acknowledge that this sample of vestry decisions are drawn from a period when the old poor law was often said to be in crisis, and hence vestries might have had a particular interest in rate-saving. Nor were harsh vestries a phenomenon confined to the north-west, as Steve Hindle shows. Yet pauper letters for other north-western townships where vestry minutes do not survive or effective vestries were never called demonstrate very clearly that overseers prevaricated on payment of relief, paid less than was needed, and regularly turned people down, prompting them to write more and more earnestly of their plight. Overseers could thus be as effective a police force as the vestry where they chose to fill this role, a point which those studying letter-writing to southern communities have also noted.[26] In short, notwithstanding rising poor law expenditure and increasing numbers on relief in the north-west there was a substantial core of people in most communities, perhaps up to 40 per cent, who were tied up in the day-to-day struggle of exploiting multiple welfare strategies at individual and family level. The competition for resources that these figures imply is a matter that we shall return to at the end of this chapter.

The economy of makeshifts at aggregate level

Let us initially take an overview of these multiple welfare strategies using data from a variety of north-western communities. Contemporary commentators were well aware of the potential richness of the economy of makeshifts in the early modern north-west.

Frederick Eden noted that 'here [Ainstable] and in most parts of Cumberland, an extensive common right is attached to most arable land'.[27] Of Bromfield in Cumberland he noted,

> there are no box clubs or friendly societies in the parish, and above all no bequests or regular annual charities bequeathed to the poor, a circumstance which, it has been observed in other districts, always has a considerable influence on the Poor Rate.[28]

A review of some of its individual parts in survey form is long overdue, and forms the bedrock of this section.

One of the most obvious responses to life-cycle need was to vary household size or structure, a point raised in the conclusion to this volume. While most census-type listings confirm that the small nuclear family and its servants has consistently lain at the heart of English household structure, these snapshot pictures tell only a partial story.[29] Over the life-cycle of a family, periods of short-term complexity were more common than census listings allow, and this observation has particular resonance when we look at the household structures of the poor. Thomas Sokoll in his 1993 book on the household sizes of paupers in Essex reconsidered the idea that the pauper household was small and simple. He was able to show that the average pauper household was quite large (4.2) and that pauper families and households were the *most*, not least, complex.[30] Eighteenth-century data for the north-west also highlights considerable diversity. The 1787 population survey of Westmorland shows that in the constablewick of Little Strickland in Morland parish, all people labelled 'poor' headed their own households. They formed 22 per cent of all households and these households were small and simple households – average 2.76 persons – of the sort which Sokoll disclaims for Essex.[31] Yet in Crosby Ravensworth just a few miles away the average pauper household was considerably larger (4.1 people) and much more likely to be complex (26 per cent). Overall, almost one quarter of all households in the Westmorland census where we find poor people (recognised and unrecognised by the poor law) were 'complex' compared to 'background levels' in the wider population excluding paupers of just 8 per cent.[32]

Spatial variation of this sort should not surprise us. Considerations of nuclear hardship, availability of servants, local variations in architecture and the degree of proximate residence amongst kin could operate in different ways on communities separated only

nominally on the map.[33] The attitude of poor law administrators
was also an important influence. Where they were active – as seems
to be the case in many north-western communities – in engineering
fluid household arrangements as part of their relief strategy,
accepted generalisations about household structure must be discarded. The story of Edmund Leatherbarrow (an old handloom
weaver, and someone already encountered in Margaret Hanly's
contribution to this volume) from Garstang is particularly illuminating. In 1816, 'The overseer to enquire what Jno Leatherbarrow
will keep his father for'.[34] Whether Edmund Leatherbarrow had any
say in this sort of bargain is unclear. The bargain for co-residence
was made but then,

> Mr John Leatherbarrow attended to say he could not afford to keep
> his father for the 2s a week any longer; he hopes that this committee
> considering his situation and the age of his father will not think 3s
> too much to be allowed him for tending his father. Allowed 3s per
> week.[35]

At the census of the poor of Garstang in 1817, Edmund Leatherbarrow was recorded in his own right as a recipient of three shillings
per week, with no indication that this was to pay for houseroom
with his son. By 1820 the stresses of co-residence were clearly
beginning to show, with the vestry minutes noting that, 'Agreed
that Edward Leatherbarrow shall have 4/ per week to himself and
1/ lodging to be paid'.[36] This sort of detailed bargaining is rarely
elaborated in the discussion over residential patterns of the old
for any area. It could be repeated both for other old people and
for those facing crisis at other stages of the life-cycle, and one is
left with a clear sense that variation of household arrangements
was an intuitively attractive part of the potential welfare mechanism
to both administrators and paupers in many localities. Lack of
coinage in the north-west may have given a particular urgency to
the attempts of overseers to foster cashless welfare options, of
which varying household structure was just one.[37]

Charitable provision was potentially a second major strand of
welfare, as several chapters in this book show, and the rural and
rural industrial north-west had a rich vein of such resources.[38]
There were four separate but potentially overlapping forms of
charity which must concern us in this context. First, formal
charitable endowments. Eighteenth- and nineteenth-century communities benefited from a considerable overhang of charitable

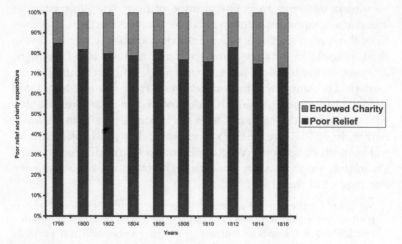

Figure 8.3 Charity and poor law expenditure in four north-western communities

endowments. Poor management, limited returns on invested capital, limited renewal of capital as it became usual to settle resources in wills on immediate kin, and the growing tide of poverty which washed over late eighteenth-century England may have served to compromise the role of charity in overall welfare over time,[39] but even by 1820 charitable provision could still make a substantial contribution to welfare in many north-western communities. Figure 8.3 relates endowed charitable expenditure[40] to poor relief expenditure in four north-western communities where records from both institutions survive side-by-side.[41] The aggregate figures are interesting, suggesting that charity significantly augmented local welfare resources in these rural communities. At individual level, access to endowed charities could be very significant for annual welfare. In Cartmel in 1750 the average pension stood at 1s. 6d. per week and yet the recipients of such pensions, as well as others not on relief, were granted the equivalent of three months of poor relief income from local endowed charities at the same date.

Of course, not all places were so well endowed, but there were also other forms of charity which might contribute to an economy of makeshifts. A second strand of philanthropy, for instance, was the charitable activity of nonconformist groups. The Quakers have attracted particular attention in north-east Lancashire, for instance, and many diarists refer to charity sermons.[42] Perhaps a more important contribution to welfare was provided by a third charitable form – the rich patchwork of irregular charitable funds which stemmed from collections by local elites to meet pressing needs associated with depression, high food prices or peculiar local circumstances. Such charitable goodwill was a vital component of welfare in the urban and rural north-west, outweighing the amount of money given out by the poor law in the years when collections took place.[43] The tendency to donate to irregular collections of this sort can be seen in most places. In Foulshaw, Westmorland, for instance, an initial extraordinary collection to help the poor at a time of high prices became a permanent accompaniment to the poor law, paying out 3d. per week to recipients (many of whom were already getting poor relief) by 1825.[44] Small money perhaps, but nonetheless a regular source of alternative welfare for those excluded from the relief process or given less than they thought they needed.

Moreover, we should also remember that much charity took the form of the occasional dispensation of money or gifts to the needy by middling people, neighbours, clergy and friends. Saints days, weddings, funerals or other local events were often an occasion for the dispensation of charity, but more significant were regular ongoing, if small, payments. These are usually closed to the historian, but the Browne family of Troutbeck fastidiously kept accounts recording in some detail the dispensation of informal charity during the early to mid-eighteenth century to those perceived to be in need. Correlating these records with overlapping poor law accounts reveals that the family recognised a circle of need some 70 per cent larger than that recognised by the overseers, and that in aggregate terms the charitable activity of this one family augmented the resources available from the poor law by between 16 and 23 per cent depending upon the year in question.[45] Few such detailed accounts survive elsewhere, but for south-west Lancashire the records of the Scarisbrick family allow us to take a different angle on this issue. Charles Scarisbrick made pension payments to his longest serving former employees of up to 6s. per month, such that his yearly expenditure on direct monetary charity by the early nineteenth century was of the order of £100. Of course, these sums acted to keep people off the relief lists in the first place, but Scarisbrick also granted more indirect forms of charity, bargaining with local poor law authorities, for instance, that widows of his former workers would be allowed to live rent free in his cottages if the poor law made monetary provision for their welfare.[46] Scarisbrick was not alone in seeing a charitable duty, as the family collections of other south-west Lancashire elites show.[47]

For those on the outside of the charity processes, and even for some recipients, other welfare avenues also beckoned. As Peter King, Sarah Horrell and Jane Humphries, and a range of other commentators have pointed out, gleaning and foraging on the wastes and commons may have made a substantial contribution to monthly or yearly welfare.[48] Such 'rights' had been under pressure in most areas for many years by the late eighteenth century, but in many north-western communities farm or industrial land was still in the 1790s located within the midst of large tracts of waste and common, where customary access to 'communal' resources had considerable longevity. Inter-community disputes over the rights of access to waste land in the north-west provides ample testimony to the perceived value of these communal resources. We should not overstate this point of course. Surveys of waste land during the late eighteenth and early nineteenth centuries suggest very clearly that in some communities the prime sites on waste land had been colonised by encroachers. Thus a survey of the waste lands around Blackburn in 1824 pointed to thatched cow-houses, coal houses, coal pits and the enclosure of land around the key water supplies, leaving 'the waste' of little use to either person or beast.[49] Such experiences find reflection in Westmorland, where most of the major landowners were, by the mid-eighteenth century, conducting surveys to find out exactly how much waste land had fallen under encroachments.[50] Even where land remained nominally open to customary rights, we should not forget that major landowners were progressively attempting to seal off access to all sorts of game, from rabbits to fish, by the later years of the eighteenth century.[51] Yet, while we are unable to place an aggregate monetary value on access to waste and common, in the psychology of the economy of makeshifts, this particular avenue may have loomed large.

In certain cases of life-cycle poverty, work continued to be a big part of welfare, as Margaret Hanly has also suggested elsewhere in this volume. Overseers' handbooks instructed them to make efforts to secure work for applicants to the community as a precursor to giving pension or other payments.[52] This may partly explain why so many pauper letters are prefaced with a detailed story of how the applicant had exhausted all avenues for ensuring welfare through work. Overseers may have been more favourably disposed to this sort of application, or to those which asked for relief at times of life-cycle crisis to supplement resources acquired through labour. Thus in July 1806 Bernard Hughes applied to the overseer of the de-industrialising township of Kirkham in the Fylde of Lancashire. The overseer noted that he,

> hath a wife and four children, wife pregnant again, is a cotton weaver and gets 13/ per week, children aged 7, 5, 3, and 1 year. Applies for some money, 1 pound 13s which he owes for rent. Allowed 1 pound 1 shilling.[53]

Work seems to have provided Hughes with the bulk of his day-to-day welfare, but not extraordinary lump sum payments such as rent. William Taylor, living in Warrington but with a settlement in Barnacre-with-Bonds near Preston, found himself in a similar predicament. He wrote to the overseers in Barnacre on 19 December 1822 in the following terms,

> Worthy gentlemen, I ham sorry that necessity obliges me in troubling you at this seasons of the year. If your own goodness still continues to me I must still trouble you as long as I ham in this life how long that will be god only knows as both me and my wife are far advanced in years and we are troubled with my infirmtys. I ham now working what I can for 3s per week and this is the only sum we have to subsist upon, what must become of us if provisions was not reasonable my work is very laborors to me for 6d per day – I ham so infirm I hope your honours will be pleased to send me. My rent is raised to 5 pounds and 5s and at the time we first came to the house the rent was not more than 2 pounds and 15s my rent is now due and I hope your goodness will be pleased to send it as yu will still oblige your obedient servant.[54]

Confirmation that there was a connection between wages and relief even in the extremities of old age is provided by the case of Martin Holmes of Garstang who was, 'aged 73; earns from 3–4/ per week. Has 2/ allowance and rent paid'.[55] Even where old age was equated with incapacity at the individual level, there might still be a role for wages in the economy of makeshifts of the residential unit. Thomas Lingart and his wife applied to the overseer of Kirkham in April 1808, and the overseer noted that,

> He is 76 years of age – she is about 50, and gets 3/ or 4/ per week when employed. Have 6 children. The oldest son Michael is married,

was apprenticed and belongs to Horwich. The second son, James, is also married, was apprentice to Blackrod and belongs there. The third son – John is apprentice in Blackrod and belongs there – 14 yr old bound September 1807. The eldest daughter, Ellen is not employed – 9 years old. The second daughter – Mary is 6yr old. The youngest daughter, Margaret, aged 5 yrs. Allowed 20/ till midsummer, and to be informed that they must not expect anything further.[56]

For younger people facing different life-cycle problems there is also a need to account for the family economy of makeshifts and the place of wages within it. In June 1822 Jane Atkinson applied to the vestry of Garstang for aid, and they concluded that the

> Overseer shall have the discretionary power of affording such temporary relief to the widow of James Atkinson as shall be necessary and that he shall make enquiry as to the amount of earning of her son employed at Catterall.[57]

Similarly, the vestry of Halliwell, an industrial township near Bolton, judged an application in December 1814 along the following lines,

> Molly Moscrop, the widow of the late Saml Moscrop applies for relief and says she has six children and the eldest is 7 years of age and the youngest is 7 months, she says she can get 3/6 per week and her eldest has had 3/6 a week as a tear boy at Kirkalls print works, so that she only has 7/ per week for the support of herself and six children.[58]

The vestry granted her an allowance to augment her wage income but later reduced her allowance as she undertook less paid work! Meanwhile, for those with illegitimate children, work and wage earning were probably integral parts of being seen as deserving of relief. In a survey of the poor of Garstang in 1817 we find, 'Mary Taylor, 34 years old earns 20d a week by winding and can weave. Has one bastard child, a boy 3 years old. 4/.'[59] No attempt to work might bring short shrift from a vestry. Such was the attitude of the Garstang vestry to a later application, 'Margaret Cundliffe wants relief for herself and her bastard – she is a young woman in health and has only one child. Refused.'[60]

For some, the connection between wages and relief at the heart of the economy of makeshifts could be a very long-term experience. Molly Moscrop provides one example of a long-term connection and Frederick Eden provides others. In the gunpowder making community of Warwick, Cumberland, he noted the case of,

M. B, a widow aged 45 has received parochial aid about 10 years, her allowance is 2 pounds a year, which added to her earnings by spinning and working for farmers is sufficient to maintain her and her children.[61]

Moreover, at about the time Eden was writing, the vestry of Colne was recording the case of Widow Stewart who,

has been these last years in receipt of an allowance of 2/ per week, but now wants 1/6 or at least 1/ more. She has 3/ per week from her work with Messrs Elliot, bleachers, and 2/ from her work with James Mghie, spinner. In consideration of her good history with the vestry, a further allowance of 1/ per week is to be granted.[62]

The day-to-day activity of the poor law itself also placed work at the heart of the economy of makeshifts in many north-western communities. For instance, overseers frequently paid for items to support work, rather than simply doling out relief. This included expenditure on things like coals for blacksmiths, looms, potatoes for seeding and cloth for selling. In terms of overall poor law budgets, these sorts of expenditure were usually small but the effect may have been disproportionate. In the Lancashire parish of Longton, for instance, the poor law authorities entered into agreement with a local merchant partnership that the parish would pay loom rents for local textile workers, keeping a whole range of people off relief who might have been otherwise dependent.[63] This group of marginal poor could also be supported in work by the creative use of poor law spending on goods given in kind. Thus, in Birkdale during the relief years 1812/13 and 1813/14, over one third (by value) of specified non-administrative expenditure in the town accounts was directed towards payments in kind, which encompassed expenditure on board and lodgings, clothing, the making of clothing, medicine, rent, coal, potatoes, turf, shoes and shoe mending, and a subvention to the local charity.[64] Where the demand created by this pattern of payments was met by awarding large money-saving contracts to a restricted range of suppliers, the externalities of expenditure in kind were limited, but with imagination the work flowing from payment in kind could be spread around individuals who were either poor themselves or might be dependent upon communal relief otherwise.

And the poor law could also be more proactive in finding work for poor people in the north-west. The strongest evidence of this comes from Lancashire, where vestry books regularly record overseers being directed to negotiate with employers for employment of people who were in, or looked like sinking into, poverty. In Garstang, for instance, the overseers had a regular dialogue with the owners of the local calico printing factory and the 1817 survey of the poor (and the decision-making process leading up to it) shows that considerable numbers of those on relief were in some form of employment.[65] In Cowpe, there was a more direct connection in the sense that mill-owners and their relatives were the biggest contributors to the local rates, owned most of the debts run up by a constant tendency for the poor law to overspend, and were the most active people in the administration of relief. There was thus a close inverse connection between net poor law expenditure in the township and levels of wages and employment.

The range of other potential coping strategies in the north-west was considerable, and there is not the space to review them here.[66] It is appropriate, however, to round off this section with a discussion of a category of welfare which we might broadly label self-help. In particular, we must make some allowance for the impact of friendly societies since it is now clear that all but the most casual or lowest paid occupations might contribute to friendly societies in the north-west.[67] Such societies were not renowned for their longevity, but some of their rules are important for this general appreciation of the economy of makeshifts. The Caldbeck (Cumberland) friendly society identified by Eden can stand for many. This society (incorporating perhaps one third of the population) promised members 4–6s. per week during bouts of sickness, with the actual level dependent on the state of the society reserves. For those who were old (defined as 70+) there was a guarantee of 4s. per week irrespective of whether the person was still working. This was at a time when Caldbeck pensioners not linked to a friendly society were receiving less than 2s. per week on average. Such entitlement was not a bar to application for relief. In Cumrew (Cumberland), Eden recorded the case of

> A. D a labourer receives occasional relief from the parish to the amount of about 10s. He belongs to a friendly society, from which he receives 4s a week. He has been long sick and has a small family of children to maintain.[68]

Such small sums would not have guaranteed subsistence for a family, but the connection between friendly society and poor relief is important. This connection is repeated in Lancashire; of the

76 people who deposited friendly society membership certificates with the overseers of Great Bolton between 1799 and 1834, 52 needed to apply for relief in addition to their friendly society benefits, and of these 17 became regular pensioners at levels of under 2s.[69] This is the sort of holistic approach to welfare strategies suggested by John Broad.

The economy of makeshifts: a community and individual view

This sort of aggregate view is a useful advance for the historiography of north-western welfare patterns. To really understand the economy of makeshifts, however, we need to pin down how the different alternative strategies were explored over time, and the exact nature of the relationship between the resources offered by these strands and those deployed by the poor law. For this, we need a detailed local study, and one concerned particularly with the key period of pressure on the old poor law (and hence the wider economy of makeshifts) in the first three decades of the nineteenth century.

The community of Cowpe (along with the hamlets of Hall Carr, Lenches and Newhallhey) was situated in the Rossendale area of Lancashire and can provide this sort of overview. Combining limited agriculture with outwork in the cotton and woollen industries, factory weaving and the finishing trades, the complex economy of the township supported a small population of 797 by 1801.[70] On the face of it, the poverty problem in the township would appear to have been substantial. The mean number of people relieved in each year 1806–30 was 73 (9.1 per cent of the entire population)[71] and in most years the poor law expenditure account was substantially overdrawn despite the raising of several extra assessments in some years. Gross expenditure which had stood at £254 in 1806 had risen to £422 by 1817 and peaked at £504 in 1826. Periodic trade crises could throw large numbers out of work in these isolated mills and finishing shops, as could extraordinary events such as the machine breaking and mill burning episodes which racked Rossendale in 1826. Moreover, there was a seasonality to employment which one does not find in lower-lying industrial areas. Snow, torrential rain and heath fires were a constant threat to communication links, and a bad

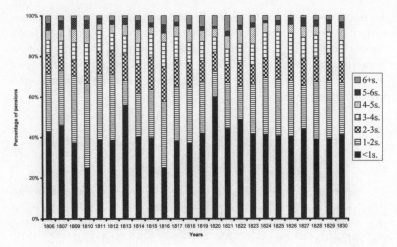

Figure 8.4 Pension payments in early nineteenth-century Cowpe

winter could upset employment patterns. And Cowpe, like other industrial communities, had a substantial core of those afflicted by life-cycle poverty problems associated with too many children, spousal death, old age and sickness or occupational accident and disease.

The role of the communal welfare system in ameliorating these needs was strictly limited. Figure 8.4 shows that the majority of all pension payments were less than 3 shillings per week by the early nineteenth century.[72] In turn, pensions accounted for between 50 and 70 per cent of all communal expenditure depending on the year, with the rest expended on payment in kind and a series of small doles to meet immediate need. The latter are particularly important. Mill-owners and their relatives were the biggest contributors to the local rates, owned most of the debts run up by a constant tendency for the poor law to overspend, and were the most active people in the administration of relief. There is thus a sense in which small and irregular money payments were used to keep the core of the local population (and hence a potential labour force in this remote area of Lancashire) in place through seasonal fluctuations, periods of falling piece and time rates, and episodes of life-cycle crises. There is more to be said about the operation and inclusivity of the poor law in Cowpe, but the key point is that the area must have witnessed a complex economy of makeshifts at both community and individual level.

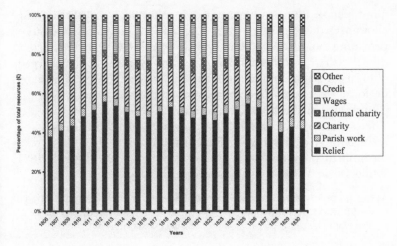

Figure 8.5 Community-level economy of makeshifts in Cowpe

In this sense, it is important that in Cowpe we can do more than simply concentrate on the poor law and narratives springing from its operation to understand the economy of makeshifts. Figure 8.5 attempts a crude reconstruction of the resources available to poor people at community level. It requires explanation and clarification of the underlying assumptions. Thus for the period 1806–30 the graph identifies 'poor' people in three sources – poor law records, the records of formal charity disbursed by the churchwardens, and the records of informal charity. The distinct individuals from these three sources (tallied against reconstitution data) form the basis for further linkage through other potential welfare sources.[73] Figure 8.5 thus takes all of the traceable income for all people classified as poor in at least one of these basic sources and aggregates it to produce a nominal township economy of makeshifts. The exercise has many drawbacks, but may nonetheless be instructive.

Within the aggregated data, 'Parish work' refers to the wages or monetary value of payment in kind, given to poor individuals by parish officers other than the overseer. The churchwarden, for instance, employed poor people to clear graveyards, ring bells or police the congregation, while the surveyors employed poor people to keep the roads open in bad weather, or to repair the roads year round.[74] For the purposes of Figure 8.5 the poor law accounts have, as far as possible, been stripped of all payments made to 'poor' people for providing services to other poor people, including allowances for nursing, care of children, making clothing, or providing board and lodging, and these have been included in this 'Parish work' category. 'Informal charity' refers to the proceeds of local collections for the poor as long as these collections resulted in local expenditure, distributions at church recorded by the churchwardens, and also the charity expenditure of local elites. The owners of Waterfoot Mill in Cowpe – the Whiteheads – kept records of the amounts of money disbursed at their door or at the mill to poor people in the locality between 1817 and 1821. While David Whitehead suggested that,

> workpeople are very poor economists when trade is good and then when trade becomes bad, having nothing beforehand, are hard up and soon in deep poverty. They blame everything but themselves.[75]

He still gave out charity, noting that 'my wife felt a great interest in the welfare of the people, particularly to the females'.[76] The graph makes two assumptions about this part of the informal charity category. First (and most reasonably) that the mean level of disbursement by the Whitehead family can also be applied to the years 1806–17 and 1822–30. Second (and less defensibly), that the two other major mill-owning families in the locality gave the same amounts in informal charity. The size of this category is small and the charity of local families just one part of it, so changing these assumptions would not change this part of the graph dramatically.[77]

Meanwhile, 'Wages' refers to the waged income of 'poor' people derived from two sources: first (and least significantly), the wage account books of Hareholme Mill;[78] second (and most importantly), the 1799–1800, 1800–4, 1820, 1816 and 1826–30 accounts of 'work put out by Rossendale mills'. These record the recipients of wages paid for tasks such as spinning, weaving, repairing faulty cloth, combing and carrying which can then be linked back to the list of those nominally poor to obtain some perspective on the work of poor people.[79] Of course, outwork of this sort was just one potential source of wages, and can thus only provide a minimal picture of the role of work in the welfare process, but they are nonetheless a useful proxy.[80]

There are also two other components of Figure 8.5. 'Credit' refers to year end debts recorded by people classed as 'poor' in the Waterfoot Mill Shop account book running from 1817–26.[81]

This shop appears to have catered not just for mill employees, but for the whole locality, not surprising in the light of the lack of a market and the fact that no shopkeepers were recorded in the rate books for the town. Indeed, David Whitehead noted in his diary that the site of his first mill

> was a small place and had no shop to sell any food. The workpeople complained of having so far to go to buy their food. So I began to sell flour and meal, and other grocery.[82]

Again, using this data involves deploying some assumptions. Most importantly, the mill shop came into existence with the firm in 1816/17, but Figure 8.5 assumes that the levels of credit found after this date also apply to the earlier period. This may be pulling the evidence too far, but such assumptions fit well with the wider culture of credit that we can observe in nineteenth-century Lancashire, and with Keith Wrightson's siting of credit at the heart of the generalised economy of makeshifts.[83] Finally, 'Other' in this framework refers to miscellaneous small sources of welfare income for the poor, such as the £3 disbursed by Colonel Dawson when he stayed in the town on his way to Manchester in 1820.

Clearly, even if one accepts the validity and usefulness of this sort of approach in the first place, key parts of Figure 8.5 are built upon a raft of assumptions. And even if those assumptions are accurate, the graph at best uncovers only part of the aggregate welfare spectrum. A range of other welfare avenues undoubtedly existed but we have inadequate records. There are also completely unquantifiable benefits which cannot be incorporated into the analysis. On 24 March 1816, for instance, the poor law authorities employed a loom master to repair the looms of local people who might otherwise be obliged to interrupt work and claim poor relief. Similarly, the overseers lent, outside the framework of the poor law accounts, money to buy looms. Moreover, the life story of David Whitehead suggests a very ingrained culture of barter in this part of Lancashire. Recalling his time as a hawker (one of a plethora of jobs he undertook before establishing his firm), he noted,

> I found it very difficult to sell for ready money. People wanted to take goods and pay so much per month ... I found a many of weavers in the country places ... who would often ask me if I took any white iron. By this they meant would I exchange my goods with them for weft which they had pilfered from their masters. I found one

shopkeeper, a grocer, who wished to exchange with me some of this kind of weft for some of my goods. He had exchanged his groceries with the weavers for this kind of weft.[84]

With these caveats in mind, it seems clear that even if this approach is only partially right we must accept that poor relief (corrected for outparish relief) was a significant source of welfare, but nonetheless a minority player in the overall resources available to the economy of makeshifts at township level during some years. In fact for Cowpe there seems little scope for placing the poor law at the centre of the welfare web in terms of its direct payments to poor people. This conclusion is interesting and goes a little way to substantiating what welfare historians have always known to be true about historical communities.

Conclusion: the state of the poor again

We might conclude with a question. If there was a complex economy of makeshifts operating in the north-west, in which ordinary people combined multiple strategies in the day-to-day business of making ends meet, what sort of living did this economy of makeshifts provide? Housing surveys of poor people in different areas of the north-west during the eighteenth and nineteenth centuries provide one way into this question. The survey of housing in Birkdale tells us much about the conditions of those trying to piece together a living from a variety of sources which offered neither generous or stable income flows. 'Little Common' in the township was largely owned by the Blundell family, who rented plots to several tenants.[85] It is here that we find the 'town cottages' for poor people. A report on these cottages in 1815 suggests that none of the inhabitants (a mixture of large families, the old and widows) were receiving direct relief from the poor law, and it highlighted a litany of poor conditions, for instance,

> The walls are nearly without plaster and almost as black as soot through the chimney smoke … The windows are nearly all out and broken. The roof or thatch is bad and rains in.[86]

Of the last cottage that the surveyor saw, he noted,

> The chamber is filled with a pair of looms and lumber. The bedding wet when I saw it by the rain coming through the roof. They enlarge the bed at night by placing stools and chairs on 2 sides of it.[87]

These perspectives must be set within the context of generally bad housing in south-west Lancashire, and perhaps within the context of a surveyor with a point to make to the township, but the survey is nonetheless a significant one. It shows the experiences of those people who were excluded, or excluded themselves, from the process of poor relief in the township, and it is clear that such conditions would have matched those of the poorest labourers in the rural south at the same time. The domestic environment was no less compromised for those turned down for relief or for those getting inadequate relief in other areas. In the Lancashire townships of Garstang, Nether Wyersdale, Ulnes Walton, Chorley and Broughton the poor law authorities actively managed the concentration of poor people into the worst township housing during the later eighteenth and early nineteenth centuries by capping the amount of rent that they would reimburse to land-lords.[88] Just how bad this sort of housing was likely to have been can be seen in the scheme to divide up the common lands of Cockerham in March 1790, where the indifferent state of the (mainly town) cottages in one parcel of land used in the allocation process attracted the comment of the surveyor and resulted in the application of a very low notional value for the acreage concerned.[89]

More stories of this sort could be deployed to illustrate the precarious domestic state of those who were engaged in the economy of makeshifts in northern and north-western com-munities. Harsh poor law decision-making exacerbated demand for the resources offered by alternative welfare avenues, resulting in limited weekly incomes and poor living conditions. The com-plex economy of makeshifts yielded, probably after much time-consuming searching, limited and potentially very unstable extra income. If we write into this equation periodic trade fluc-tuations which could throw whole regions on to relief, degrading such alternative welfare strategies, then one can see that endemic poverty was alive and well in the north-west. Where Eden thought of the economy of makeshifts in the eighteenth-century north-west in positive terms, this analysis suggests that in terms of resource yield, if not in terms of the symbolism of semi-independence, the economy of makeshifts was more an expression of despair and communal failure than the triumph of individual ingenuity over the forces of increasing risk and uncertainty marshalled by agrarian and industrial capitalism.

Notes

1 The data for this chapter were collected with the generous support of the Scoloudie Foundation and British Academy, and much of the writing was undertaken during my time as visiting professor at the University of Trier in 1998. I am grateful to the foundation and to Professor Dr Dietrich Ebeling of the University of Trier for their support. I am also grateful to Alannah Tomkins, for her perceptive commentary on earlier drafts of this chapter.

2 D. Thomson, 'The welfare of the elderly in the past: a family or community responsibility?', in M. Pelling and R. M. Smith (eds), *Life, Death and the Elderly: Historical Perspectives* (London, Routledge, 1991) and M. Daunton, *Progress and Poverty: An Economic and Social History of Britain 1700–1850* (Oxford, Oxford University Press, 1995).

3 See T. Wales, 'Poverty, poor relief and the life-cycle: some evidence from seventeenth century Norfolk' in R. M. Smith (ed.), *Land, Kinship and Life Cycle* (Cambridge, Cambridge University Press, 1984), and P. Thane, 'Government and society in England and Wales 1750–1914', in F. M. L. Thompson (ed.), *The Cambridge Social History of Britain 1750–1950* (Cambridge, Cambridge University Press, 1990).

4 R. M. Smith, 'Ageing and well being in early modern England: pension trends and gender preferences under the English Old Poor Law 1650–1800', in P. Johnson and P. Thane (eds), *Old Age From Antiquity to Post Modernity* (London, Routledge, 1998).

5 P. King, 'Pauper inventories and the material lives of the poor in the eighteenth and early nineteenth centuries', in T. Hitchcock, P. King and P. Sharpe (eds), *Chronicling Poverty: The Voices and Strategies of the English Poor 1640–1840* (Basingstoke, Macmillan, 1997).

6 S. Hindle, 'Power, poor relief and social relations in Holland Fen, c. 1600–1800', *Historical Journal*, 41 (1998).

7 This chapter is particularly concerned with responses to life-cycle poverty problems.

8 For an early example, see Cumbria Record Office, Kendal (hereafter KRO) uncatalogued, 'The great end book of Ravenstonedale'. My thanks to Professor R. W. Hoyle for bringing this source to my attention in 1995.

9 K. Wrightson, *Earthly Necessities: Economic Lives in Early Modern Britain* (New Haven, Yale University Press, 2000), pp. 270–313.

10 B. Stapleton, 'Inherited poverty and life-cycle poverty: Odiham, Hampshire, 1650–1850' *Social History*, 18 (1993).

11 E. H. Hunt, 'Paupers and pensioners past and present', *Ageing and Society*, 9 (1990).

12 J. Broad, 'Parish economies of welfare, 1650–1834', *Historical Journal*, 42 (1999).

13 Smith, 'Pension trends'.

14 E. C. Midwinter, *Social Administration in Lancashire* (Manchester, Manchester University Press, 1969), p. 62.

15 See S. A. King, *Poverty and Welfare, 1700–1850: A Regional Perspective* (Manchester, Manchester University Press, 2000).

16 The sources for this figure are Rawtenstall Library (hereafter RL), Rc 352 RAW, 'The poor law accounts of Cowpe 1806–1831', Lancashire Record Office (hereafter LRO) PR2095, 'Account book of Aughton, 1784–1838', LRO DDX 1852/4, 'Ulnes Walton poor law accounts 1800–36', LRO PR795 and 796, 'Accounts of Greenhalgh 1741–1838', LRO DDLi (uncatalogued), 'Poor law accounts of Warrington', KRO WPR/81, 'Overseer account book for Temple Sowerby, 1765–1837' and WPR/89/01, 'Old poor law accounts for Cartmel, 1761–1832'. The years chosen for analysis are deliberately located within the supposed crisis of the old poor law. This chapter eschews a discussion of the socio-economic, topographical or institutional structures of these communities because its aim is to highlight similarities of welfare experience at the individual and aggregate level.

17 These years were chosen because they encompass a sustained upsurge in national relief expenditure. The communities are KRO WPR/9/VI, 'Orton vestry minutes 1790–1902', LRO MBCO/7/1, 'Colne ratepayers minutes', and Bolton Local Studies library (hereafter BL) HTB 1/2, 'Halliwell township minutes'.

18 LRO MBCO/7/1, 'Colne ratepayers minutes'.

19 *Ibid.*

20 LRO DDX 386/3, 'Garstang vestry minutes'.

21 *Ibid.*

22 *Ibid.*

23 *Ibid.*

24 LRO MBCO/7/1, 'Colne ratepayers minutes'.

25 BL HTB 1/2, 'Halliwell'.

26 See J. S. Taylor, 'Voices in the crowd: the Kirby Lonsdale township letters 1809–1834' in Hitchcock *et al.*, *Chronicling Poverty*, pp. 109–26. The best Lancashire collections are LRO PR2391/2–46, 'Overseers letters for Billington' and LRO DDNw 9/8–12, 'Petitions for relief in Newton with Scales'.

27 F. M. Eden, *The State of the Poor*, vol. 2 (London, 1797), p. 46.

28 *Ibid.*, p. 49.

29 P. Laslett, *Household and Family in Past Time* (Cambridge, Cambridge University Press, 1972).

30 T. Sokoll, *Household and Family Among the Poor: The Case of Two Essex Communities in the Late Eighteenth and Early Nineteenth Centuries* (Bochum, Verlaag fur Regionalgeschichte, 1993). We should beware of focusing exclusively on co-residence. Where kin lived nearby there may have been little need to vary household structure.

31 Small household sizes do not reflect source weaknesses. Richard Wall's discussion of regional differences in household size has highlighted consistently low figures from the late eighteenth century to the time of the first census: see R. Wall, 'Regional and temporal variations in English household structure from 1650', in J. Hobcraft and P. Rees (eds), *Regional Demographic Development* (London, Croom Helm, 1979); R. Wall, 'Characteristics of European family and household systems', *Historical Social Research*, 23 (1998).

32 See L. Ashcroft (ed.), *Vital Statistics: The Westmorland Census of 1787* (Berwick, Curwen Archives Trust, 1992). No general guidelines were issued by the justices other than the order that constables should 'Make returns of the names and number of inhabitants within their different constablewicks distinguishing their occupation, sex and of what each family severally consists'. Interestingly, most places make a distinction between those who were poor and those who were poor and supported or partly supported by the poor law. The latter group were always a small minority of the former group, adding weight to the contention that there was a considerable level of 'background' poverty.

33 See R. M. Smith, 'Charity, self-interest and welfare: reflections from demography and family history', in M. Daunton (ed.), *Charity, Self Interest and Welfare in the English Past* (London, UCL Press, 1996) and P. Laslett, 'Family, kinship and collectivity as systems of support in pre-industrial Europe: a consideration of the nuclear hardship hypothesis', *Continuity and Change*, 3 (1988).

34 LRO DDX 386/3, 'Garstang vestry minutes', June 1816.

35 *Ibid.*, August 1816.

36 *Ibid.*, September 1820. By July 1821, the allowance had risen to 6s. 6d.

37 See S. A. King and J. C. Muldrew, 'Cash, wages and the economy of makeshifts in England, 1650–1800', in P. Scholliers and L. D. Schwarz (eds), *Worlds of Wages* (Oxford, Berghahn, 2003). Payment of relief in kind rather than cash is a similar example.

38 For the most recent survey see H. Cunningham and J. Innes (eds), *Charity, Philanthropy and Reform From the 1690s to 1850* (Basingstoke, Macmillan, 1998).

39 See J. A. Johnston, 'Family, kin and community in eight Lincolnshire parishes 1567–1800', *Rural History*, 6 (1995), and W. Coster, *Kinship and Inheritance in Early Modern England: Three Yorkshire Parishes* (York, Borthwick Institute, 1993). The trend was least marked in the distant rural counties such as Westmorland and Cumberland. In the Westmorland communities of Undermilkbeck and Applethwaite, for instance, Thomas Dixon left 20s. per annum to the poor in 1730, James Sattherwaite left the interest on 100 pounds to the poor in 1785, and Margaret Williams left the interest on 67 pounds to the poor in 1789. If we combine these with existing historical legacies,

we can see that the capital for these two townships amounted to over 1,500 pounds by the later eighteenth century. At 5 per cent interest, this would eclipse the formal poor relief bill for the townships at this date.

40 Using the records only of endowed charities that gave out cash or made other provision that might be considered part of a practical economy of makeshifts.

41 The communities are Cartmel, Crosby Ravensworth, Whalley, and Treales. See LRO PR 2777/5, 'Whalley St George's day charity', KRO WPC/11/4, 'Ed Thwaite's charity, Crosby Ravensworth, 1751–1840', KRO WPC/12, 'Crosby Ravensworth charity book', KRO WPR 17/4, 'Overseers accounts for Crosby Ravensworth', KRO WPR 14, 'Charity accounts for Cartmel', KRO WPR 89/01, 'Old Poor Law accounts for Cartmel 1761–1832', KRO WPR/Chapelwardens 3, 'Accounts for Cartmel 1721–98' and LRO DDX/1910/1–2, 'Accounts of Boultons charity, Treales'. The graph deals with poor relief expenditure net of administration costs and excludes charity money which was administered by the parish and included in records of poor relief expenditure.

42 See R. Watson, 'Poverty in north-east Lancashire in 1843: evidence from quaker charity records', *Local Population Studies*, 55 (1995).

43 Midwinter, *Social Administration*.

44 KRO WD/D/D6/68, 'Donations to the poor in Foulshaw'.

45 KRO Wd/Te/8/3, 'The diary of Benjamin Browne', KRO WD/Te/16/4, 'Account book', KRO WD/Te/24, 'Poor law accounts for Troutbeck', and KRO WPR/62/W2, 'Overseers accounts'.

46 LRO DDSc/24/10, 'Bargain'.

47 See, for instance, LRO DDHe/104/9, 'Accounts of Thomas Hesketh re poor'.

48 S. Horrell and J. Humphries, 'Old questions, new data and alternative perspectives: families' living standards in the industrial revolution', *Journal of Economic History*, 52 (1992), and J. Humphries, 'Enclosure, common rights and women: the proletarianisation of families in the late eighteenth and early nineteenth centuries', *Journal of Economic History*, 50 (1990). Also P. King, 'Customary right and women's earnings: the importance of gleaning to the rural labouring poor 1750–1850', *Economic History Review*, 44 (1991).

49 LRO DDCm/2/177, 'Particulars of tenants of the waste lands of the township of Blackburn, April 1824'.

50 See, for instance CRO WD/Big/1/64/36, 'Plan of encroachments in Beetham'.

51 See, for instance, LRO DDGa/17/88–89, 'Correspondence regarding trespassing', LRO DDHe/82/18, 'Correspondence on the taking of game, 1804', LRO DDHe/79/104a, 'Memorandum regarding trespassing in Hesketh fisheries, 1821', and LRO DDB/acc 6685/Box 176, 'Game preservation, 1818–1819'.

52 See R. Wall, 'Work, welfare and the family: an illustration of the adaptive economy' in L. Bonfield, R. M. Smith and K. Wrightson (eds), *The World We Have Gained* (Oxford, Oxford University Press, 1986).

53 LRO PR810, 'Kirkham order book'.

54 LRO PR1332–1334, 'Accounts of Barnacre with Bonds'.

55 LRO DDX 386/3, 'Garstang vestry minutes'.

56 LRO PR810, 'Kirkham order book'.

57 LRO DDX 386/3, 'Garstang vestry minutes'.

58 BL HTB 1/2, 'Halliwell'. For an instructive view on the role of work in the household economies of widows, see E. Musgrave, 'Women and craft guilds in eighteenth century Nantes', in G. Crossick (ed.), *The Artisan and the European town* (Aldershot, Ashgate, 1997).

59 LRO DDX 386/3, 'Garstang vestry minutes'.

60 *Ibid.*

61 Eden, *The State*, p. 92.

62 LRO MBC0/7/1, 'Colne ratepayers minutes'.

63 LRO DDHe/83/84, 'Cottage and loom rents'. In 1820 the overseers spent £16 hiring looms for 27 people.

64 LRO DDIn/63/37, 'Accounts of Birkdale township',

65 Overseers and recipients sometimes conflicted over the relationship between work and welfare where there were moves forcibly to apprentice the children of poor families, undermining the fragile household economies of paupers. Resistance was strong and women seem to have been adept in northern communities at moving their children around households in communities to avoid the scrutiny of the overseer.

66 One potentially important avenue was to run up rent arrears. In the Lancashire township of Longton, pauper cottages with a nominal annual rental of £365 18s. in 1820 had accrued rent arrears of £209 18s. 6d. See LRO DDHe/83/84, 'Cottage and loom rents'.

67 Though this is a perspective which seems to escape the most recent contribution to the debate: see M. Gorsky, 'The growth and distribution of English friendly societies in the early nineteenth century', *Economic History Review*, 51 (1998).

68 Eden, *The State*, p. 69. See also LRO DDX/28/51, 'The rules and regulations of the Chatburn friendly society'.

69 BL PGB/2/1–76, 'Friendly society membership certificates', and LRO DDX/153, 'Friendly society membership certificates'.

70 Manchester Central Reference Library (hereafter MCL) L 75/8/1, 'Parish records 1790–1830'.

71 However, the accounts conflate those receiving relief from the township itself, those who were sent their relief whilst living away in other townships (but who are still listed in the accounts), and those who received relief from other townships while living in Cowpe (and who are also listed in the accounts). In the overseer records

out-township and in-township relief recipients are distinguished and stripping the former group from the relief lists suggests that no more than 4 per cent of the population were likely to have been dependent on relief in any one year.

72 RL Rc 352 Raw, 'The poor law accounts of Cowpe'.

73 This procedure biases the reading of the graph in two ways. First, those struggling to maintain independence on the margins of economy and society will be missed if they do not appear in these sources. Second, all of those who appear in the three sources are treated as nominally poor, no matter how many or how few times they appear. On record linkage procedures, see S. A. King, 'Power, representation and the self: problems with sources for record linkage', *Local Historian*, 27 (1997), and *idem*, 'Historical demography, life-cycle reconstruction and family reconstitution: new perspectives', *History and Computing*, 8 (1996).

74 For these records, see RL uncatalogued, 'Accounts'.

75 RL RC 921 WHI, 'Diary of David Whitehead'.

76 *Ibid*.

77 See RL RC 921, 'Family papers' and RL RC 942 CRA, 'Diary'.

78 RL RC 677 CLO, 'Mill accounts, with wages and medical certificates'.

79 RL RC 677, 'Wage account book for outworkers 1799–1800', RL RC Ros, 'Sale and subcontracting book 1826–30', RL RC Ros, 'Cash account book 1800–1804', and RL RC Clo, 'Outworker account book 1820'.

80 Figure 8.5 incorporates an important assumption about the contribution of work – that the mean figure for outwork by value to poor people in the years of detailed accounts can be applied to the years during the period 1806–30 where we do not have detailed breakdowns.

81 The category is misleading in a number of senses. Most importantly, it records debts only at year end when the shop formally balanced accounts – a sort of net credit. An alternative option would have been to aggregate the monthly debts and apply them. See RL RC 658, 'Accounts'.

82 RL RC 921 WHI, 'The diary of David Whitehead'.

83 S. A. King and J. G. Timmins, *Making Sense of the Industrial Revolution* (Manchester, Manchester University Press, 2000); Wrightson, *Earthly Necessities*.

84 RL RC 921 WHI, 'The diary of David Whitehead'.

85 LRO DDIn/66/30, 'Birkdale rental 1814'.

86 LRO DDIn/45/14, 'Report on the town cottages of Birkdale'.

87 *Ibid*.

88 King, *Poverty*.

89 LRO DDCm/13/3, 'Scheme'.

9
Conclusion
Steven King and Alannah Tomkins

Observations and questions

We started this volume with the observation that English welfare historians have developed an increasingly sophisticated theoretical framework within which to analyse the economy of makeshifts. Some of our contributors have explored the nuances of this framework. Sarah Lloyd, for instance, suggests that the texture of encounters between those applying for and those dispensing charity invite us to step beyond the material aspects of the economy of makeshifts and to locate and interpret the 'cultural imperatives' that wound through the makeshift economy. Steve Hindle has encouraged us to consider not only the economic angle of the economy of makeshifts, but also the socio-political significance of the construction, reconstruction and exploitation of the makeshift economy in any locality. And his term 'economy of diversified resources' adds a further, and very interesting, strand to the linguistic definition of the complementary or contradictory welfare strands viewed from the perspective of poor people and their communities. We also suggested, however, that the empirical base from which an analysis of the practicalities of the operation of the economy of makeshifts would have to spring was strictly limited. A range of unasked or unanswered questions suggested themselves: at a given point in time or for a given community, what was the range of the economy of makeshifts? How did the value of individual elements of the economy of makeshifts change over time? Was the economy of makeshifts quite fragile and in need of constant remoulding or was it resilient in the face of changes in land tenure and work location? How did the poor and the poor law balance the different elements of the economy of makeshifts in response to different life-cycle stages or different causes and durations of poverty? Were there regionally distinct economies of makeshifts or were the similarities greater than the differences? How did the constellation of coping strategies employed by those who obtained poor relief differ from that assembled by those denied relief or too proud to apply? In particular, what impact did access criteria have on the usefulness of the economy of makeshifts? What impact did the rapid transition of the English population from a rural to an urban industrial population have on the value and composition of the economy of makeshifts? Did the cause of poverty or marginality have a bearing on the coping strategies assembled? In particular, did sudden need associated with sickness or trade cycles generate a distinctive economy of makeshifts? Did those at different life-cycle stages seek out and exploit very different (particularly demographic?) coping strategies, or was the economy of makeshifts immune to considerations of life-cycle? And did middling people recognise the importance of an economy of makeshifts and go out of their way to create extra strands to this economy?

Our contributors have allowed us to begin to think about providing answers to some of these questions. Steve Hindle, Margaret Hanly and Steven King all effectively point to an 'economy of diversified resources', though with charity, work and poor relief at its heart. Around this core they highlight a (potentially very valuable but ultimately inadequately quantifiable) range of peripheral avenues which might be uncertain, contested and constantly under pressure at the same time as they retained a psychological value to the poor and their communities. This said, our contributors do not always agree on the composition of the welfare net; Steve Hindle suggests, in effect, that exploitation of common rights in Geddington was too certain for this to be regarded as part of the economy of makeshifts, while Steve King regards exploitation of waste and common land as an integral feature of the economy of makeshifts in Rossendale. This difference highlights the importance of location and regionality in any approach to the economy of makeshifts. Factors such as differential elimination of the commons, differences in land tenure and the presence or absence of a charitable elite could generate very important variations in the composition and robustness of the makeshift economy within and between counties. Differences in natural resource and employment patterns might have the same effect, though Sarah Lloyd's discussion of the role and character of London-based charity should warn us that the economy of makeshifts has more than a local flavour. Most importantly, though, we should not forget the very important intra- and inter-regional cultural variations which could impact heavily on the composition of makeshift economies and the order in which makeshift strands were put together at different life-cycle stages.

Such observations allow the marginal poor some agency. However, we should not ignore the fact that one of the enduring themes to come out of the preceding chapters is the actual or perceived fragility of makeshift economies in most areas. At one level, Alannah Tomkins's analysis of pawning practices opens up in a unique way a much neglected strand of the makeshift economy for urban dwellers in particular. However, the existence of that 'welfare avenue' is itself testimony to the fragility of the coping strategies employed by individuals and families to deal with the strains of everyday life. The same might be observed in Heather Shore's excellent linkage of crime into the makeshift economy.[1] Even where they were not fragile, the access conditions for certain avenues in the 'economy of diversified resources' could, as both Margaret Hanly and Sarah Lloyd suggest, prove onerous. Moreover, such conditions made the resources to be garnered dependent upon a cultural or political contest that might implicitly or explicitly reduce their value.

The process of obtaining access to poor law resources was also contested, as several of our contributors have pointed out. The role of those resources in the economy of makeshifts differed greatly between and within regions and between urban and rural areas, but in Lancashire at least the poor law was a minor player in the makeshift economies of most people and at most times. As vestry evidence shows, those who controlled and executed poor law policy had a keen appreciation of the outlines and value of the economy of makeshifts and, at least in some regions, maintained an expectation that these avenues would be explored. Barrett's review of the links between aggregate poor relief spending and kinship density in different Yorkshire communities demonstrates this very effectively indeed. This said, from an opposite angle, Steve Hindle demonstrates that some elements of community or county elites actively argued for a bolstering of the different resource avenues in the 'economy of diversified resources' through the donation and manipulation of charitable funds.

Clearly, then, our contributors have made important advances.

At the same time, there are some aspects of the economy of makeshifts that have received inadequate attention thus far, and part of the rationale of this conclusion is to draw out the writing on three of these areas – demographic strategies, self-help and institutionalised welfare – with a view to generating a platform on which to base a future agenda.

Demographic strategies

We might start with one of the coping strategies that informed the original economy of makeshifts concept – migration and demographic realignment. Historical demographers have in the last two decades been busy exploding key myths about the propensity of eighteenth- and nineteenth-century people to move and their reasons for doing so. While early commentators such as Arthur Redford lumped most poor migrants together as 'subsistence migrants' caught in an inexorable drift towards towns, the work of Pooley and Turnbull in particular has led to a more complex assessment of the nature of, and motivations for, movement.[2] Thus, it is now clear that almost all migration throughout the period covered by this volume was local and circular. Most people moved several times over a life-cycle, but relatively few ended up more than 10–15 miles from where they were born. A spell as an urban resident was probably included in many life-cycles, but the idea that people went to towns and died or stayed there has been shown to be a fallacy. In practice, the return traffic from towns as servants, skilled workers and others returned home was considerable and is testimony to one coping strategy that requires further elaboration.

Motivations for movement appear to have been varied, though work and marriage dominate the schema developed by Pooley and Turnbull, and while migration was a constant feature of entire life-cycles it was children and young adults who numerically dominated in the migration stakes. Apprenticeship – an obvious coping strategy for a family with too many mouths and an inability to put older children to truly productive work, and for a poor law wishing to cut long-term bills – was one factor in child movement, but the majority of child migrants went in tow with their families. Of course, migration carried material costs (travel, selling and re-buying of furniture or tools, etc.) and also cut migrants off from some of the potential coping strategies that would have been available to them had they stayed, for instance access to charity or credit. Thus one of the most important advances in the migration literature has been a renewed emphasis on the way in which the poor law could reduce the actual and potential costs of movement (and hence influence which part of the economy of makeshifts paupers turned to) by financing the money cost of movement and agreeing to pay out-parish relief. As pauper letters make clear, access to such out-parish relief was an important part of the economy of makeshifts in both the north and the south, though it was more prevalent in the former.[3]

These are important advances, but in terms of the economy of makeshifts many stones are left unturned. We still know almost nothing, for instance, about the issue of temporary/seasonal migration even though it is clear from poor law accounts (where men would sometimes agree with the community for care of their family, to be reimbursed on their return) that it happened. And while historical demographers have reconstructed the theoretical economic benefits accruing to movement to towns[4] there have been no detailed nominal studies relating individual migration decisions to family survival strategies of the sort which are being conducted by Paul André Rosental and his collaborators on the continent.[5] Moreover, while we know the broad age distribution of migrants between the seventeenth and nineteenth centuries, this is not enough to tell us about the place of migration in the life-cycle of coping strategies. Thus, did sudden trade-cycle crisis make physical movement more likely, and was there a relationship between need associated with having too many young children and migration? Contemporary commentators often drew such connections, but more empirical work is needed on such questions. Further work is also needed on the issue of whether migration was more likely to be adopted as a coping strategy in some types of community than in others. It is clear, for instance, that the upland communities which were to become broadly proto-industrial by the later eighteenth century lost disproportionate numbers of people to migration prior to rural industrial development. People in town hinterlands may also have seen migration as the easiest of coping strategies in the face of individual and family poverty.[6] Such observations point up very clearly the potential disparity between the composition and richness of the economy of makeshifts in urban areas vis-à-vis rural areas, a theme which has been implicit in the chapters of Alannah Tomkins, Sarah Lloyd and Heather Shore.

Another aspect of demographic realignment – marriage and remarriage – has been better covered by historical demographers and cultural historians. While the economic circumstances of men allowed them to remain solvent and single for longer than most women,[7] ultimately couples are usually thought to have had greater access to material resources and a wider range of potential coping strategies than singletons. We might query whether such hard material considerations figured obviously in the decision of when and who to marry, but three things about the marriage market and process which emerge from the recent historiography are important for this discussion. The first is that both male and female marriage ages fell during the course of the eighteenth and early nineteenth centuries.[8] Exactly why they did so remains a matter of debate,[9] but what the falling age must have meant is that many couples marrying for the first time in the later eighteenth century were unlikely to be economically independent of family, kin and friends. In other words, most marriages must have been undertaken firmly in the grasp of the economy of makeshifts, though few historical demographers have carried through this logic of their observation of falling marriage ages.[10]

The second important observation is that the rate of marital dissolution probably fell for much of the period covered by this volume, as life expectancy improved and industrialisation in much of the north and midlands cut down migration distances still further. The corollary of this observation is that one of the classic seventeenth-century coping strategies – marrying or remarrying a wealthy widow or widower – was likely to have been less and less important over time. This is even more the case when we take account of the recent work of cultural historians such as Elizabeth Foyster and Pam Sharpe who show, through the skilful use of case studies, that the remarriage process for widows in particular was one fraught with hurdles and uncertain outcomes.[11] Sharpe suggests that because of their privileged access to poor relief and informal relief (gleaning, work for the parish, etc.) women may have had little incentive to remarry. This said, chronological gaps between widowhood and remarriage for those widows who eventually did get remarried tended to be narrow, something which perhaps reinforces the idea that marriage and remarriage was an important coping strategy in certain life-cycle positions.[12]

Meanwhile, the final key aspect of marriage historiography is that English society in our period never resolves the core paradox that while couples were (and were acknowledged to be) more economically secure, commentators from Malthus backwards were persistently afraid of the consequences of pauper marriages for the moral state of communities and classes. We see this paradox reflected in poor law records, with some poor law officials actively encouraging and paying for marriage while others, sometimes in the same communities at different points in time, actively discouraged pauper unions. One of the logical extensions of this observation is that whatever the nominal shape of the local economy of makeshifts, paupers were not always in a position to make choices about the way that they combined coping strategies. This is not about access conditions but active constraint, offering further weight to the contentions of Sarah Lloyd and Steve Hindle that an 'economy' of makeshifts was actually shot through with cultural and socio-political judgements on the part of poor people and their communities. We might also consider the idea that the 'economy' of makeshifts had an emotional angle. We know, for instance, that remarriage for women was most likely in two brief windows of the life-cycle – for women who had relatively few young children and for women with grown-up children but who had not yet reached old age – and more work is needed not only on how remarriage for women fitted into a life-cycle of makeshifts but also on the emotional questions that prompted them to take the remarriage path. Men notionally found it easier to remarry at all ages, but we need to ask searching questions about how far remarriage represented a conscious coping strategy as opposed to a desire for companionship. The answers to these sorts of questions almost certainly varied by community type – remarriage rates at all ages were much higher in rural industrial communities than either towns or rural areas, for instance – and more widely the role of marriage and remarriage in the overall welfare package assembled by early modern families may have varied according to the prevailing causes of poverty and marginality.

A further and overlapping literature that we must address is the increasingly sophisticated discussion of early modern propensities to vary household structures and to be tied into complex neighbourhood, friendship and occupational networks which could be energised when sudden and short-term or gnawing and long-term poverty overtook an individual. Margaret Hanly hints at the importance of these networks in her contribution to this volume. The earliest literature saw these as discrete coping strategies. Peter Laslett, for instance, stressed from the 1960s that English households were both small and simple.[13] Sam Barrett deals with the details of this literature in his chapter, but in essence there have been few credible challenges to Laslettian orthodoxy. Rather, more recent historiography has moved the goalposts, asking whether the form of the nuclear family really matters and in the process combining issues which Laslett saw as discrete. Thus one strand of thinking which is important for an understanding of the economy of makeshifts is the idea that what matters is not the form of the family and household at any point in time, but its changing size and composition over the whole life-cycle of the family. Thomas Sokoll, for instance, has been able to compare pauper listings for Essex communities to suggest that far from pauper households being small and simple, they were actually large and complex. Few were solitary, many had children (single or married) to help them out, others took in servants, lodgers or (in particular) grandchildren, and still more resided together under the same roof as a collective coping strategy.[14] In other words, at particular times of life-cycle stress, households showed a distinct propensity to split and reform. By using population listings that combine the experiences of family units at all life-cycle stages, we miss this basic characteristic, and thereby potentially gloss over important differences in the coping strategies employed in different regions or socio-economic environments.

A second strand of thinking is that whether people lived together is less relevant in understanding the cohesiveness of the family and its role in things such as welfare than whether kin, good friends and occupational or religious colleagues lived proximate to each other and could thus offer day-to-day aid to those in need.[15] And a final theme in the modern historiography of the family which is relevant here is the idea that understanding the operation of families has less to do with ties of blood or marriage, and more to do with 'fictive kin' – the friends, neighbours, occupational colleagues and religious brethren who could be as close in emotional and financial terms as family were tied into similar systems of expectation and obligation, and who might be better resourced than family members when poverty or the need to invest in a business loomed large. As Tadmor and others have pointed out, such fictive kin frequently took kinship titles,[16] though neither social nor welfare historians have taken the next logical step and included such networks (other perhaps than ill-specified 'neighbourhood networks') into discussion of the shape and vibrancy of economies of makeshift at local level. Partly this reflects problems of source and language, but historians such as Pat Thane are by no means alone in suggesting that kinship and friendship may have been one of the great unseen props to the early modern economy of makeshifts. This in turn raises important questions for future research, notably the extent to which emphasis on such networks varied over the life-cycle and according to the exact cause of poverty. We might also ask whether there were regional differences in emphasis here, with Barrett and others suggesting persuasively in this volume that kinship density was somewhat higher in the industrial and urban north than has often been found in the rural and urban south or east. By inference, we also need to ask whether certain socio-economic community types generated a greater role for kinship and other networks in the overall economy of makeshifts than did other community types.

Self-help

In some ways, of course turning to kinship, neighbourhood and occupational networks might be classified as a form of self-help, and this part of a potential economy of makeshifts has attracted a good deal of commentary too. The role of friendly societies, not elsewhere given sustained attention in this volume, is worthy of particular consideration. The literature on the subject is considerable.[17] By 1803 there were almost 10,000 official friendly societies with over 700,000 members, but the true figure is probably nearer 1 million when we take account of small local societies that escaped registration. Growth in the rest of the nineteenth century was to be exponential, reaching 5.5 million by 1903. In 1850 the Manchester Oddfellows alone could boast a membership of 500,000 and the organisational form had proved its appeal to women as well as men, with the foundation of over 1,000 female-only friendly societies. These figures notwithstanding, friendly society membership has rarely been integrated into the framework of the wider economy of makeshifts. Fees are held to have been too high for the poorest sections of the labour force (and thus those most likely to need the economy of makeshifts on a regular basis) to afford, many friendly societies were financially unstable and could provide only brief and short-term benefits and there was a massive disparity in the distribution of friendly society membership, recently highlighted again by Gorsky.[18] Lancashire in particular, and urban industrial areas more generally, dominated aggregate friendly society memberships, and so even if friendly society membership was important as a coping strategy it played this role only for a limited section of the population.

Yet such commentary is misleading. Relatively few people spent their entire lives in poverty defined as dependence upon poor relief or charity. It is thus conceivable that almost everybody would at some point have had the resources to become friendly society members and that the benefits of membership could be an important part of the economy of makeshifts at certain life-cycle stages.[19] The fact that the majority of friendly society members were on the books for a relatively short time and showed some propensity to drop out and then come back again, is surely testimony to this.[20] Moreover, the idea that poor law officials saw friendly society membership as an important alternative coping mechanism can be seen in the fact that they collected membership certificates against the event of a poor relief application by a member and that they often paid subscription arrears if people applied for this form of support from the old poor law.[21] Such practices reflect the fact that, as Steve Hindle shows us in his contribution to this volume, communities could take an active interest in supporting the wider economy of makeshifts. Moreover, while it is true that there were wide spatial disparities in membership, it is also important to remember that membership wherever it was taken out conferred more benefits than just monetary payments at times of sickness or old age. Friendly society membership was thus often a foundation for vibrant neighbourhood networks, with fellow members visiting each other at time of incapacity and probably offering additional emotional and material support. It is not surprising, therefore, to find Gorsky suggesting that friendly society membership was most dense where poor law systems were weakest and that friendly societies took over much of the role of communal welfare, though even he fails to link such conclusions into a wider discussion of the economy of makeshifts.[22] The pressing need for such integration will be clear from the foregoing discussion. This is particularly true of the role of friendly society provision in the economy of makeshifts of female members and their families.

A further makeshift on which we have plenty of indirect discussion – and one which again falls under the general head of self-help – is modification to the income and expenditure nexus. That poor people were supposed to work even if they received poor relief is acknowledged by a wide variety of commentators, and by contributors to this volume. That poor people did work is confirmed by poor law records and letters back to their parish by or for paupers themselves. But locating the role of work in making ends meet for poor people is often problematic, and it is for this reason that we come back to the issue of work here. Snell, Lee, Valenze and others have identified long-term trends in national and regional employment patterns and they, along with Sarah Horrell and Jane Humphries,[23] have identified equally important long-term trends in the differential labour force participation of men, women and children. Contributors to the proto-industrial literature too have been active in tracing regional employment patterns and identifying influences on employment within regions such as technological redundancy.[24] Much of this overlapping literature highlights the decline in formal labour force participation amongst women in various regions, with inevitable knock-on effects to the robustness of the family economy.[25]

How such broad changes manifested themselves at local level and influenced the composition or strength of the economy of makeshifts, though, is not always or usually clear. Specific local influences modified these broad trends. Moreover, the poor themselves were often the most dynamic of local groups in creating work opportunities in the service or manufacturing sector or on the margins of the legitimate and illegitimate economy. Because of the nature of our sources, much of this sort of activity goes unrecorded so that we miss a potentially important response to local pressure on the economy of makeshifts. The poor law itself could also create short-term employment opportunities, blurring the distinctions between poor relief and the economy of makeshifts in the eighteenth and nineteenth centuries in the same way that the overlap between charity and poor relief had blurred the same distinctions in the seventeenth century.[26] Nursing, laying out the dead, boarding the children of others, training the children of others, working on the parish roads and buying goods from those who might otherwise be dependent upon poor relief[27] were common themes in the accounts of the overseer of the poor even before the more formal wage and employment subsidies of the late eighteenth century such as the roundsman system. So were entries for direct support of those in work such as coals for blacksmiths, looms, potatoes for seeding and cloth for selling. And, in the north and midlands in particular, it is common to find vestries ordering parish officials to negotiate actively with employers to subsidise employment and to provide work opportunities for more deserving and able-bodied paupers. Friends and neighbours, tied into relationships of obligation and trust through neighbourhood networks, might also bargain for employment on behalf of the poor.

The problem with this coping strategy is that it is difficult to pin down the local range of work opportunities available for those facing sudden or life-cycle crises, a problem exacerbated by the tendency for employment capacity of a local economy to fluctuate considerably over time and for some people to work elsewhere for all or part of the time as a coping strategy. It is even more difficult to pin down the level of individual and family remuneration from the work process, and thus to locate the role of work in generating yearly income. This is not simply a matter of lack of record survival; some income certainly came from illegal (poaching, selling stolen clothes) or semi-legal (selling or pawning goods given by the poor law) activity and would never have been recorded, while for much of the eighteenth century and even into the nineteenth century a shortage of coin encouraged barter (as Steven King has shown in his chapter) and credit economies in many regions, making it difficult to quantify the economy of makeshifts.[28] For other aspects of income generation records are slightly better, but historians do not agree on how to interpret them. On common rights, for instance, we now have a fairly good understanding of the dynamics of their decline but there is little agreement on how we should value them at different stages of this decline.[29] For other elements of 'work' of course we have an opposite problem – a fairly good understanding of who earned what from an activity, but then little genuine understanding of how widespread or robust the activity was. Income from gleaning (widely defined) is a case in point. Peter King has shown convincingly that gleaning could bolster household income in the midlands and south-east by an average of 12 per cent, more for female-headed households. He has also suggested some of the chronology of decline in this aspect of the economy of makeshifts.[30] We are still very far, however, from an understanding of the nature and speed of decline in gleaning, and it is becoming ever clearer that gleaning in its widest sense was a core element of the economy of makeshifts in the early modern north whereas most historiography stresses the paucity of opportunities for gleaning in this region.

More work is clearly needed. In the meantime, household budgets of the sort constructed in the 1790s by Frederick Morton Eden and assembled and used by Sarah Horrell and Jane Humphries can help us to locate a baseline for the contribution of work to the economy of makeshifts and to understand the degree of flexibility which early modern families had to manipulate expenditure and income as a *specific strand* in the economy of makeshifts.[31] While the data are not always consistent and showed more regional difference than has thus far been acknowledged, little has changed since Eden showed the majority of families to be fundamentally incapable of meeting even basic expenditure requirements through work alone. Indeed, there is probably a sense in which, for the majority of the potentially poor urban and rural population, work at the individual level became a less and less important strand in making ends meet. This was particularly true in the south and midlands. The opposite side of the coin is that poor and marginal people probably invested much more of their time over the eighteenth and nineteenth centuries in modifying expenditure. Credit networks were one aspect of this, as were pawnbrokers. More widely, as Margaret Hanly points out in her chapter, it becomes possible from the 1760s to locate well-defined cycles of accumulation and dis-accumulation in the material lives of the potentially poor. Selling household items that were also a store of wealth had become an established plank of the rural and urban economy of makeshifts by the 1820s in a way which was not the case in the 1720s. In this sense, welfare historians might do well to remember that the development of national and regional markets meant that what was defined as saleable and what was not changed radically from the 1760s. The fact that the poor used such changes to their advantage is testimony to the regenerative capacity of the economy of makeshifts against the backdrop of local and national adversity in some of its traditional key strands.

Institutionalised welfare avenues

One of the welfare strands sometimes seen to have been subject to most pressure is formal charity, and several of our contributors have dealt directly or indirectly with this theme. As with work, however, charity is revisited here because it must be set in its widest context if we are to construct an agenda for future research. Thus the level of resources devoted to endowed, institutional and subscription charities and to informal giving to beggars or at church in urban and rural England in the eighteenth century was very considerable. Colin Jones, for instance, suggests that informal charity probably exceeded the scale of resources transferred through poor relief in most years.[32] Formal charitable giving dwarfed even this in capital terms. However, the relative importance of charity and communal welfare is usually held to have shifted decisively in favour of the latter during the eighteenth century. This reflected spiralling need, the fact that bequests in wills became more and more restricted, the tendency for old charity capital provisions to be overtaken by inflation or bad management, and a tendency for the range of poor people with access to charity to shrink in the face of its institutionalisation. Prochaska has also pointed out the different levels of imbalance in eighteenth- and nineteenth-century charitable provision, with London dominating the league tables and the existence of a wide difference in charitable provision between and within regions.[33]

Yet while it *might* be right to suggest that in an aggregate sense the potential contribution of charitable resources to the economy of makeshifts dwindled after 1750,[34] when we arrive at the local level no such generalisations are possible. Despite the work of Alannah Tomkins, Donna Andrew and Barry Stapleton,[35] we still have a very poor understanding of trends in the level of even formal charitable resources in most communities. We know even less about the complexities of access conditions to charitable resources, and what we do know comes from the rules of charities themselves. Welfare historians have yet to link up family reconstitution evidence of the sort used here by Sam Barrett with charity data to see whether in fact those rules were followed. Nor have they, by and large, linked up poor law and charity records to look at individual and familial overlap in claiming these two resource strands. Stapleton has used charity records to look at the issue of inherited poverty, but he was unable to tie up charity and poor law expenditure records for Odiham in Hampshire.[36]

Moreover, there is also a sense in which welfare historians with particular local interests have failed to appreciate just how much charity money was available from sources outside the locality, a point also made by Sarah Lloyd in her contribution to this volume. When, in 1770, the overseers of Greystoke in Cumberland sent a petition to the trustees of John Nicholson, bookseller of London, asking for an annual pension for Sarah, the widow of Nathan Nicholson of that parish, who was in need of charity by virtue of her tender and weak constitution and her age, they were employing a mechanism of resource acquisition which was familiar to many parishes in the eighteenth-century north-west. In this particular case the pension was granted, and Nicholson does not appear on the poor law accounts or in local charity accounts. More work on this area needs to be done, while the research of Shapley on the subscription funds which exploded on to the scene at times when seasonal or trade-cycle stress intersected with life-cycle stress in Manchester further highlights the need for welfare historians to appreciate the degree to which the role of charity in the economy of makeshifts could be continually reinvented.[37]

The economy of makeshifts: ways forward

Of course, we could have discussed more of the disparate strands of the economy of makeshifts in this chapter. The work of Craig Muldrew on the operation of, and access to, credit networks is one example.[38] The vigorous literature on food riots and the tendency for people to assert their customary rights in the face of pressure on their living standards also has a place in a discussion of the form and function of the economy of makeshifts. The same might be said of the non-financial lending and borrowing networks that nineteenth-century antiquarian historians identified in villages and towns up and down the country.[39]

There is clearly a need for a properly holistic approach, incorporating more than just the charity-poor law axis that has largely figured in the literature so far. Before we collect the data, however, we need a better theoretical understanding of how we might expect the economy of makeshifts to have operated in the English context. Thus there are likely to have been subtle life-cycle, regional and

community-type (particularly urban-rural) differences in the composition of the aggregate and individual economy of makeshifts.
We probably need to make a distinction between short-, medium-
and long-term welfare strategies on the part of an individual or
family, and between those families that had *choices* in this sense
and those that did not. And we probably also need to understand
how those who were poor and marginal *thought about* the economy
of makeshifts and its individual components. Certainly we must
pin down what was considered 'normal' and thus outside the idea
of an economy of makeshifts in the contemporary mind. The
selling of goods as opposed to their pawning, for instance, may
have lingered differently in the contemporary mind when thinking
about survival strategies than in the minds of modern historians.
And above all we need to think about just how individuals and
families got a map of the local and regional economy of makeshifts.
How did they know about charities, work opportunities or remarriage opportunities, how did they know what routes were open,
which were closed and which might be opened by adopting a
particular moral stance or getting a particular type of support in
the locality? Was the economy of makeshifts at individual or family
level the outcome of chance or the outcome of planned response,
and how did this balance change according to life-cycle stage or
the particular cause of poverty?

Such questions and ideas represent the beginnings of a complex
practical agenda. This agenda can be made more explicit if we
return to the key questions of the opening section of this chapter:
how did the poor and the poor law balance the different elements
of the economy of makeshifts in response to different life-cycle
stages or different causes and durations of poverty? While nominal
linkage of sources cannot provide all of the answers, some of our
studies have suggested that a proliferation of this technique might
significantly advance our understanding of the economy of
makeshifts, especially where projects systematically sample communities within and between regions. And if the key factor in the
economy of makeshifts is the nature of individual and family
life-cycles rather than the size and constellation of the coping
avenues available at community level, then it would make sense
within and between regions to try and reconstruct economies of
makeshift in communities with very different life-cycle dimensions. A good proxy for this is likely to be levels of mortality. We
have plenty of infant mortality data available for the eighteenth

and nineteenth centuries and, while there is no necessary link
between infant and childhood or adult mortality, reconstructing
the economy of makeshifts in similar communities but at either
end of the mortality spectrum would surely be an excellent place
to start?

Does gender matter in understanding the value, assembly or
longevity of an economy of makeshifts? Continental historians
such as Catharina Lis suggest that it does. So does Lane with her
work on the informal economy, Valenze with her analysis of *The
First Industrial Woman* and the oral historians working in the late
nineteenth century. Our studies have hinted at the same conclusion, but the detailed community level analyses of female coping
strategies, both within and outside the nuclear family context,
needed to reinforce this view have yet to be undertaken. We also
need to understand in a rather more refined way the sort of living
that engagement with the economy of makeshifts yielded at individual and family level. Linking censuses of the poor and household
budgets to poor law accounts, vestry minutes and family reconstitution would be a good start in this direction. For the north-west
alone it is possible to link several surveys of this type to other
substantial databases.

Was the economy of makeshifts quite fragile and in need of
constant remoulding or was it resilient in the face of changes in
land tenure, work location or age structure? Both the historiographical literature and our own contributors are divided on this
issue and only sensitively chosen case studies will allow us to reach
a consensus. We might also ask how the constant tension between
supply of welfare from a widely conceived economy of makeshifts
and potentially wide demand, notably at times of trade cycle stress,
was reconciled by the gatekeepers to alternative resources. For a
few locations we know something about the changing rules which
governed access to gleaning or commons. For rather more places
we know, at least in outline, the rules that governed who could
get charity or who could become a member of a friendly society,
but no one has yet put together the access criteria for a single
community or attempted to model who was thus left out, even
though the reconstitution studies exist to do it. A similar and
related point about the need to advance our understanding of the
speed with which different elements of the economy of makeshifts
could respond to different sorts of individual and family need
might also be made. The poor law could, depending upon the

sentiment of the officials in charge for the year, be fast or slow acting. Whether fast or slow in its own terms, it is a fact that being recorded in the books of the overseer of the poor was the tail end of a potentially long and uncertain process. Resort to the pawnshop was more immediate, as was outright sale of goods. But what about other avenues in the local economy of makeshifts, and when we assemble all of the makeshifts ranked according to potential speed of response, what can we learn about the position of the poor?

Most of the contributions to the economy of makeshift historiography implicitly accept that the poor had relative freedom of choice, subject to obvious access conditions, in where they deployed effort in the economy of makeshifts, but how far was this true? In particular, we might ask what the role of the poor law was in directing paupers in particular ways. Through their employment practices, the relative balance of payment in cash/kind or regular/irregular relief and through their manipulation of local employment and residential arrangements, overseers and vestries had the power to direct paupers, both those on relief and those not. Even their practices with regard to providing clothing for paupers could determine where effort was applied by well or poorly clothed paupers in the localised economy of makeshifts. Linkage between vestry minutes, poor law accounts and charity records would help to resolve such questions and remains entirely feasible.

Did middling people recognise the importance of an economy of makeshifts? An analysis of the rise of institutional charity or the urban subscription charity suggests that they did. However, analysis of the literature on gleaning or common rights and on the opposition to allotments [40] suggests a contrary picture. Which perspective is right? And how did poor people themselves perceive the economy of makeshifts in different socio-economic settings, at different life-cycle stages or in different periods? In particular was navigating a yearly living when on the margins of poverty an acquired skill and one which required familiarity with the seasonal and life-cycle manipulation of different welfare avenues? The more sophisticated use of pauper letters employing typologies like those suggested by Sokoll may help here,[41] and, when combined with family reconstitution, will allow us to confront the equally intriguing question of whether there was any difference between the culture of poverty and the culture of makeshifts between those who were caught in grinding whole-life poverty and those who only experienced the odd incident.

While we have achieved much, as this complex practical agenda demonstrates, much remains to be done.

Notes

1 We have not really explored the complementary theme of the ability of the poor to constantly remould the economy of makeshifts, except perhaps in the chapter by Sarah Lloyd, but pauper letters frequently hint at the resourcefulness of the poor in this direction.

2 A. Redford, *Labour Migration in England, 1800–1850* (3rd edn, Manchester, Manchester University Press, 1976); C. G. Pooley and J. Turnbull, *Migration and Mobility in Britain Since the 18th Century* (London, UCL Press, 1998).

3 See J. S. Taylor, 'A different kind of Speenhamland: non-resident relief in the industrial revolution', *Journal of British Studies*, 30 (1991).

4 J. G. Williamson, *Coping With City Growth During the British Industrial Revolution* (Cambridge, Cambridge University Press, 1985).

5 C. Lemercier and P. Rosental, 'Pays ruraux et découpage de l'espace: Les reseaux migratoires dans la région Lilloise au millieu du XIX siècle', *Population*, 55 (2000); J. Bourdieu, G. Postel-Vinay, P. Rosental and A. Suwa-Eisenmann, 'Migrations et transmissions inter-générationelles dans la France du XIX et du début du XX siècle', *Annals*, 4 (2000).

6 See S. King, 'Sharing the urban graveyard: Sterblichkeitsdynamik im stadtischen Hinterland, England 1680–1820', in J. Voegle and W. Woelk (eds), *Stadt, Krankheit und Tod* (Berlin, Drucker and Humbolt, 2000).

7 P. Sharpe, 'Literally spinsters: a new interpretation of local economy and demography in Colyton in the seventeenth and eighteenth centuries', *Economic History Review*, 44 (1991).

8 See E. A. Wrigley, R. S. Davies, J. E. Oeppen and R. S. Schofield, *English Population History From Family Reconstitution, 1580–1837* (Cambridge, Cambridge University Press, 1997).

9 See the debate in *International Review of Social History*, 44 (1999).

10 The fact that few young workers appear to have managed to save anything towards their marriages reinforces this point. See J. Styles, 'Involuntary consumers? Servants and their clothes in eighteenth century England', in S. A. King and C. J. E. R. Payne (eds), *The Dress of the Poor, 1700–1900* (London, Pasold, 2002).

11 See E. Foyster, 'Marrying the experienced widow in early modern England: the male perspective', in S. Cavallo and L. Warner (eds), *Widowhood in Medieval and Early Modern Europe* (Harlow, Longman,

1999), and P. Sharpe, 'Survival strategies and stories: poor widows and widowers in early industrial England', in *ibid.*, who notes that getting rid of a bad money manager through death of a spouse and/or obtaining a good money manager through remarriage could actually be a core plank of a coping strategy.

12 Sharpe, 'Survival'; for those who did not remarry, prostitution was an alternative option. On this matter in London see T. Henderson, *Disorderly Women in Eighteenth Century London* (London, Longman, 1999).

13 For the classic statement of this view, see P. Laslett, 'Mean household size in England since the sixteenth century', in P. Laslett and R. Wall (eds), *Household and Family in Past Time* (Cambridge, Cambridge University Press, 1972).

14 T. Sokoll, *Household and Family Among the Poor: The Case of Two Essex Communities in the Later Eighteenth and Early Nineteenth Centuries* (Bochum, Verlaag fur Regionalgeschichte, 1993).

15 For a good review of the debate on this theme, see B. Reay, *Microhistories: Demography, Society and Culture in Rural England, 1800–1930* (Cambridge, Cambridge University Press, 1996).

16 N. Tadmor, *Family and Friends in Eighteenth Century England* (Cambridge, Cambridge University Press, 2001).

17 For key contributions, see P. Gosden, *The Friendly Society in England, 1815–75* (Manchester, Manchester University Press, 1961); D. Neave, *Mutual Aid in the Victorian Countryside, 1830–1914* (Hull, Hull University Press, 1991); B. Supple, 'Legislation and virtue: an essay on working class self-help and the state', in N. McKendrick (ed.), *Historical Perspectives: Studies in English Thought and Society* (London, Europa, 1974); G. D. H. Cole, *A Short History of the British Working Class Movement 1789–1947* (London, Allen and Unwin, 1966) and E. Lord, 'Weighed in the balance and found wanting: female friendly societies, self-help and economic virtue in the east midlands in the eighteenth and nineteenth centuries', *Midland History*, 22 (1997).

18 M. Gorsky, 'The growth and distribution of English friendly societies in the early nineteenth century', *Economic History Review*, 51 (1998).

19 See E. Hopkins, *Working Class Self-Help in Nineteenth Century England* (London, UCL Press, 1995).

20 See D. G. Green, 'The friendly society and Adam Smith liberalism', in D. Gladstone (ed.), *Before Beveridge: Welfare Before the Welfare State* (London, IEA, 1998).

21 Payment of subscriptions was technically forbidden under the new poor law. However, archival evidence suggests that subscriptions did continue to be paid in certain localities after 1834. This was particularly the case where the establishment of the new poor law was contested.

22 Gorsky, 'The growth'.

23 S. Horrell and J. Humphries, 'Women's labour force participation and the transition to the male breadwinner family, 1790–1865', *Economic History Review*, 48 (1995) and S. Horrell and J. Humphries, 'The exploitation of little children: child labor and the family economy in the Industrial Revolution', *Explorations in Economic History*, 32 (1995).

24 For a review of this literature, see P. Hudson, 'Proto-industrialization in England', in S. Ogilvie and M. Cerman (eds), *European Proto-Industrialisation* (Cambridge, Cambridge University Press, 1996).

25 On this, see J. Long, *Conversations in Cold Rooms: Women, Work and Poverty in Nineteenth Century Northumberland* (Woodbridge, Boydell, 1999).

26 P. Slack, *From Reformation to Improvement: Public Welfare in Early Modern England* (Oxford, Oxford University Press, 1998).

27 It is too often overlooked that net poor law expenditure in places, even in the north, was high and growing during the eighteenth century. This may have led to a net redistribution of income, but it also meant that the poor law became the largest single source of demand for goods and services in many places.

28 See S. King and J. C. Muldrew, 'Cash, wages and the economy of makeshifts in England 1650–1830', in P. Scholliers and L. Schwarz (eds), *Worlds of Wages* (Oxford, Berghahn, 2003).

29 On common rights and their value, see J. Humphries, 'Enclosures, common rights and women: the proletarianisation of families in the late eighteenth and early nineteenth centuries', *Journal of Economic History*, 50 (1990), and J. M. Neeson, *Commoners: Common Right, Enclosure and Social Change in England 1700–1820* (Cambridge, Cambridge University Press, 1993).

30 P. King, 'Customary rights and women's earnings: the importance of gleaning to the rural labouring poor 1750–1850', *Economic History Review*, 44 (1991); *idem*, 'Female offenders: work and life-cycle change in eighteenth century London', *Continuity and Change*, 11 (1996).

31 S. Horrell and J. Humphries, 'Old questions, new data and alternative perspectives: families' living standards in the industrial revolution', *Journal of Economic History*, 52 (1992), and F. M. Eden, *The State of the Poor: A History of the Labouring Classes in England* (New York, Blom, 1971).

32 C. Jones, 'Some recent trends in the history of charity', in Daunton, *Charity*.

33 F. Prochaska, *The Voluntary Impulse: Philanthropy in Modern Britain* (London, Faber, 1988); *idem*, *Women and Philanthropy in Nineteenth Century England* (Oxford, Clarendon, 1980).

34 We must, though, make important distinctions between north and south in terms of charity and its relationship to relief. Parts of Durham, north Lancashire and large parts of Cumberland and Westmorland frequently failed to raise a poor rate, or if they did

raise one it was so nominal that the magnitude of relief is dictated by the scale of the collection, not the scale of need.

35 D. Andrew, *Philanthropy and Police: Charity in Eighteenth-Century London* (Oxford, Princeton University Press, 1989); B. Stapleton, 'Inherited poverty and life-cycle poverty: Odiham, Hampshire', *Social History*, 18 (1993); A. Tomkins, 'The experience of urban poverty – a comparison of Oxford and Shrewsbury, 1740–1770' (unpublished DPhil, University of Oxford, 1994).

36 Stapleton, 'Inherited poverty'.

37 P. Shapley, *Charity and Power in Victorian Manchester* (Manchester, Chetham Society, 2000).

38 C. Muldrew, 'Credit and the courts: debt litigation in a seventeenth century urban community', *Economic History Review*, 46 (1993).

39 J. Lawson, *Letters to the Young on Progress in Pudsey Over the Last Sixty Years* (Chichester, Caliban, 1977).

40 J. Burchardt, 'Rural social relations, 1830–50: opposition to allotments for labourers', *Agricultural History Review*, 45 (1997).

41 T. Sokoll, *Essex Pauper Letters, 1731–1837* (Oxford, Oxford University Press, 2001).

Index